SPYING FOR THE
FÜHRER

SPYING FOR THE FÜHRER
HITLER'S ESPIONAGE MACHINE

Christer Jörgensen

CHARTWELL
BOOKS, INC.

This edition published in 2014 by
CHARTWELL BOOKS, INC.
A division of BOOK SALES, INC.
276 Fifth Avenue Suite 206
New York, New York 10001
USA

ISBN-13: 978-0-7858-3087-0

Produced by
Windmill Books
First Floor
9-17 St. Albans Place
London N1 ONX

Senior Managing Editor: Tim Cooke
Editors: James Murphy, Anthony Hall
Picture Researchers: Andrew Webb, Becky Cox
Designer: Anthony Cohen
Production Director: Alastair Gourlay

Printed in China

Contents

Abbreviations

AA — Auswärtige Amt – German Foreign Office.

Abwehr — German Militayry Intelligence Service; meaning "defence" in German.

Abteilung — German for Section or Department.

AO — Abwehr Officer.

AO — Ausland Organization. A rival of the established German Foreign Office. Set up by Hitler to promote Nazi influence among Germans settled abroad.

Apparat — Russian spying term meaning spy ring or network.

Anst — Abwehrnebenstelle – Abwehr sub-station.

Ast — Abwehr stelle – Abwehr station in Germany or a German-occupied country.

B-Dienst — Funkbeobachtungsdienst – German Naval Monitoring and Deciphering Service.

Bundesheer — Austrian Army before 1938.

Bupo — *Bundespolizei* – the Swiss Federal Police or Secret Police.

Bureau Ha — Swiss intelligence *Bureau Haussmann*.

Bureua Zychon — Polish Intelligence Service (PIS) station in Poznab, western Poland, spying on Germany. Headed by Major Zychon.

"C" — Head of the British SIS.

Centre — Soviet Military Intelligence (GRU) headquarters in Moscow.

Chetniks — Yugoslav royalists led by Colonel Drazha Michailovitch and loyal to King Peter II.

CI — *Centrale Inlichtingdienst* – Dutch Central Intelligence Service.

CIS — Czech Intelligence Service. (My own abbreviation for the Czech Chief of Staff Section II.)

Cobbler — Abwehr slang for a forger of documents.

Comintern — Communist International set up by Lenin in 1919 to promote, by any means, the furtherance of the communist world revolution. Its headquarters was in Moscow.

Cut-out — Agent used as middleman between spies to avoid personal contact and risk of detection.

Deuxiéme Bureau — French Military Intelligence or General Staff Section II.

DMI — Director of Military Intelligence (British).

Einsatzkommando — Special Action unit of the SS.

Falange — Spanish fascist movement.

FBI — Federal Bureau of Investigation (US).

FHO — Fremde Heere Ost –Foreign Armies East. A special German Army intelligence service set up to spy on Poland, Czechoslovakia, the USSR and Eastern Europe's armed forces.

FHW — Fremde Heere West – Foreign Armies West. As above only detailed to spy on Western Europe.

Forschungsamt — Telephone and telegraph monitoring and tapping service under Göring's special patronage and protection.

Forschungstelle — Service set up to tap Allied calls across the Atlantic during the war from a monitoring station in the northern Netherlands.

Funkabwehr — German Radio Security Service.

Gauleiter — Provisional Governor in the Third Reich and head of a Gau (district).

Gestapo — Geheime Staatspolizei – German Secret State Police.

GSP — Gibraltar Special (or Security) Police.

GRU — *Glavno Razvedyvatelno Upravlenie* – Fourth Section of the Soviet General Staff (Stavka), i.e. Soviet Military Intelligence Service.

Heimwehr — Austrian conservative Catholic defence organization aimed at preventing either a socialist or Nazi takeover.

HO — Home Office (British Ministry of the Interior).

Ic — Intelligence officer attached to a German Army division, corps or army, often in frontline duty.

ILO — International Labour Organization.

IMRO — Macedonian Internal Revolutionary Organization, set up to create a union between Macedonia and Bulgaria.

IN6 — Section of the German General Staff dealing with the development of armoured forces and headed by Colonel (later General) Heinz Guderian.

INF III — Ribbentrop's AA intelligence service set up in 1941.

NSA — International Socialist Agency. Swiss Socialist News agency set up to spread propaganda and real news.

Kapelle — Abwehr slang for a ring or network of spies; literally means musical orchestra led by a conductor.

KdP — Karpaten deutsche Partei – Carpathian German Party. Active in Slovakia to promote ethnic German interest.

KO	Kriegsorganization. An Abwehr station in a neutral or overseas country.
KPD	Kommunistische Partei Deutschlands – German Communist Party.
LAF	Lithuanian Activist Front. A nationalist and anti-Soviet organization set up to fight the Soviet occupation in 1940–41.
LIU	Letter Interception Unit of the British Letter Censorship Office.
MI5	Military Intelligence Section 5 (British Counter-Intelligence Service).
MI6	Military Intelligence Section 6 (British Espionage Service). More commonly known as the SIS.
MO5	Military Organization Section 5. Precursor of MI5 until change of name in 1916.
ND	Nachrichtendienst – Imperial German Secret Service.
NF	*National Front* – Swiss Nazi organization.
NKVD	*Narodny Kommissariat Vnutrennich Dyel* – The People's Commissariat for Internal Affairs. The Soviet Secret Police.
NNSP	*Norsk National Socialistisk Parti* – Norwegian Nazi Party and rival of Colonel Quisling's *National Samling* (NS) party.
NSDAP	National Socialistische Deutsche Arbeiter Partei – German National Socialist Workers' Party, i.e. the Nazi Party.
OD	*Orde Dienst* – Dutch Resistance Group.
OGPU	*Objedinennoje Gosudarstvennoje Polititjeskoje Upravlenije* – Soviet State Security Service. Precursor to the equally feared NKVD and named thus from 1923 to 1934.
OKH	Oberkommando der Heeres – German Army High Command.
OKW	Oberkommando der Wehrmacht – German Armed Forces High Command.
O.Qu.III	Oberquartiermeister – Quarter Master General's Office or the ND section.
Orpo	Ordnungspolizei – the uniformed, ordinary German Police.
OSS	Office of Strategic Services. US Sabotage and Subversion Service equivalent to the British SOE.
OUN	Ukrainian Nationalist Organization.
OT	Organization Todt – the German Army's Construction Corps led by Dr. Fritz Todt, an emminent German engineer
Ovpo	Norwegian Secret Police.
Pers Z	Central Staff office at the AA but in reality the German Foreign Office's own deciphering and monitoring service.
Pianist	Abwehr slang for a clandestine radio operator.

PIS	Polish Intelligence Service (my own abbreviation for the Polish General Staff Section II).
PVDE	Portuguese Secret Police.
RFK	Rot Front Kämpfer. Paramilitary wing of the KPD and street-brawling opponent of the SA.
RPO	Radio Observation Post. SD monitoring and deciphering service.
RSHA	Reichssicherheitshauptamt – Supreme State Security Department. Set up in 1939 to supervise the Gestapo, Sipo and SD.
SA	Sturmabteilung – Stormtroopers. The "Brownshirts" led until 1934 by Ernst Röhm.
SAI	Swiss Army Intelligence under Colonel Roger Masson (my own abbreviation).
SD	Sicherheitsdienst – Secret Service. A branch of the SS; the Nazi secret intelligence service set up in 1933 to parallel that of the Abwehr.
SdP	Sudetendeutsche Partei. Sudeten German Party led by Konrad Henlein.
Siguranza	Romanian Security Police.
SIM	*Servizio Italiano Militare* – Italian Military Intelligence Service.
Shoes	Abwehr slang for forged documents.
Schupo	Schutzpolizei – Ordinary German Police.
Sipo	Sicherheitspolizei – Security Police. The sister organization of the Gestapo and SD.
SIS	Secret Intelligence Service. British intelligence service also known as MI6.
SOE	Special Operations Executive. A branch of the SIS known as Section D, but made into its own organization under Sir Hugh Dalton in the summer of 1940.
SPD	Sozialdemokratischen Partei Deutschland – German Social Democratic Party.
Special Branch	A section of Scotland Yard (British Police) that dealt with matters of state security or politically related crime.
SS	Schutz Staffel – Protection Squad. The original title for Hitler's small personal bodyguard led by Heinrich Himmler.
Suréte	French Secret Police.
Tirpitz Ufer	Abwehr GHQ in Berlin at Tirpitz Ufer 76–76 along the Landwehr Canal Embankment.
Treff	Abwehr slang for secret rendezvous by agents or spies.
UPA	Ukrainian Insurgency Army led by Stephan Bandera.
Ustashe	Croat nationalist/fascist movement led by Dr. Ante Pavelic.
Volksdeutsche	Ethnic Germans living outside the Greater German Reich.

Introduction

The Importance of Intelligence

INTELLIGENCE IS AT THE VERY HEART OF WARFARE. To know what the enemy intends to do and how he intends to do it remains the single most valuable commodity for military and political leaders in wartime. It is the duty of intelligence services to obtain this information by any means, fair or foul. The role of espionage operatives in turn is to discover the enemy's dispositions, intentions, strengths and weaknesses, in order to put the armed forces in the best possible position to exploit this intelligence. It would be a mistake to argue, as some idealists and cynics have done, that intelligence is not worth the effort or resources expended on it. As will be shown, these ideas are not only entirely false, but in wartime can prove to be dangerous and potentially catastrophic.

Few intelligence services are as surrounded by myth and lack of understanding as those of Nazi Germany. The German military intelligence service, known by its acronym Abwehr, is shrouded in falsehoods and contradictory facts. This is due in no small part to one figure, who towers above the rest of Germany's spymasters: Admiral Wilhelm Canaris, the head of the Abwehr from January 1935 until March 1944. Canaris began his career as an enthusiastic supporter of Hitler, only to grow disillusioned with the Nazis as World War II progressed. Canaris sought to play the role of loyal spymaster to his Führer, while at the same time trying to maintain a modicum of civilized behaviour towards his enemies and support the dormant but ever-present German opposition movement. It was one of the strange paradoxes of the Third Reich that the very organization that sought to realize Hitler's grandiose ambitions, the Wehrmacht, was also the heart and soul of the opposition against him. No part of the Wehrmacht was more strongly opposed to Hitler's regime, or had more conspirators present in its ranks, than the Abwehr. In the end, Canaris, and most of the men loyal to him, paid with their lives for their opposition to Hitler.

Hitler's Nationalist Socialist revolution did not destroy the traditional pillars of monarchical, conservative Germany after the seizure of power in

BELOW: *The Nazi internal intelligence service in action. The man in the centre in the trilby is a member of the Gestapo, the dreaded state security body.*

1933. This left centres of opposition, including elements of the Wehrmacht and Abwehr, intact and ready to take any opportunity to undermine the Nazis, as evidence of their tyranny grew.

Hitler never entirely trusted his military intelligence service, and sought in this field, as in others, to rule by the disastrous Roman maxim of "divide and rule". The Führer endorsed a young and ruthless intelligence officer from the SS, to form the Nazi's own secret service, the dreaded Sicherheitsdienst (SD). That man was the most feared and ruthless operator in the Third Reich: Reinhard Heydrich, who had begun his career in the German Navy under Canaris but ended up as the admiral's deadliest enemy. By the time of his assassination in May 1942, Heydrich was probably plotting to launch a coup against the Abwehr, an organization he both feared and held in deepest contempt. Under Heydrich, the SD became a sort of dirty tricks department that did all the jobs Hitler wanted done, but which Canaris refused or avoided undertaking.

The SD's operations enjoyed varying degrees of success, though both the SD and Abwehr wasted time and resources intriguing and plotting against each other, which had a very damaging effect on Germany's intelligence performance. When they cooperated, as they did in Holland in 1942 against the British, their combined efforts against the

enemy's agents were most impressive. The overall effect of this secret war between intelligence services, however, meant abject failure in many areas. What triumphs there were during the war, such as the SD-Abwehr success in Holland, Agent "Cicero" in Turkey and Colonel Gehlen's formidable intelligence organization on the Eastern Front, have to be set against equally spectacular failures in other fields.

Hitler's Espionage Machine is above all a story of betrayal, plots, deceit, cowardice, double dealing and treason, but also of enormous heroism, intelligence, shrewdness and cool nerves. If the intelligence war seems comparatively pleasant by comparison to the brutality and violence of the slaughter that took place on the battlefield, it should be remembered that the life expectancy of an agent during World War II was very low. Little mercy was shown to an agent caught by the enemy, and sooner or later most agents were detected. This is their story. The story of Adolf Hitler's network of Nazi spies and agents that operated around the world and spread terror and fear across Europe.

Chapter 1

The Nachrichtendienst (ND)

"Espionage is the world's second oldest profession and just
as honourable as the first"[1]

Michael J.Barrett, Assistant General of the Central Intelligence Agency (CIA)

THE GERMAN INTELLIGENCE SERVICES OF WORLD WAR II were founded upon the intelligence services of the Prussian and Imperial eras. Well before World War I, this service, known as the Geheime Nachrichtendienst (Security Intelligence Service, abbreviated to ND) was a much feared weapon. Prior to 1914, the British worried that the ND had infiltrated their country, and this fear was based on the ND's inflated reputation for omnipotence and efficiency.

Although British concerns were exaggerated, the ND did score some major intelligence coups before and after World War I, but these must be set against some equally spectacular failures. The ND was the forerunner of the Abwehr, whose chief, Admiral Canaris, served as an ND agent.[1]

Humble Beginnings

The roots of the German intelligence services lie with the High Command of the Army (Oberkommando der Heeres or OKH), commonly known as the General Staff, which formed the core of first the Prussian, and then the German intelligence services from the early nineteenth century until the collapsing Nazi state disbanded the Abwehr and OKH in 1944.

LEFT: *General Kurt von Schleicher (left, in uniform) and Count Franz von Papen. Both were predecessors to Hitler as German Chancellor.*

Historically, there was no special peacetime intelligence branch in the Prussian Army, and the General Staff officers were dubious about the value of intelligence. However, during the 1860s the great German commander, General Count Helmut von Moltke, had no such doubts about military espionage. He made good use of spies during the war of 1866 against Austria, and demanded that the intelligence branch recruit an agent to find out about the Austrian order of battle. Such an agent existed in the shape of a young but disgruntled Austrian officer who resigned his post in 1863, and under cover as a journalist gained entry to the Austrian General Staff. This agent, Baron August von Schluga, turned up in Berlin in April 1866 with the entire Austrian order of battle, profiles of the main commanders and a general outline of the Austrian plans. Moltke defeated the Austrians in a brilliant seven-week campaign that culminated in the legendary Battle of Königsgrätz in July that sealed the Prussian victory.

No small share of Moltke's success was due to Schluga, who remained in Prussian and later Imperial German service as Agent No. 17. As a consequence, Moltke decided to make the intelligence branch a permanent section of the OKH, but it was not until 1889 that it was placed under the control of the Quarter Master General's Department. The service was to be known as Department O.Qu.III, III Oberquartiermeister section, or Department IIIb. It was to be better known as the

ABOVE: *General Count Helmut von Moltke, Prussia's master strategist, owed his victory over the Austrians in 1866 in part to good intelligence, and especially the work of Agent 17.*

Nachrichtendienst (ND), a contraction of its full title, Geheime Nachrichtendienst der Heeres (Army Security Intelligence Service). Before this reorganization, the service had been divided, and German military intelligence continued to be separated into two large sections. These sections reflected Germany's vulnerable geographical situation, numerous potential enemies and the need to plan for a two-front war, problems that were to haunt Germany in both world wars. One section was earmarked to watch developments in the west (primarily France), and the other section the east (exclusively Russia).

Colonel Nicolai's Nachrichtendienst

By smashing Napoleon III's France in 1871, Prussia paved the way for the unification of Germany under her aegis, and the domination of European international politics by Germany's chancellor Otto von Bismarck. During the next three decades there was peace in Europe. When Bismarck was fired in 1890, the new Kaiser, Wilhelm II, replaced him with an army of political place men, with the result that military intelligence suffered. Department IIIb mothballed its main agent in France, No. 17, until he could be of use again. Little did he or his controllers in Berlin realize that it would be more than 40 years before his services were required again. He continued to report to Berlin, but he did not engage in active espionage and only met his controller, for reasons of security, once a year. The ND had no idea whether Schluga lived in Paris or what he did there.

In 1894 France formally allied herself with Imperial Russia, which fed Germany's fear of encirclement. This fear and sense of insecurity benefited the ND immensely, as Department IIIb was expanded to become the largest military intelligence service outside Russia. Special NOs (Nachrichtenoffizier – intelligence officers) were posted to stations in cities close to the threatened western and eastern frontiers. In the west these posts were established in Münster, Koblenz, Metz, Saarbrücken, Karlsruhe and Strasbourg to keep a wary eye on France. In the east, against Imperial Russia, NOs were placed in Königsberg, Allenstein, Danzig, Posen and Breslau; all locations well-situated to spy on Poland and Russia's western marches.

The NOs sent out to spy on Russia and France were quite alone since they were expected to do all the work themselves without proper staff. Officers of the OKH, always mindful of costs, were chary of paying for spies and agents to undertake espionage in what was then only potential enemy territory. The rising international temperature during the late 1890s, however, forced the penny pinching General Staff to pay for an expanded ND. By 1901 the service comprised a large central staff located in Berlin, NO officers on the borders, and 124 paid agents working for posts in Britain, Belgium, Switzerland, Italy, Spain, Luxembourg, Denmark, Sweden and Romania. This was quite an impressive network, and it gave Germany early warning of enemy preparations for war, including plans for mobilization.

The impact of this degree of professionalism should not be exaggerated, since much work was still being undertaken by the German military attachés in legations and embassies scattered across Europe. France proved the hardest intelligence nut to crack since the French viewed Germany as an out-and-out enemy come peace or war. German officers, including the military attaché in Paris, were forbidden, on pain of expulsion, to attend French Army manoeuvres, a legitimate method of picking up military intelligence at the time. This forced military attaché Major Max von Schwartzkoppen, to engage in espionage which exposed him and the embassy to great danger of detection and diplomatic scandal.

Britain's naval power only came under the scrutiny of German military intelligence in 1901, when by reciprocal agreement naval attachés were appointed to London and Berlin. This allowed the German naval attaché to begin collecting information on the Royal Navy. Until then the Imperial Navy's entire stockpile of information on its formidable enemy was gathered from British Parliamentary papers, House of Commons debates and the free British press. Nevertheless, this process needed six naval officers in Berlin to accumulate, sort and analyze the stream of data being sent out. In 1903 the German Admiralty ordered the ND to appoint a naval officer to each major sea port in Britain to spy and make detailed reports to the German naval attaché in London. This move increased the tension in Anglo-German relations and unleashed a wave of spymania first in Britain and later on in Germany, that swept through the two countries, creating intense suspicion and paranoia.

In 1908 German Army manuals still held that intelligence could be efficiently gathered from the observations of officers in the field, while reconnaissance could be left entirely in the hands of the army's 10 cavalry divisions. It was typical of the sort of anachronistic thinking prevalent in all the armies of Europe prior to World War I. Nevertheless, the ND was expanding, and was now organized into divisions: Division 1 (Russia), Division 3 (France and Belgium), Division 9 (Italy), Division 10 (Austria-Hungary), Division 4 (Foreign

BELOW: *One of Krupp's large-calibre siege guns. The ND managed to keep the existence of these weapons secret from the French and Russians before World War I.*

Fortresses), and finally the "Cinderella" of the ND: Division 7 (Technical Developments).

Nicolai and ND Divisions 1 and 3

Russia posed then, as it would later, a formidable intelligence problem for the Germans. The Russian state had the most effective and sinister internal security organization of the time in the *Ochrana*, which was not only effective at hunting down and eliminating terrorist revolutionaries but also in catching foreign spies. The Russians in general, given their expertise and professionalism in the area of espionage and counter-intelligence, were also very aware of security issues. The otherwise indiscreet Imperial Duma (1906–17), the Russian parliament, did not, for example, hold any open debates on defence issues as was the usual procedure in the British parliament. Division 1 was therefore forced to scan the press for reports on defence matters. Fortunately for the Germans, they had a most competent and intelligence-minded military attaché in St. Petersburg, Captain Bernhard von Eggeling, who kept a sharp eye on Russian military affairs. As a result the ND did not rate the Imperial Russian Army very highly and considered it slow, cumbersome and defensive-minded.

Division 1 was headed for much of this pre-war period by Colonel Walter Nicolai who spoke fluent French, Russian and Japanese, which was quite an accomplishment for an officer in the German Army where a smattering of French passed for "language skills". During his time at the staff college (1901–03) Nicolai had been sent on a spying mission to Poland to investigate Russian defences and mobilization capabilities. He spied out the locations and layouts of the Russian border forts of Novo-Georgievsk, Grodno, Kovno and Warsaw. When Nicolai returned to Germany, the General Staff was so impressed with his work that he was promoted to the rank of junior major and put in charge of ND Division 1. Despite the size of the task facing him, Nicolai had only a budget of £15,000 and a full-time staff of four officers. This was a puny force to pit against the largest enemy Germany

Before 1914, Germany left military intelligence gathering to its army officers in the field

faced. The Russian threat, as seen by increasingly concerned observers in Berlin, was growing almost by the day, which forced the ND to revise its hitherto unflattering assessment of the Imperial Russian Army. Not only did this enormous empire have a population twice that of Germany,[3] and an industrial production rate higher than that of the USA, since 1905 it had increased its mobilization rate to such an extent that frontline troops would be assembled and ready to march by the fifth day of the mobilization order. It was also strengthening its border defences with Germany, a move made possible by the French, who had helped the Russian colossus by pouring some 1.2–1.5 billion francs into the building, modernization, extension and double-tracking of Russia's railway system. This added yet another danger to the Germans, namely that the Russians could now reinforce their western borders with some six divisions from Siberia. All these developments exposed Germany to the risk of a prolonged two-front war.

The "Avenger" strikes

Colonel Nicolai was sure that the French and Russian intelligence services were collaborating closely against Germany, and that the French *Deuxiéme Bureau* (General Staff Section II, or French military intelligence) had spies inside the German Army. These spies had provided France, Nicolai believed, with details of the Schlieffen Plan, the German Army's strategic blueprint to win a two-front war. In fact the *Ochrana*, in cooperation with Russian military intelligence, had acquired copies of the Schlieffen Plan. Prior to the outbreak of war, a French intelligence officer, Captain Lambling, had three meetings with a German working for the Russians who called himself "Le Vengeur" (the Avenger). As if his name was not melodramatic enough, the Avenger met Lambling in Paris, Nice and again in Brussels, each time in secluded spots with his entire face bandaged. Whatever Lambling may have thought of this masquerade, the Avenger handed him the entire Schlieffen Plan and details of the deployment, concentration and battle order of

ABOVE: *A new German battle-cruiser is guided out of port prior to World War I. Germany's decision to build a High Seas Fleet increased tension between London and Berlin.*

the Imperial German Army. Lambling found the intelligence most credible and confirmed it through other sources.

The plan and the Avenger's intelligence were passed on to Paris where the GHQ of the French Army, with an inflated reputation for logic and brilliance, dismissed the Schlieffen Plan as unrealistic and decided the Avenger was an ND plant. This rejection of such gems of intelligence emphasizes a number of important points. Firstly, the common failure of the military to make use of the information supplied by their own intelligence services, and their scepticism about intelligence that seems too good to be true. Secondly, with regard to the Schlieffen Plan, it showed clearly that the French maintained a most unhappy record of basing their strategic planning on the experiences of the past. During the war of 1870–71, the Germans had respected Belgian neutrality and invaded France through Alsace-Lorraine. The French High Command banked on the Germans repeating this move in a future war. They countered it by building a formidable line of forts from the Belgian frontier to the Swiss border, deploying their entire frontline strength along the German frontier, and devising Plan XVII to counter any German invasion with an offensive of their own.[4]

With the Schlieffen Plan compromised, what saved Germany from a total intelligence debacle was Nicolai's superb counter-intelligence efforts, keeping the *Deuxiéme Bureau* from guessing what Germany's behind-the-front strengths and weaknesses were. For example, Nicolai and the ND managed to conceal from prying French and Russian eyes the existence of the heavy Krupp railway guns. These played a crucial role in pulverizing the Belgian and French fortress defences in 1914 and came as a nasty surprise to the enemy. Another secret that provided momentum during the autumn offensive in 1914 and almost overwhelmed the French was the German method of deploying her reserve divisions in the frontline. This gave the Germans a formidable advantage both numerically and in the element of surprise. The ND was also aware of the close military cooperation that existed between France, Britain and supposedly neutral Belgium. The Belgians had allowed the French to establish a widespread network of agents in their country. Its purpose, as shown by ND reports, was simple: to spy on Germany.

ND Divisions 9 and 10

Germany's alliance with Austria-Hungary was the pillar of its diplomatic system. But the polyglot and weakened Hapsburg Empire was probably more of a military burden than an asset to Germany. From an intelligence point of view the Austrian secret service did not inspire much confidence either, since the

ABOVE: *The Easter Rising in 1916, a republican insurrection in Ireland against British (these are Irish republican fighters). In an attempt to prevent such uprisings, in the nineteenth century the British had established the Irish Special Branch.*

head of Austrian counter-intelligence, Colonel Redl, was exposed as having been a Russian agent in 1909. At least Austria's commitment to Germany could be relied on. Italy, on the other hand, though officially an ally, was in fact committed to staying out of a war and not siding with Germany. The ND found this out by observing the redeployment of French troops away from the Italian frontier, which could have only one meaning: the Italians had made a deal with Paris not to attack France whilst she was engaged in hostile action against Germany. This had of course been kept from the German politicians and generals.

The organization of the ND and its work against France and Russia reflected Germany's geographic and political position as that of a continental state whose military power was primarily land-based. It should therefore have been the most logical thing for Britain to have been Germany's ally in the latter's struggle with France and Russia, Britain's traditional enemies. The fact that such an alliance did not occur was due to a grave and most costly strategic mistake. At the turn of the twentieth century, Germany sought, eagerly encouraged by

Kaiser Wilhelm II and his aggressively minded Grand Admiral, Count Alfred von Tirpitz,[5] to build the second-largest and most powerful battle fleet in the world: the High Seas Fleet (Hochsee Flotte). This move posed a direct challenge to the global supremacy of the Royal Navy and Britain responded with her own massive shipbuilding programme.

The British convinced themselves that they were under direct threat, and during the years leading up to the war several well-known writers created an atmosphere of fear, suspicion and hostility towards Germany. It was claimed that the Germans, using their sheltered North Sea coast, could attempt an invasion of East Anglia. It was also claimed that before the German troops, transported and protected by the Imperial Navy, descended on England's undefended shores Britain would be undermined from within by an army of collaborators and spies. In 1909, when the British Joint Intelligence Committee met to discuss the establishment of a permanent intelligence service, one of its advocates, Colonel James Edmonds, pointed out that the Germans were formidable spies, since they viewed espionage as a legitimate and integral part of warfare. He attributed Germany's string of victories during the previous century in no small part to her efficient and professional military intelligence services. The absence of such a service in France in the war of 1870–71 had greatly contributed to the French military debacle. Edmonds was convinced that unless a similar military intelligence service, professionally manned and funded, was set up in Britain she would share the fate of France at the hands of the growing threat of Imperial Germany. He also believed there were ND agents all over Britain, each with a district to cover. Under each ND officer were paid German agents and British traitors reporting to the German Embassy in London or directly to the ND in Berlin.[6] Edmonds contrasted the strict control, surveillance and registration of all foreigners in the Reich with the slack or even non-existent control in liberal Britain. The colonel's fears were not without foundation, despite some modern authors' claims to the contrary.[7]

Britain had in fact already taken steps in this regard. Faced with an Irish terrorist threat posed by the Irish Republican Brotherhood (IRB) and other violent nationalist groups, Scotland Yard had set up the Irish Special Branch during the previous century to provide an internal security organization that, on a much smaller scale, resembled the *Ochrana* in Russia. Most Britons would have been outraged at such a comparison, but there were similarities.

Another good reason for creating a new secret service was that Britain's military failures during the Boer War of 1899–1902 were in no small measure due to a decided lack of accurate and timely intelligence.[8] For both political and military reasons therefore there seemed a compelling need to set up a proper intelligence service within a more professional and structured system.

It would be wrong to assume that Britain did not possess something like an intelligence service before 24 July 1909, when both MI5 and the Secret

BELOW: *The newly widened Kiel Canal that enabled German warships to be transferred from the North Sea to the Baltic unhindered. It proved an obvious target of British espionage conducted by MI6 (SIS).*

ABOVE: *During World War I the British interned "enemy aliens" to prevent espionage. Here, a long column of mainly German residents in Britain are conducted under armed guard to prison barges at Southend-on-Sea in 1915.*

Intelligence Service (SIS) were founded. In 1887 the British had created the post of Director of Military Intelligence (DMI) and the more powerful Director of Naval Intelligence (DNI). The Naval Intelligence Division (NID) was the only properly organized secret service that Britain had before 1909. In May 1909, Captain Reginald "Blinker"

Hall organized a most successful "photographic trip" to Kiel conducted by himself and Captain Trench (RN) and Lieutenant Brandon (Royal Marines). A year later Brandon and Trench returned for some spying on the coastal forts on the East Frisian island of Borkum, but the vigilant German police found the two "tourists" just a measure too keen to find out about military objectives. They were both arrested and later sentenced to four years in prison.

While the SIS was to prove a major problem to the ND during World War I, it was Sir Vernon

Kell's Military Organization Section 5 (MO5), responsible for counter-intelligence, that was to prove a major obstacle to German spies in Britain. In the summer of 1910 the British tried to convict Lieutenant Siegfried Helm of spying, but failed. Two years later a German defector named Karl Hentschel volunteered information that led to the apprehension and conviction of a Royal Navy gunner, George Parrott. In 1909 Special Branch had established that the suspected ND "post office" for agents in Britain was run by a London barber named Karl Gustav Ernst, from his shop at 402A Caledonian Road. The Letter Interception Unit (LIU) checked all post, and the identities of the members of the Ernst spy ring were established. This surveillance confirmed MO5's worst fears: the barber shop was indeed the ND's "post office" in Britain, and it was extremely active.

> *The British counter-intelligence service, MO5, was a highly effective obstacle to German spies*

Enemies of the Fatherland, 1914–18

On 28 June 1914, the heir to the throne of Austria-Hungary, Grand Duke Ferdinand, was shot in Sarajevo, the capital of Bosnia-Herçegovina, by a member of the Serbian terrorist and spy organization known as the "Black Hand". A month later World War I erupted. This allowed MO5 to move against German spies and agents in Britain. At the crack of dawn on 4 August 1914, the first operation in the Anglo-German "war of the shadows" began when members of the Special Branch broke down the doors to Ernst's barber shop. Ernst was arrested and during the day some 20 other German spies followed him into prison. Ernst was sentenced to death at the Old Bailey in November 1914. On 5 August, the day after the barber shop raid, the Alien Registration Act came into force. This enabled MO5, with the assistance of Special Branch, to round up about 200 suspected German agents. It also allowed the Home Office to round up and intern 32,000 "enemy aliens" resident in Britain. The British Government was to pursue the same thorough and effective policy in World War II. The internment of enemy aliens has come under severe criticism, but from a counter-intelligence point of view it made sense. It deprived Germany of a pool of possible agents. All aliens, neutral, friendly or enemy, that remained at large had to be registered by the police. British fears of enemy spies lurking in the midst of the foreign-born population were not unfounded, as we have seen.

As the process of alien registration got under way, the General Post Office (GPO) began keeping a vigilant eye on all telegram traffic. One telegram that struck officials as suspicious was from an American, Charles Lody, to a certain Adolf Burchard in Stockholm congratulating him on Germany's military setbacks. The GPO censors kept a watch on all correspondence going to Burchard, while MO5 put Lody under surveillance. Lody, who had arrived in Scotland from America under an American passport, was arrested in early October 1914. He turned out to be Carl Hans Lody, a lieutenant in the German Navy Reserve. Most of his coded reports by telegram to Burchard had been intercepted, all except one telling Burchard of rumours that Russian troops were in Scotland, en route to Belgium, to assist their hard-pressed allies on the crumbling Western Front.[9] Not surprisingly Lody was found guilty of espionage and on 6 November 1914 he was stood against a wall in the Tower of London and shot. He was shot, rather than hanged, because he had acted out of patriotism and was a serving German officer, and was therefore spared the humiliation of being hanged like a common criminal. Whether Lody appreciated this gentlemanly gesture the story does not tell.

Those who criticize the conduct of the British authorities towards their resident foreigners should keep in mind that Germany did exactly the same with their foreign guests who were, without ceremony, thrown into prisons or temporary holding camps.

The Germans, reacting to British Germanophobia, in turn were gripped by spy fever from 1912. French, Russian and British visitors, journalists, businessmen and tourists were treated with scant respect since they were viewed, even by the general public, as potential spies and enemy agents. ND counter-intelligence, in close collaboration with the Imperial Police, kept a sharp lookout for anything suspicious. During the war some 235 British agents were found and imprisoned for spying inside Germany; of these only three were actually British, one was Peruvian but 46 were in fact, surprisingly enough, French.

"Ostfront": On the Eastern Front

Colonel Nicolai made good use of what the Germans called Spannungsreisende or "observer-travellers" who were civilians, volunteers, tourists, reserve officers (like Lody), and businessmen who were in enemy territory when the war broke out. One such Spannungsreisende was a representative of the Pyrene Company, an American businessman, Wilbert E. Stratton, who was travelling in Russia during the summer of 1914. On his way back to St. Petersburg Stratton noticed trains filled with Russian troops moving towards the East Prussian border. He got to a telegraph station and sent back reports to Berlin of his observations. Stratton continued to serve the ND as a valued agent in Stockholm and St. Petersburg, but he refused to risk an assignment in Britain. Even if the ND had scored a major point with Stratton this was cancelled out, as Nicolai pointed out to his ND subordinates, by the fact that the *Ochrana* and Russian intelligence services probably knew more about Germany's eastern frontier lands than the Germans did themselves.

There was only a single army to defend the whole Eastern Front, the Eighth Army under Generals Hindenburg and Ludendorff. If this army was to have any chance of stopping the Russian offensive into Eastern Prussia then the two commanders needed accurate intelligence. Thanks to the development of the wireless for military communications just before the war, the Germans were able to score a major success by tapping into this rich source of information. The Eighth Army had a diligent and well-trained radio staff that monitored Russian wireless communications, and these intercepts revealed, in detail, every move the Russians made. General Samsonov's Second Army was destroyed at the

Battle of Tannenberg at the end of August, while the First Army, under General Pavel von Rennenkampf, was badly mauled before it was pulled back across the frontier in mid-September. Infuriated nationalists in Russia suspected treason (rather than lax radio procedures or incompetence), and hanged Rennenkampf in effigy, calling him "rehnen-ohne-kampf" – "ran without a fight". Russia's German community, which was even larger and more well-established than Britain's, also became the scapegoat of nationalist and xenophobic mobs and the target of official

LEFT AND ABOVE: *Mata Hari, a femme fatale who proved an irresistible symbol of the eternal allure of the female spy. In reality she was a clumsy real-life German spy who paid with her life for dabbling as a double agent. She faced a firing squad in October 1917 in the Bois de Vincennes.*

retribution from the state authorities, including the police and secret services.

The Western Front

The Schlieffen Plan called for a massive sweep through Belgium to avoid the French forts and installations along the border with Germany, so as to take Paris in a giant scythe-like move. As a result the British were forced to evacuate their NID station in Brussels at 7 Rue Gachard as the Germans advanced and occupied the city. In one move the entire British intelligence network in western Europe had been disrupted. SIS chief Admiral Mansfield Smith-Cumming,[10] the legendary "C", was forced from late 1914 to rebuild his networks using neutral Holland as a base from where 300 agents worked under the control of four departments. Most of his agents were Dutch and slipped, undetected to begin with, across the frontier into occupied Belgium. To stop this infiltration, the ND set up its major station on the Western Front at Antwerp in Belgium, under a female spymaster, "Fräulein Doktor", Dr. Elsbeth Schragmüller. The Antwerp station became the most effective of Nicolai's ND networks in the West, and controlled 62 out of a total of 337 agents.

No spy of any time or epoch has achieved the fame or infamy as that of the tragic figure of Mata Hari, Germany's "master spy" of World War I, who was shot by the French in October 1917. The French prosecutors, at her trial a few months earlier, had claimed this amoral and infamous beauty had won the confidence and favours of some of France's top generals and politicians in order to betray their secrets to the enemy. By having Mata Hari executed the French believed that they had eliminated one of the most dangerous and proficient spies operating inside their country.

The truth behind the legend of Mata Hari is far more mundane and tragic. Mata Hari was in fact a Dutch woman, Gertrude Zelle, who had acquired her exotic stage name of Mata Hari during a six-year sojourn with her estranged husband on Java, in what is now Indonesia. She arrived in Paris, with her daughter in tow, in 1905 and took the city by storm with her erotic dancing act and her after-stage "services" for discerning, rich gentlemen. There are doubts whether this dancer/prostitute really was a spy. Colonel Gempp, head of the post-war successor to the ND, the Abwehr, was certain that Mata Hari was quite innocent of being anyone's spy, least of all Germany's.

In fact Gertrude had loyalty to only three loves in her otherwise unhappy and sordid life: her daughter, her young Russian lover, and, finally, her adopted country, France. Gertrude wished to serve France as an agent, but as a Dutch neutral the *Deuxiéme Bureau* did not deem her reliable enough. Gertrude therefore set out to prove herself by her own means. In early 1916, she allowed herself to be recruited by the ND chief in

Cologne, Baron von Mirbach. Mirbach passed her on for initial training to Captain Rössler of the Düsseldorf ND. Designated agent H-21, Gertrude was passed on for intensive training under Herr Habersack of the Antwerp ND.

With her training completed Gertrude was sent to Madrid, the capital of Spain, a key neutral in World War I. Its minerals and metals were essential for the production of arms on both sides, and its ports were needed by Germany to conduct its U-boat campaign against the Allies in the Mediterranean. Madrid, like Berne in Switzerland and other neutral European cities, became one of the spy centres of Europe.

Into the Lion's Den

Into this hotbed of intrigue stepped the rather naïve and inexperienced Gertrude, who set out to conquer the bed and mind of Madrid's German military attaché, Hans von Kalle, thinking he would provide intelligence that she could then pass on to the French. However, Kalle saw through her game from the start. He was neither charmed by her fading beauty, nor convinced she was serving only Germany. He wrote an open letter to Berlin, knowing it would pass through the hands of the French censors and be read by the French Security Police. He wrote that agent H-21 would soon be arriving in Paris and the French promptly put two and two together.

As she stepped off the train from Madrid, in Paris, Gertrude was arrested by agents of the French *Surité*, who refused to believe her story of wanting to serve France as a double agent. She was put on trial on 24 July 1917, and despite her protests of innocence and a singular lack of hard evidence on the part of the prosecution, was sentenced to death for espionage. On a grey morning in October that same year Mata Hari met her fate at the hands of a French firing squad in the Bois de Vincennes outside Paris.[11]

A secret war was also conducted behind the German trench lines on the Western Front. Despite early difficulties between SIS and the Belgians, the British established a fully functioning agent network in Belgium and northern France. They sent questionnaires across the lines fastened to balloons, a simple but effective method of intelligence gathering.[12] The Allies established the so-called "railroad transport groups" that kept an eye on German troop movements. One such network, "Frankignoul", was broken when the ND grew suspicious of certain activities along the line between Belgian Lanaeken into Dutch Maastricht and German-occupied territory.

Infiltrating the POW Camps

The Germans were also adept at infiltrating resistance groups in the occupied territories with double agents and informers. They also managed to infiltrate the ranks of the prisoners of war (POWs) with English-speaking ND agents. One such agent pretended to be an escaped British POW and gained access to a prisoner rescue network run by a British nurse, Edith Cavell, and her Belgian deputy, Philippe Baucq. The ND did not hesitate to strike and the two were sentenced to death by a German military court. Both were shot on 10 October 1915. The British press whipped up the public into a frenzy of hatred for the "bloody Krauts" and the even bloodier Kaiser. It was a public relations disaster of the first order for the already deeply hated Germans and their feared Secret Service.

The Germans were active, in some cases pioneering, in other intelligence fields. A number of new inventions proved interesting tools for the ND. After the success of the Eastern Front campaign in 1917, the Germans set up, under 32-year-old Captain Ludwig Voit, not only a GHQ (West) Radio Station but also a Cryptanalytic Station West within it. The results were quite good since both the British and the French, having learnt nothing from their Russian allies about poor radio procedures, were indiscreet and very informative about their movements, deployments and plans. Unfortunately for the Germans, the French and British were better at deciphering coded transmissions, and the legendary Room 40 at the

Despite the allure and glamour of Mata Hari, she was in reality a rather tragic figure

British Admiralty proved adept at breaking German codes. The Germans hit back by attacking the Allied use of field telephones. Otto Arendt, a 32-year-old telegraph inspector, invented a clever listening device that picked up and amplified the telephones' returning earth currents. This enabled the Germans to listen into the Allied field telephones By 1918 the Germans had 292 such devices in operation along the Western Front.

Intelligence gathered by these methods was put to good use by the Fremdes Heeres Abteilung (Foreign Armies Department – FHA) under Major von Rauch. The Germans predicted the British Somme offensive of 1916 through surveillance of British field telephone lines, the interrogation of captured prisoners and the use of aerial reconnaissance.

So, in addition to the ND, the frontline commands in the West and East had their own Intelligence Branches. Furthermore, the German Navy had its intelligence service similar to the NID. Its headquarters was at Neumünster and was headed by Lieutenant Martin Braune with almost 500 officers and a large staff. Braune also set up some 24 listening posts along the German North Sea coast.

ABOVE: *Vessels of Germany's ultimate weapon of deterrence and threat: its powerful Imperial High Seas Fleet. There were intelligence officers on board every German warship during World War I.*

There were also intelligence officers aboard each and every German warship. It was the combination of these factors that kept the German High Seas Fleet informed of the British Grand Fleet's movements during the Battle of Jutland in 1916.

One cannot simply say that the ND was a success or a failure. It succeeded well in some parts but failed in others. On the whole Nicolai could be proud of his own and his service's record before and during World War I. After all, the Abwehr tried to imitate the earlier élan and style of the ND with varying results. German intelligence, although its efforts did not lead to victory for Germany in 1914–18, learned valuable lessons that were put to good use in the future. The pity was that Nicolai was not to see the new service in action, especially as it was his service upon which the Abwehr was built. He fell foul of the Nazis and ended up as one of their many victims when they achieved power in Germany.

Chapter 2

Preparations for War

"An American joke has it that there are only three alternatives for a middle-age man: get a mistress, buy a red sports car or become a spy. Every time one sees such a man drive down the road in a bright red sports car one should be thankful he is trying to kill himself in style rather than trying to commit adultery or treason"[1]

AFTER IMPERIAL GERMANY'S DEFEAT IN 1918 AND THE END OF THE SECOND REICH, the Weimar Republic that was founded on the ruins wanted to make a break with the past. A new Germany needed a new intelligence service not devoted to being a tool of an openly aggressive state. Instead it was to be one that concentrated on counter-intelligence, and as far as was practical was not to engage in active espionage. On 21 January 1921 the German military intelligence service was officially reborn as the Abwehr[2] under the leadership of Colonel Gempp. The colonel was an old ND hand who had been trained by Nicolai personally, and was the right man for the job. But compared to the wartime ND, the new intelligence service was tiny with only three General Staff officers, six other officers, and a small clerical staff working in its HQ offices. The Abwehr also had an officer in each of the seven military districts that covered Germany. The new service was so poorly equipped that it had no radios, no document-producing workshop (in other words a forgers' department) nor any of the other resources a proper intelligence agency needed in order to function. In 1933 Gempp was replaced by Captain

LEFT: *A German military column enters the Sudetenland German city of Friedenland on 3 October 1938 to an enthusiastic welcome from the local populace.*

Conrad Patzig from the German Navy, who was not enamoured with his new task at all. He got the job because the Abwehr was so unimportant and, from a career point of view such a dead-end, that no German Army officer wanted it. The navy, almost by default, thus came to head the Abwehr.

Patzig was a blunt, no-nonsense officer who was a non-political naval professional at heart, and way out of his depth heading a military intelligence service. He openly showed his detestation of the Nazis, their leader and their methods, which did not bode well for the service's cooperation with the Nazi authorities. Ethical and honest, Patzig constantly clashed with Heinrich Himmler, the Reichsführer-SS and head of the Gestapo, and his deputy Reinhard Heydrich. They complained about Patzig first to Hitler and then to General Blomberg, head of the army. Blomberg yielded to pressure and fired Patzig. But who was to replace him? Grand Admiral Raeder, head of the German Navy (Kriegsmarine), was determined to keep the Abwehr in the navy's sphere of influence. His problem was finding the right candidate. Few young officers wanted the post; and in addition whoever was chosen had to be someone with an intelligence background. Raeder, however, found his man in Captain Wilhelm Franz Canaris, who was due to retire from the navy and had been appointed to command the naval fortress of

at such arrogance and told Canaris: "If that is what you think, Captain Canaris, then I am sorry to say that this day is the beginning of your end."[3] Unfortunately for Canaris, Patzig's gloomy prediction would prove chillingly accurate.

Secret Headquarters

Patzig then continued his tour. The Abwehr's headquarters were not particularly impressive by the standards of the Third Reich. They were made up of two town houses on the Tirpitz embankment, or the Tirpitz Ufer Nos. 76–78, by the Landwehr canal in central Berlin. These quarters were quite cramped and likened to a warren, with dark corridors and small offices. But the houses served well as the inconspicuous headquarters of a secret service. Furthermore, the Abwehr HQ was connected with the General Staff building on the Bendlerstrasse around the corner. So if an Abwehr official wanted a meeting with OKH, this was possible without having to leave the building and be seen in the street. It was an open secret that foreign agents, especially French and Polish, loitered on the Bendlerstrasse to keep an eye on who entered or left the building. These "loiterers with intent" would also try to eavesdrop on conversations. The precaution of keeping quiet during walks around this quarter was both necessary and justified. Canaris installed himself in a small and poorly decorated office in the building. It contained his old desk and a filing cabinet and would later include two paintings. One was a signed portrait of General Franco and the other was that of a Japanese demon, a gift from the Japanese ambassador in Berlin, Baron Oshima.[4]

That was the Abwehr's famous headquarters, but what of the men who served inside the building and the Abwehr's various sections? Section I (Abwehr I), headed by Colonel Piekenbrock, ran a huge espionage network in the Low Countries, France, Austria, Poland and Czechoslovakia not only to acquire intelligence, but also to make contact and promote pro-German elements within

Swinemünde. When Raeder asked him to head the Abwehr the still ambitious and active Canaris jumped at the proposal. He sped to Berlin to take charge, and turned up at the snowbound Abwehr headquarters at Tirpitz Ufer on 1 January 1935, which meant summoning Patzig back from what was an official holiday. Patzig turned up at 10:00 hours and showed the new intelligence chief around. They ended up in Patzig's office for a chat, Patzig pointing out the mess that Canaris was getting himself into, especially on account of Himmler and Heydrich. Canaris, exuding supreme if misplaced self-confidence, replied with a faint smile on his lips: "I'm an incurable optimist. And as far as those fellows are concerned, I think I know how to get along with them." Patzig stiffened

those countries. The largest and most active department during the coming war was Abwehr II which was charged with "special duties", such as commando raids and sabotage. This was headed from early 1938 by Colonel Erwin von Lahousen, an Austrian intelligence officer with the Bundesheer (the Austrian Army). Then there was Major-General von Betivegni's counter-intelligence section (Abwehr III), which was to prove an extremely effective part of the service. It had subsections specializing in disinformation, such as Abwehr IIID, aimed at confusing the enemy. There was also Abwehr IIIF that sought to infiltrate its agents into foreign intelligence services, and was also charged with the main task of counter-intelligence. In 1942 IIIF was to play a major role in unearthing and crushing the "Red Orchestra" of Soviet spies operating in the heart of Berlin and Western Europe. The administration of the Abwehr, or Z Section, was housed on the top floor of the Tirpitz Ufer and was headed by Colonel Hans Oster. He was an extrovert and committed anti-Nazi, who did not hide his feelings about Hitler and his crew of misfits. Oster took it upon

himself, with and without Canaris' permission, to keep the British and French intelligence services up to date with what "Emil" (one of Hitler's many nicknames) was up to.

Hitler's Own Secret Services

It is rarely understood that Hitler was a revolutionary at heart, and that he never liked or trusted the German High Command or its representatives. In order to provide himself with an alternative source of intelligence to that of the Abwehr, the Führer turned to his trusted "black guard", the SS (Schutz Staffel – defence unit), for assistance. The security and intelligence service of the SS, the Sicherheitsdienst (Security Service) or SD, was set up before Hitler came to power, and from 1931 was run by Reinhard Heydrich. After Hitler became chancellor in 1933, the SD became part of the Sipo, or Sicherheitspolizei (Security Police), which cooperated with the feared Geheime

BELOW: *Abwehr headquarters in Berlin, located at 76–78 Tirpitz Ufer on the pleasant Landwehr canal in central Berlin, just around the corner from the Bendlerstrasse.*

Staatspolizei (Secret State Police), better known as the Gestapo.

These three organizations were part of Himmler's three-headed monster of a secret service that was to strike fear not only into the German people but every other nation in Europe that had the misfortune to fall under the heel of the Nazi boot. The symbiosis between the Gestapo and the SD was seen in the location of their respective offices. It was an open secret that the Gestapo's HQ was housed at No. 8 Prinz Albrecht Strasse. To threaten a Berliner or a German with a trip to that notorious address was taken very seriously and could make even the toughest of men lose their nerve. Less well-known was the fact that Heydrich's SD headquarters backed on to those of the Gestapo in the Hohenzollern Palace of 102 Wilhelmstrasse. Heydrich recruited his staff from the ranks of the Orpo (Ordnungspolizei – Order Police: the regular police force of the Third Reich) and the Kripo (Kriminalpolizei – Criminal Police).

The SD's Responsibilities

The SD was divided into two broad areas of responsibility: Office I (Inland) cooperated closely with the Gestapo in keeping a watch on those groups the Nazi regime particularly loathed, such as Jews, socialists, freemasons, communists, committed Christians, conservatives and anyone even remotely connected with them. Office I, Section II dealt with Jews, which paralleled the work and investigations of Gestapo Department IIB. Similar sections existed for each of the other groups. On the domestic scene the SD agents' reports were heavily supplemented by voluntary denunciations from the general public.

As Hitler began to expand the Third Reich into Central Europe, it became important to compile lists of German exiles resident in Austria and Czechoslovakia where many of them had taken refuge. SD Office II (Ausland) was responsible for espionage abroad, mainly in the neighbouring states on Germany's borders. It was charged with sabotage, subversion, espionage and, on certain occasions, assassination. SD Ausland was supposed to work in collaboration with the Abwehr, but these two organizations were in fact bitter rivals. Furthermore, Canaris refused to use his agents for some of the tasks that the SD undertook, and he was especially opposed to the assassination of German political exiles. An additional office was set up, SD Office III, to compile lists of enemies of Germany abroad who were to be arrested or liquidated by the SS after the conquest or annexation of that country.

The SD and the Gestapo: Partners in Crime

The SD-Gestapo nexus penetrated every aspect of private and public life in Germany, creating an oppressive atmosphere of fear, suspicion and terror. In 1936 the SS, which had been granted sweeping powers in 1933 after Hitler's declaration of a state of emergency, was given even more authority over internal security and became in effect an organization above the law. The police force was divided into the civilian Orpo and the security Sipo, of which the Kripo, SD and Gestapo were all a part. When the Reichssicherheitshauptamt (RSHA – Reich Security Main Office) was created in 1939, the police were no longer formally under the civilian Ministry of Interior but placed under the SS and the

ABOVE: *The dreaded Gestapo was ever-present in Nazi Germany. Here, a group of suspects are about to be carried off to the local Gestapo HQ for questioning.*

RSHA. This reorganization made Himmler one of the most powerful men in Germany.

Heading the Gestapo was SS General Heinrich Müller, better known as "Gestapo Muller", who had not been a Nazi before 1933 and whose sympathies were more with the communists. After Hitler's ascendancy to power Müller quickly switched allegiance but continued to have an abiding admiration for the Communists, the Gulag[5] Stalin personally and his secret police, the feared NKVD.[6] Müller tried to model the Gestapo on the NKVD, and with the establishment of torture chambers, agent networks, informers and a vast prison system he achieved his goal. Unlike the SD, the Gestapo was only concerned with domestic counter-intelligence and the destruction of enemies within. As Hitler conquered more and more of Europe, however, the role of the Gestapo, like that of the SS, expanded massively, to keep in step with that territorial expansion. By 1944 Müller headed an organization with 40,000 agents and full-time staff that was organized into two dozen different sections, and was represented in every occupied and neutral country in Europe.

Although the Gestapo was a sinister organization, neither the SD or the Abwehr could have done their counter-intelligence work without it. The Gestapo men became, even more so than the members of the SS, the most feared and loathed henchmen of the Nazi regime in occupied Europe.

The Red Menace

Hitler had come to power partly due to his strong rhetoric about the threat the communists posed to the fabric of life in Germany. After the Nazis took control, therefore, a priority for the Gestapo, in cooperation with the SD, was to crush the huge German Communist Party (KPD) led by Ernst Thälmann. The KPD was the largest communist party outside the USSR, and Berlin was the centre of Soviet espionage in Europe. After February 1933 Soviet operations were moved to Amsterdam, Prague and Paris. Meanwhile, the Gestapo and SD set about demolishing the communist underground. Although a huge number of communists were apprehended and put into custody in the growing numbers of concentration camps that were being built, the KPD's network was never exterminated. Beneath the surface it continued to offer the regime continuous and sometimes fierce resistance. Most communists, however, chose to abandon their Marxist version of socialism for Hitler's more nationalist one. Many Nazis post-1933 were old Red Front (RKF) fighters, or members of the KPD. As long as they showed the right amount of loyalty they were not questioned about their past. In the light of events revealed later, the Gestapo and SD should have delved deeper into the past of some Nazis and critically questioned where these Red Nazis' real

BELOW: *The remains of the offices and headquarters of the feared RSHA in Berlin. The photo was taken in mid-1945 after Nazi Germany's defeat.*

allegiances lay.[7] The truth is that Nazi Germany was riddled with communists and their sympathizers. These sympathizers proved willing and able to assist Moscow in its intelligence war with Germany; a war where the Soviets proved to be far more able and professional than their German counterparts.

An Uneasy Partnership

During the 1920s, both the USSR and the Weimar Republic, successor regimes to empires that had been defeated in World War I, were regarded with suspicion by other European states. In 1922 they acknowledged their mutual status by signing the Treaty of Rapallo, in which each side renounced any territorial or financial claims against the other, and agreed to closer military and technical cooperation. This meant Germany could develop its arms and military equipment with the help of the Soviets, while the USSR, starved of investment and Western technology, got both from German sources. In return the Soviet armed forces were given access to German military professionalism while the Weimar government, which was dominated by socialists for much of the republic's brief life, tolerated the Soviet intelligence service's use of its territory to spy on Poland, France and the surrounding countries. Students, businessmen, advisers, consultants and German diplomats were given unusually open access to travel in the USSR which was denied to other foreigners. This proved to be an invaluable source of intelligence for the German authorities. Both sides tolerated one another's activities, but only up to a certain limit, which if crossed brought swift retribution. When Soviet agents collaborated with the KPD to try to overthrow the German Government they were apprehended and deported. Similarly, some German "tourists" or "students" caught snooping in Russia in 1932 were severely punished by the Soviet authorities.

The strange partnership of Germany and the USSR survived the coming to power of Hitler, at least in the field of intelligence. In February 1933, less than a month after Hitler became chancellor, a mysterious fire took place in the Reichstag. The arsonist was a lone Dutch communist, Marius van der Lubbe, who had acted on his own initiative. The German police arrested three Bulgarian officials from the *Comintern* (Communist International), the organization tasked with spreading communism around the world. They included Gregori Dimitrov, later head of the *Comintern,* and one of Stalin's most trusted associates. The Bulgarian officials were carrying false papers and had made no attempt to hide their presence in Berlin. They were accused at their trial of directing Lubbe and his assumed accomplices in burning down the Reichstag. To the surprise of the world the three Bulgarians were acquitted and never during the trial feared for their lives. They were deported from Germany and given a hero's welcome in the USSR.[8] This suited Hitler, since he was not after the blood of these communists but wanted only an excuse to crush the KPD and introduce emergency powers. By March 1933 political opposition to the NSDAP (National-sozialistische Deutsche Arbeiterpartei – National Socialist German Workers' Party, better known as the Nazis) had been banned and the the life of the constitutional Weimar Republic was over. Stalin had helped Hitler secure power by sending him subsidies to aid the Nazi efforts. This was done in the hope that Hitler would prove to be an opponent of Britain and France. Similarly Stalin ordered Ernst Thälmann and the KPD not to cooperate with the Social Democrats (SPD) against the Nazis, thereby giving Hitler one less rival to worry about.

In June 1934, Ernst Röhm and his SA followers were purged with brutal ferocity

Ernst Röhm

The secret collaboration did not end there. Some of the main obstacles to Stalin's aim of reviving the old Soviet-German Rapallo pact were the right-wing elements that opposed Hitler's rule. These included one of Hitler's most senior supporters, Ernst Röhm, the commander of the one-million-strong SA (Sturmabteilung), also known as the Brownshirts. Röhm was a genuine Nazi radical who wanted a real social revolution in Germany. This made Röhm an opponent of the German Army, since he wanted to replace it with an armed and militarized version of the SA. Röhm was also hated by many industrialists and right-wing conservatives who gave their grudging support to Hitler, because Röhm wanted to nationalize German industry and much of the privately owned economy. In addition, several Nazi leaders (including Göring, Göbbels and Himmler) wanted him removed as an obstacle to their own power and influence. The Soviets also wanted Röhm out of the way because the SA leader favoured an alliance with France rather than the USSR.

"Night of the Long Knives"

Rumours that Röhm was preparing a coup were circulated and believed. These stories were probably the work of the Soviet intelligence services. Hitler decided to act, and act with violence. On 30 June 1934 Röhm, his senior SA staff and hundreds of other opponents of the regime were rounded up and shot by the SS and army in a series of killings that became known as the "Night of the Long Knives." A shared obstacle and threat had been removed forever. The only place abroad where the Röhm Purge was greeted with approval was the Kremlin, where Stalin believed that the suppression of the SA signalled that Hitler was now master in his own house, which made him a more useful ally for the USSR.

In 1937 it was Hitler's turn to repay Stalin's favour by letting the SD take part in Stalin's plot against the Soviet Red Army. In early 1937, a report from a White Russian émigré based in Paris named Skoblin reached Heydrich suggesting Marshal Mikhail Tukhachevsky was plotting to overthrow Stalin. Heydrich believed the report to be genuine and brought it to Hitler's attention. Hitler agreed with Heydrich's analysis, and chose to back Stalin against Tukhachevsky. He kept the whole matter secret from his own generals, whom he suspected of maintaining contact with high-ranking Red Army officers. Heydrich ordered two SD squads to break into Tirpitz Ufer and Bendlerstrasse where they gathered documents to incriminate the Red Army generals. In Prague, SS-Standartenführer Böhme

destroying the British Empire which he admired so deeply. His ambitions in territorial terms lay in Central and Eastern Europe and not in the West, and especially not at the expense of Britain's colonies. He hoped that the diplomat Joachim von Ribbentrop would be able to steer the British and their pro-German future king, Edward, Prince of Wales, towards an alliance. But Ribbentrop was a disaster as Germany's Ambassador in London. He was loud, boorish, humourless and fanatical in his views, which did nothing to endear him to his hosts. The British Foreign Office (FO) began shortly after his first diplomatic gaffes to refer to him as "von Brickendrop" for his uncouth and undiplomatic conduct. In turn Ribbentrop returned to Berlin a bitter Anglophobe.

German Agents in Britain

Meanwhile in London, both the German Embassy and the local Auslands Organisation (AO) office became active centres of espionage and even knew where the Ministry of Information was located, despite the fact that was this was supposed to be a secret. But how could it be when even the GPO used to call the German Embassy to find out addresses of British organizations no-one had heard of!

The reason why German espionage services were so well established in Britain before 1939, was that Germans had agents working in the country even before Hitler came to power. In 1932 the LIU opened a suspicious-looking letter to an officer cadet serving at the Royal Military Academy at Sandhurst by the name of Lieutenant Norman Baillie-Stewart. The letter sent from Berlin contained £50 and a note from a supposed sweetheart in Germany. More letters with money arrived from Germany, and in January 1933 Baillie-Stewart was confronted with this evidence by MI5. He was accused of travelling to the Netherlands to hand over information on British tanks and arms to his Abwehr employers. Baillie-Stewart denied the charge but was court-martialled, cashiered and given a five-year sentence for espionage. The British were shocked that a young officer could betray his country. But there were others. German agents in Britain posed as journalists or officials of semi-governmental organizations. Max Knight

ABOVE: *The publicity shy head of the Gestapo: Heinz Müller. An admirer of the NKVD, he modelled his own fearsome police force on that dreaded Soviet organization.*

handed the documents via Czech middlemen to President Benes of Czechoslovakia, who passed on the intelligence to his ally Stalin. A Soviet courier arrived in Prague to pick up the documents, which were in Moscow by May. Tukhachevsky was arrested on 4 June; he and several other officers were tried *in absentia* on 11 June 1937. They were shortly thereafter shot. This set off Stalin's huge folly, the murder of 40,000 officers that left his armed forces leaderless and in a complete shambles. The plot was Soviet but Heydrich had played his role to perfection.

Although Hitler kept his options open as to who he would make his ally, one of his preferred choices was Britain. After all, he did not see the sense in

headed a special section of MI5 simply to watch these spies, and in May 1939 Sir Samuel Hoare, the Home Secretary, expelled six prominent German journalists on suspicion of spying.

In 1935 a landlady in Broadstairs, Kent, reported that a continental guest had left an unpaid bill and the police came to investigate. The gentleman had left papers and documents behind which seemed quite suspect to the police. Special Branch and an MI5 officer, Edward Hinchley-Cooke, turned up and found maps, diagrams and an assortment of documents about the Royal Air Force (RAF) and its airfields in southern England. The guest was Dr. Hermann Görtz who had been a member of the Abwehr since 1931, and had been given the task of spying on Britain's airfields. He was accompanied by his "niece", Marianne, who was his helper and secretary. On 8 November 1935 Görtz returned to Harwich, Essex, where he was promptly arrested and taken to Broadstairs. He claimed that it was all a misunderstanding about the bill, and as for the documents, the wily Görtz explained, these were for a novel he was writing. The judge at the Old Bailey did not believe him and in March 1936 Görtz was sentenced to three years in prison.

A Dangerous Enemy to Underestimate

One German spy who would never have left unpaid bills was Baron Robert Treeck[9] and his Chilean-German mistress, Baroness Violetta von Schröders, who arrived in Britain in early 1936. The wealthy German rented two country houses and a town house at 12 Cheyne Walk in the heart of London's political establishment. One of his country properties was Luckington Manor, which was close to the estate of Sir Stewart Menzies. This gave the baron access to the exclusive Beaufort Hunt, an event patronized by none other than his Highness the Prince of Wales. Menzies believed that Treeck was an Abwehr agent sent to Britain to keep in touch with and influence the prince in Germany's favour.

On 20 January 1936, King George V died, and one of the first to congratulate Edward on becoming king was Hitler's personal emissary the Duke of Coburg. Edward VIII proved a valuable asset to Germany during the ensuing Rhineland Crisis of March 1936, when the king, quite unconstitutionally, intervened with the government to prevent Britain from supporting France. He even phoned the German Ambassador, Leopold von Hösch, to tell the diplomat he was strongly opposed to any British interference in German affairs. When Hösch died unexpectedly, Mrs Wallace Simpson, Edward's future wife, influenced the king to ask for her friend Ribbentrop, who left Berlin in October 1936. However, by December the king had abdicated, and with his departure a strong advocate for the appeasement of Hitler was gone. But Hitler did not lay to rest his ambition to use Edward for his own ends.

RIGHT: *The convenient Reichstag fire in February 1933 was blamed on the communists by the Nazis, and by the communists on SS-controlled arsonists.*

ABOVE: *Ribbentrop the diplomat in Britain. He is seen here on 30 October 1936 in diplomatic top hat and white gloves, having had an audience with King Edward VIII.*

Like Britain, Poland became the target of Nazi espionage operations prior to World War II. The Poles, however, were not passive victims in this field: "The Poles, in the realm of intelligence work, are the most gifted people in the world, and what the Polish Intelligence Service had accomplished became clear to the Germans when Warsaw was taken."[10]

Germany and Poland have a most complex and troubled recent history of relations, not least in the twentieth century. Poland's recreation as a sovereign state in 1918 was a shock to the Germans and its territorial expansion at Germany's expense rankled.[11] The Abwehr of the Weimar Republic, with its limited resources, gave the lion's share of its attentions to this new threat on Germany's eastern frontier. As the

Polish press was quite secretive and yielded only small amounts of intelligence, the Abwehr used travelling Germans or Poles willing to spy for money to keep it informed, or simply used volunteer agents who proffered their intelligence for a symbolic sum.

The Polish Intelligence Service (PIS),[12] also known as Section II of the Polish General Staff, was probably the most talented and most dangerous adversary that the Abwehr faced beside the Soviet GRU and the NKVD. It was led by military men whose careers before and after Poland's independence had been spent in clandestine operations or intelligence work. Unlike their German colleagues they were steeped in a culture of secrecy, since they had been hunted for years by the imperial secret services of both Russia and Germany. That they had survived was testimony to their skill and professionalism in the arts of the "secret game", and no-one was more skilled at the game than Major Zychon. He was the head of the PIS main post in Bydgoszcz (Bromberg) in western Poland. Bureau Zychon, as it was called, was charged with espionage against Germany that Zychon undertook in person or through his 11 substations situated along the long German frontier. Zychon was Germany's most dangerous PIS adversary. Through his main station and substations Zychon ran a remarkable network of agents that penetrated into the very heart of the German state. In Danzig (Gdansk) one of his agents, Madame Shebinska, received intelligence about sensitive Abwehr operations through normal social contacts with Abwehr officers stationed in the international port. This gave the PIS a remarkable ability to block or sabotage almost every operation launched against Poland.

Count Jurek Sosnowski

Zychon had working for him the most spectacular foreign spy to work in pre-war Germany. Count Jurek Sosnowski was stylishly handsome, dashing in the way only a Polish aristocrat could be, very rich and had a lavishly decorated flat in central Berlin. He posed as a disaffected Polish officer who had left his country to escape persecution. In reality Sosnowski was working for the PIS and Zychon. For reasons of combining business with pleasure, Sosnowski conducted a series of affairs with women in high

social positions. This gave him access to the most important circles in Nazi Germany and intelligence of every kind, much of it gained through indiscreet pillow talk. Considering the sensitivity of the information they carried in their heads, and the nature of the paranoid regime which they served, it is remarkable that these Germans were so disastrously open and indiscreet with their secrets.

Sosnowski soon had an entire harem of enraptured German women providing him with intelligence, but when he met Baroness von Berg, who was married as Frau von Falkenhayn, he found a partner in passion and espionage that matched his own talents. They were seen everywhere that members of Berlin society were supposed to be seen: horse races, balls, dinners and night clubs. Falkenhayn was divorced so there was no jealous husband to worry about. Frau von Falkenhayn recruited Frau von Natzmer, who worked as a secretary in the General Staff's Section IN6, under Colonel Heinz Guderian (who was working to create the German Army's new armoured forces). IN6 was the most secret section in the whole of Bendlerstrasse. Falkenhayn soon realized Sosnowski's real purpose and that she was working indirectly for the PIS. Nevertheless, in love with

Sosnowski and enamoured of the thrill of playing the spy, she prevailed upon Netzmer to get her information. Netzmer handed Falkenhayn a sketch of the IN6 offices, Guderian's duties, schedule and work methods, every detail of the build-up of Germany's panzer army, and even blueprints of the tank designs. Sosnowski was very pleased with Falkenhayn and her agent. In turn Netzmer recruited Fraulein von Jena and three other secretaries to help in acquiring secrets in a sort of chain of agents that spread inside the Bendlerstrasse. Sosnowski, meanwhile, was busy spreading his charms by seducing the wife of a Colonel Biedenfuhr, while he bribed Lieutenant Rutloff at the German War Ministry to give him a series of sensitive documents. By the end of 1934 Sosnowski had acquired over 150 secret documents, the key to Guderian's safe and even an outline of German plans to invade Poland.

But like many other spies Sosnowski made one fatal error. In his case it was in typical fashion; he

ABOVE: *Poland's "James Bond": Count Jurek Sosnowski (right), seen here having lunch in a Berlin restaurant in 1934 with his mistress – Baroness von Berg.*

slept with one woman too many. He had become the lover of a fiery Hungarian dancer, Rita Pasci, even going on a vacation to Hungary with her. Pasci, however, was not too pleased to discover that her handsome Polish lover was also sleeping with a whole army of Berlin society women and soon realized that he was a spy. Out of jealousy she walked into the Abwehr HQ at Tirpitz Ufer and told the Abwehr that Sosnowski was a Polish spy and that he had Netzmer and Jena working for him. The Abwehr was shocked since they knew these secretaries worked in the IN6 section and that this leak could be disastrous. The Abwehr immediately handed the matter over to Richard Protze of the newly constituted Gestapo, who barged into Sosnowski's Berlin flat in the middle of a champagne dinner. Sosnowski was, it seems, packing his bags. Despite Protze screaming at him that he was a low-down spy, the Pole flatly denied the accusation.

In the People's Court no mercy was shown to Sosnowski's female agents. Both Netzmer and Falkenhayn were sentenced to death. Sosnowski chivalrously kissed Falkenhayn's hand as she was dragged out of court screaming. Both women were beheaded by axe in February 1935 after Hitler refused to grant an amnesty.[13] Jena spent the rest of her life in a German prison. Sosnowski, however, with last-minute timing that James Bond himself would have been proud of, was rescued by Canaris.

The Abwehr chief went to see the Polish Ambassador in Berlin, Jozef Lipski, and suggested an exchange of Sosnowski for a Polish agent who worked for the Abwehr in Warsaw. Lipski, without knowing he was talking to the head of the Abwehr, agreed to the deal. When Sosnowski turned up in Warsaw his story and the documents he had smuggled out were not believed. They were deemed too good to be true and Sosnowski found himself suspected of being a double agent. Whilst the count cooled his heels in prison, the Polish General Staff and the PIS assessed whether his documents were genuine. They were and provided the Poles with an outstanding insight into Germany's military expansion. In 1939 after the invasion of Poland, Canaris charged Lahousen, the head of Abwehr Section II, with finding Sosnowski, but the elusive count escaped and was finally caught by the Soviets.

Polish Agents in German Pay

The Abwehr's successes in Poland were neither as frequent or spectacular as the Poles' operations inside the Reich. Two Polish Abwehr agents spied out the Polish Navy's Baltic bases on the Hela Peninsula (north of Danzig) and at Oxthöft. An even greater coup could have been achieved had the Abwehr taken a more positive shine to a potential agent that literally turned up on its doorstep. In 1930 a PIS officer, Tolodzietzki, who worked under Zychon, offered his services to the Abwehr's Polish Section. However, the Germans believed the officer was a plant, sent in their direction by the cunning Major Zychon. Tolodzietzki was, in fact, the genuine article and his intelligence could have been invaluable. In the end, Zychon got suspicious of his errant officer and had Tolodzietzki arrested, sentenced and hanged. Another PIS officer also fell under suspicion and was arrested. He was later found by the Abwehr in October 1939, after the German invasion, and turned loose on the USSR.

"Peaceful" Conquests

An independent Austria was an affront to Hitler, who wanted to incorporate this small German-speaking nation into his growing Reich. The SD spearheaded the subversion of Austria, and it was the SS which was behind the bungled coup against the Catholic conservative dictatorship of Chancellor Dolfuss in July 1934. Dolfuss was killed by his Austrian Nazi assailants, but the coup faltered and eventually failed when the conspirators were confronted by the Austrian Heimwehr (Home Defence) and the Austrian Army (Bundesheer). Austria remained independent until early 1938, when the Germans were ready to strike again. Hitler mobilized the Wehrmacht and the Austrian Nazi fifth column to undermine Chancellor Kurt von Schuschnigg's regime, through a combination of military and political blackmail. In March 1938 Canaris, who had helped in the subversion work but who wanted the Austrians to resist the German occupation, activated Operation Otto to grab the staff and documents of the Austrian intelligence services before Heydrich could acquire these for the SD. Canaris succeeded in obtaining, through Vienna, an intelligence avenue into Switzerland, Italy, Hungary, Czechoslovakia and the Balkans.

After March 1938, the next independent state to be consumed by Hitler's territorial expansionism

Polish intelligence units were some of Germany's most formidable and dangerous adversaries

was Czechoslovakia, whose strategic situation had been deeply undermined by the German acquisition of Austria. Both the Abwehr and the SD were involved in the subversion and undermining of this democracy. The SD set up a station in Dresden to screen Sudeten German refugees from Czechoslovakia and prevent the Czech Intelligence Service (CIS) from infiltrating Germany. This station, headed by SS-Sturmbannführer Wilhelm Krichbaum, sent its agents into the Sudetenland, the ethnic German part of Czechoslaovakia, to gather intelligence and stir up trouble for the Czech authorities. Himmler had allowed the SD a free hand against the Czechs.[14] For its part, the SD felt free to indulge itself in activities which included cross-border murder.

One particular target was Rudolf Formis, a German supporter of the disgraced radical Nazi Otto Strasser, who had set up a radio station in the Sudetenland that broadcast anti-Hitler propaganda. Heydrich called in his hatchet man, Alfred Naujocks, and gave him the job to solve the Formis problem permanently and silence the embarrassing radio station. During the night of 23 January 1935 Naujocks, Werner Göttsch and several other SD assassins crossed the frontier into Czechoslovakia. They located Formis in a hotel a short distance from Prague and killed him.

Activities in the Sudetenland

Heydrich had found a special role for the SD: not only to crush the internal opposition within Germany, but to pursue the Führer's enemies abroad and to extend the reach of the Reich by subversion and terror against neighbouring states. Himmler was an ardent supporter of the concept of a Greater German Reich that not only included Austria but also western Czechoslovakia. This meant meddling in the complex and chaotic politics of the Sudeten Germans. Most supported the Sudetendeutsche Partei (SdP) led by Konrad Henlein, who passed for a moderate among the disaffected minority of Volksdeutsche (ethnic Germans). The SD funnelled arms, supplies and

cash to support the Sudeten Nazi faction within the SdP. The SD hoped that it could subvert the party, remove Henlein and make the SdP thoroughly Nazi. It was no coincidence that Henlein, the moderate, and his nationalists were supported by the Abwehr. Henlein was probably an Abwehr agent himself and the armed militants of the SdP were subsidized, armed and supported by the Abwehr in setting up training camps on German soil. The Abwehr hoped to defeat the SD-led Sudeten Nazis and dominate the Sudetenland itself. And so intelligence operations in the Sudetenland became an extension of the SD-Abwehr struggle for primacy in Germany's internecine intelligence war.

The "Ten Commandments"

According to the deal struck between Canaris and Heydrich in 1936, set out in what became known as the "Ten Commandments", the duties and areas of authority of the Abwehr and the SD had been firmly established. It was of course a deal that the SS/SD did not respect, and the Abwehr was forced into a losing battle to maintain its position. The SD had the upper hand in the Sudetenland with agents such as Friedrich Brehm working for it, undermining Henlein and spreading SS influence at the expense of the SdP. Brehm organized much of the SD network in the Sudetenland, or so he

claimed, though SD agent Otto Liebl was probably just as important. Putting both to shame was Rudolf Kasper, an expert on Sudetenland labour questions who was financed by Robert Ley's Labour Front (Deutches Arbeitsfront – DAF), essentially a Nazi state-controlled trade union. This did not stop Kasper from also working for the SD Dresden station and for SS-Obergruppenführer Fritz Tittmann. These agents were part of a massive SD network of some 65 known agents, but they were in turn only the tip of the iceberg. This larger organization of intelligence moles extended into the German legation in Prague where Press Secretary Fritz von Chamier and Sigismund von Bibra, the Legation secretary, worked for the SD. They worked to keep the SS informed not only about Czech and Sudeten politics but also, to the fury of foreign minister Ribbentrop, Germany's foreign policy towards Czechoslovakia. The SD had one final weapon in its war of subversion: its own paper, the *Rumburger Zietung*, whose editor, Heinz Pfeiffer, was an SD agent. He was dismissed by Henlein as an *"eitler Querkopf"* (vain crank) but attempts to shut down the paper, whose threats had a curious tendency of being carried out, all failed despite Canaris' support.

The SD and the Czech Problem

In May 1938 the CIS, aware of various plots, warned President Benes that the Germans were planning to invade Bohemia in western Czechoslavakia. Hitler, whose preparations were incomplete, had to furiously deny these accusations and allow his temper to cool during the summer. But by October 1938 he was back on the offensive and had forced France and Britain to accept the disgraceful Munich Accord. Germany, without shedding a drop of blood, occupied and annexed the German-speaking Sudetenland. However, this was not enough for the Führer of National Socialist Germany. Hitler felt that Munich was no victory, since he wanted the whole Czech state smashed and broken up. In January 1939 Reinhard Heydrich called his subordinates to a meeting where he told them: "The foreign policy of Germany demands that the Czechoslovak Republic be broken up and destroyed within the next few months, if necessary by force. To prepare and facilitate the moves against Czechoslovakia, it appears expedient to support and stimulate the endeavours of the Slovaks in their movement for autonomy."[15]

Heydrich was as good as his word and put his SD chief in Austria, Ernst Kaltenbrunner, in charge of the task of making Slovakia "independent" of the Czechs. Kaltenbrunner had a valuable contact in Franz Karmasin, head of the KdP (*Karpatendeutsche Partei*),[16] who, in 1937, introduced the SS chief to leading Slovak politicians Ferdinand Durcansky and Karl Sidor. When Karmasin was made Head of German Affairs in Slovakia he kept Kaltenbrunner informed about Slovak politics in the republic. In October 1938 Kaltenbrunner also established so-called SS "volunteers", who on his orders staged a series of attacks on the German minority in Slovakia in late February 1939. In mid-March Kaltenbrunner tried to prevail upon the Czech-appointed Slovak Premier, Karl Sidor, to declare Slovakia independent. When this failed, other SD agents contacted a fiery Catholic priest, Dr. Joseph

ABOVE: *Konrad Henlein (right), leader of the Sudeten German Nationalists, seen here by Hitler's side at the German Führer's retreat at Berchtesgaden.*

Tiso, who headed the Slovak opposition. Tiso was more than willing to oblige the Germans, and on 14 March 1939 Tiso declared Slovakia independent of Prague's control. On 15 March 1939 what remained of the truncated Czech state was occupied and incorporated into the Reich Protectorate of Bohemia-Moravia under the puppet President Dr. Emil Hacha (who had visited Berlin in March 1939 to plead with Hitler not to invade). Hitler had won the subversion war by subjugating Czechoslovakia, but the consequences of these actions opened the road to a general European war, and ultimately his own demise. However, in March 1939 Hitler, with the aid of his intelligence service, had achieved another bloodless victory.

Chapter 3

The Spymasters

"Spying might perhaps be tolerable if it were done by men of honour"[1]

C. Montesquieu (eighteenth-century French philosopher)

AN INTELLIGENCE SERVICE TAKES ITS CHARACTER FROM THE PERSONALITY of its leaders and their personal quirks, strengths and weaknesses.[2] It is quite an interesting coincidence that the two first leaders of the British Secret Intelligence Service (SIS) were naval officers,[3] as was the leader of the World War II Abwehr, Admiral Wilhelm Canaris. It was due to his personality and leadership that the Abwehr ended up as the effective agency it became, though it was his personal weaknesses that also damaged the service. This said, all intelligence services have their fair share of outstanding successes and failures. The SD, a far more sinister, ruthless and arguably the more effective service of the Third Reich, also reflected the personality of its founder and leader, Reinhard Heydrich, until his assassination in Prague in May 1942. While Canaris was a monarchist and something of a dreamer, Heydrich was his absolute opposite. He was an amoral careerist, and there were no depths to which he would not stoop to advance to the very top of the Third Reich. It has been suggested that Heydrich even aimed to step into Hitler's shoes one day. The two men did share one characteristic. Both knew how to survive in Hitler's Nazi jungle and

LEFT: *Admiral Canaris, head of the Abwehr. He hated not only Hitler and Himmler, but the entire Nazi system, a system that eventually executed him.*

thrived on the conflict. As spymasters, however, they were both outshone by the most effective intelligence head that Germany produced during the Nazi era, and possibly the whole of the twentieth century: General Reinhard Gehlen, head of the Fremde Heere Ost (FHO). Gehlen not only survived the war, unlike the other two, but went on to set up the Gehlen Organization. Immediately after the war it worked for the US Central Intelligence Agency (CIA), and later formed the basis of the West German, or Federal, Secret Police.

If there was anyone who qualified as the chameleon of the Third Reich then that was Wilhelm Canaris. William Shirer, the famous pre-war American journalist who was resident in Berlin, commented that no two men had the same opinion about Canaris. The admiral's Austrian subordinate, Erwin von Lahousen, claimed that:

"Canaris was a personality of pure intellect. We relied on his inner very unique and complicated nature for this reason. He hated violence and therefore hated Hitler, his abominable system and particularly his methods. Canaris was, in whatever way you may look upon him, a human being."[4]

Although he did not leave everyone in such a lyrical mood, the overall impression that Canaris left on people was a positive one. The otherwise very cynical, deeply suspicious and cold-hearted head of Swedish military intelligence, Colonel Carlos

ABOVE: *A German cruiser of the Emden class, similar to that of the* Dresden *on which both Lieutenant Heydrich and Captain Canaris served during the 1920s.*

BELOW: *A British cruiser of equivalent type to the Emden class of cruiser. In this case HMS* Bristol.

Adlercreutz, while not glowing in his praises of the Abwehr chief, believed that Canaris was a decent, upright and very humane man. General Franco, whom Canaris had known since World War I, was another of his admirers who had every reason to trust and be grateful for Canaris' assistance during World War II. Without Canaris and his timely "leaks" of intelligence regarding Hitler's plans to compromise their neutrality, it is unlikely that Spain or Sweden could have kept out of the conflagration which engulfed Europe.

Even Heydrich, no admirer of the admiral or his service, had to admit that Canaris was "a cunning old fox".[5] If these were the opinions of his supposed allies, then what of his enemies in the "game of foxes" (as the American journalist and author Ladislas Farago called espionage)? Allen Dulles, Office of Strategic Services (OSS) officer and later head of the CIA, believed that Canaris was "one of the bravest men of modern history", and saw to it that the admiral's widow got a decent pension to live off after the war. Sir Stewart Menzies, head of SIS/MI6, called Canaris "damned brave and damned unlucky", which was probably more to the point. Others, like SIS agent Samuel Lohan, were not so generous. Lohan dismissed Canaris as an "inefficient, intriguing, traitorous, lisping queer".[6] Clearly Canaris was a man who inspired partisan views. Outsiders found him a strange and a paradoxical character who was difficult to fathom, while his subordinates and employees adored him as a caring and paternalistic chief.

An Enigmatic Man

Loyalty did not stop his subordinates from making fun of him behind his back, and for exactly the same reasons they adored him as a superior; his kindness, mercy and generosity towards those weaker or less fortunate than himself. This earned

him the nicknames "Father of the Unfortunate" or "Father Christmas", the latter nickname being bestowed due to his white hair as much as for his kindness. Even in 1935 when he took over the Abwehr, aged 48, Canaris was prematurely white-haired which made him seem much older than he was. He wore his heavy woollen uniform all year round, was an abstemious workaholic, and a pill-popping hypochondriac who had a strange aversion to tall men. As his workload increased he grew more distant from his small but loving family, although his two daughters adored their father. While Canaris could be distrustful of people and at times brusque towards subordinates, he was very fond of his dogs. "My dog is discreet and never betrays me. I can't say the same about any human."[7]

Canaris' family, because of the similarity in name, claimed to be descendants of the nineteenth-century Greek independence leader, Admiral Konstantin Kanaris. This gave rise to rumours and speculation about the Abwehr chief's racial and national background, and gave rise to yet another nickname: "the Levantine." Perhaps in his subtle and devious intellect there was something of the Greek in Canaris. The family, in fact, like so many other German noble or leading families, was of decidedly foreign descent.[8] The Canarisi family hailed from near Lake Como in northern Italy, and emigrated to Germany in the eighteenth century, changing their name to Canaris in 1789. A decade later they converted to Protestantism. Wilhelm Canaris was born into a wealthy industrialist's home in Aplerbeck outside Dortmund on New Year's day 1887. He joined the German Navy in 1905 where he established a solid reputation for being good-natured, humane and efficient. He served on the cruiser *Dresden*, which survived the Battle of the Falklands in 1914, after which she managed to escape to Chile where HMS *Glasgow* found and cornered her. It was here that the young junior officer, Canaris, showed his guile and nose for an agent's craftiness. While he went over to parley and protest to the British that the *Dresden* was in neutral waters, which meant she could not be attacked, his colleagues scuttled her. Canaris was already fluent in Spanish and made his way to Santiago, the capital of Chile, where he gained entry into the Imperial German Embassy. With a brand-new Chilean passport Canaris travelled across the Andes to Buenos Aires where he boarded, undetected, a British ship bound for England. Despite the supposed vigilance of MI5, Canaris escaped their agents and checks unscathed. He arrived in neutral Netherlands, still with his Chilean passport, and then travelled on to

BELOW : *A British convoy in formation. Canaris, as a young spy in Madrid, caused significant damage to Allied shipping in the Mediterranean during World War I.*

Hamburg where he took the opportunity of calling on his aunt, Dorothea Popp, who got an enormous shock. In Berlin on 17 September 1915, the authorities pinned the Knight's Cross on his chest.[9] He was first-rate spy material, and was prevailed upon to join the ND under Captain von Krohn of the ND Etappe (purchasing agency). In 1916 he was the sent to Madrid. There the young and dashing German spy was in his element since this was where the SIS, with the help of the French *Suréte* and *Deuxiéme Bureau*, locked horns with the ND. The German naval and military attachés also had an extensive network of spies and informers reaching far into the Spanish Government. Canaris' task was far more mundane but no less deadly for Allied vessels in the Mediterranean: to provide the German U-boat base at Pola in the Adriatic (in what is now Croatia) with accurate intelligence about Allied shipping. When Allied shipping losses soared the SIS became aware that there was a German agent in Spain giving the enemy accurate intelligence. During the summer of 1916, the SIS sent a young Scottish agent by the name of Stewart Menzies to Spain to liquidate this agent. But Menzies, the future head of SIS, was unable to find, let alone kill, the crafty naval officer. A far more congenial contact Canaris made during this period was that of a Spanish Army officer from Galicia who was as inscrutable and phlegmatic as Canaris himself: Don Francisco Franco.

A Lucky Escape

Suffering from malaria and seriously overworked, Canaris, still holding a Chilean passport, was sent back to Germany disguised as a Catholic monk.[10] He made his way through France without a hitch, but was arrested at the Swiss border and handed over to the Italian police. The Italians, fooled by Canaris' claim that he was suffering from the virulent, lethal form of malaria, gave in to Spanish protests that the "dying" young German officer should not be handed over to the French and returned him to Spain. On his way back, Canaris persuaded the captain of the

ABOVE: *Karl Liebknecht, German communist leader, who sought to topple the German Government in November 1918, shown here giving a fiery speech to his supporters. Canaris was implicated in Liebknecht's violent end.*

vessel taking him to Cartagena not to call in on Marseilles, where he risked being arrested by the French and shot. Menzies, with his Spanish contact Juan March, found out that Canaris was in Cartagena but before he had a chance to act, the elusive young man had hitched a ride to Pola in a German U-boat, *U-35*.

Upon his return to Germany Canaris married Erika Waag. His role during the 1920s is shrouded in some mystery. He was not a field agent as he had been during World War I, but he was still involved in clandestine intelligence work. During the aborted attempt by communists to take over Germany in 1918–21 Canaris, an outright and sworn enemy of the communists, worked hard to thwart their revolution by harbouring and protecting the assassins of the communist leaders, Rosa Luxembourg and Karl Liebknecht. He was also linked to an extreme right-wing organization based in Kiel that had the support of the local naval station.

The overt communist threat to Germany ended after the failure of an uprising in Saxony in 1923. Canaris then reverted to other duties linked to trips to Japan, Spain and Sweden where he secretly purchased new naval vessels and weaponry for the much-reduced German Navy. Canaris' task was to hide these from the Allied control commission set up to verify that Germany conformed to the terms of the Treaty of Versailles.

It was during his time at Kiel, in about 1922, that Canaris, with the rank of kapitänleutnant and with a legendary wartime record for his exploits as an agent, met and befriended a very tall, young and shy naval officer by the name of Reinhard Heydrich. It was not so unusual that the two men, despite the considerable age difference, became companions. They were both loners and outsiders and shared a love for music. Heydrich became a family friend and was included in the Canaris' music evenings when he played the violin with Canaris' musically talented wife Erika. Professionally Canaris fired the young Heydrich's love of agents, codes and spying. This relationship of apprentice and master was to continue throughout Heydrich's naval service. Their subsequent relationship after Heydrich joined the SS was far more complex, and changed over the years until Heydrich had manoeuvred himself into the ascendancy. But in those early years Canaris had a friend and disciple to instruct in all the secrets of spying. He convinced Heydrich of the importance of communications, and as a result Heydrich trained as a telecommunications officer.

Entry Into The SS

Under mysterious circumstances, Heydrich was dismissed from the navy in 1931. The official reason was that he had made a girl pregnant but refused to marry her. Heydrich claimed that he was dismissed because he had joined the NSDAP in May 1931, and that it had nothing to do with his relationship with the "disgraced" girl. Neither reason sounds plausible. The German Navy, unlike the German Army, was relatively pro-Nazi

Reinhard Heydrich was utterly detested by his enemies, and feared even by his friends

and riddled with Nazi sympathizers. Heydrich's contact with the Nazis would not have been unusual, nor would his fornication. Heydrich, who was as amoral as he was ambitious, would have been unlikely to resign because of a matter of honour. Unlike Canaris, Heydrich was not a "man of honour", but he was a born spy. Trained in code-breaking and trade craft by Canaris himself, Heydrich's first assignments had been to the port cities of Hamburg and Bremen where he kept watch on left-wing activists for the navy. It is perfectly possible that his exit from the service was engineered by Grand Admiral Raeder, the head of the navy, who fired Heydrich so that he would be free to join the SS under Himmler. The latter obliged Raeder by recruiting Heydrich to head the SS intelligence service in 1931. What the two navy conspirators, Canaris and Raeder, no doubt hoped to achieve was to have Heydrich as a mole inside the ranks of the SS if, or when, the Nazis took power. They hoped to control and manipulate Heydrich just as the German industrialists and conservative leaders hoped they could control Hitler. On both counts these calculations proved wrong. Hitler became Germany's master and Heydrich became head of the SS's own intelligence service, the SD, and one of Canaris' worst enemies.

The Beast: Reinhard Heydrich

If few had a bad word to say about Canaris the same could not be said for Reinhard Heydrich. No-one had a word to say in his favour as a human being. Most, especially his associates, were keen to denigrate him in the most blunt terms. Canaris, who by 1941 walked in fear of being toppled as head of the Abwehr by Heydrich, called him "most impressive of the beasts". Walter Schellenberg, who worked under Heydrich in the SD, described him as a "tall, thin man behind a huge desk, with small, shifty eyes set

RIGHT: *Heydrich the sportsman. Seen here in his fencing outfit, he was an able swordsman. He had a fiercely competitive nature and had to win and excel in everything.*

too close together on either side of a fine, long aquiline nose. He had long spidery fingers and exuded a sinister aura through a combination of ruthless energy and extreme hunger for power." Yet Schellenberg also noted that Heydrich had an artistic side. Indeed, he was an accomplished violinist and seemed, for a careerist, devoted to music. He was also very intelligent and perhaps the most impressive leader in the whole of the Third Reich. He was truly, as both Schellenberg, and Wilhelm Höttl, head of the SD Balkan Section, put it, the spider in the web of the Nazi empire. He was an expert at seeing the weaknesses of others and exploiting them. His only weakness, in Schellenberg's opinion, was his uncontrollable sexual appetite. Himmler, his boss, had almost as complex a relationship with Heydrich as did Canaris: a combination of fear, admiration and respect. He admired Heydrich for his tall, blonde Aryan look and his sharp brain, but when he was annoyed with his pushy and ambitious deputy, he would call him a Mongol from the hordes of Genghis Khan, on account of his slanted eyes. The final word perhaps should go to Heydrich's deputy, Werner Best, who simply called the SD chief, "the most demoniacal personality in the National Socialist leadership".[11]

Reinhard Heydrich

Heydrich was a complex and quite tortured character who may have experienced, like most Nazi leaders, a great sense of inferiority.[12] He was born in 1904 into a cultured and artistic middle-class German family. His father, Bruno Heydrich, was an accomplished musician by profession, who encouraged his sons, Reinhard and Heinz, to take up music at least as a serious hobby. At school the boys were taunted for their supposed Jewish ancestry, based simply on their father's "Jewish" look and their step-grandfather's Jewish-sounding name. Despite this flimsy evidence Heydrich, when he came into power, went to extraordinary lengths to remove any trace of his step-grandfather's existence because he was worried that he might, by some remote chance, be Jewish. The question remains whether Heydrich was Jewish or not, though ultimately the question remains unanswered. Perhaps this odious architect of the Holocaust was Jewish, or even suspected that

ABOVE: *Reinhard Gehlen (centre) shared Heydrich's love of sports but loved this activity for its own pleasure. He was also, unlike his Nazi colleague, a good and caring, if very demanding, superior. He is shown with his men at the FHO.*

he was. Many other prominent Nazis could not be sure of their ancestry. Not even Hitler himself.[13]

This unrelenting taunting and teasing hardened Heydrich to the point of making him, in time, lose empathy with humanity. He was extremely competitive and took up sport, not for the relaxation or healthy training it brought, but for the sheer competition it engendered. It was an arrogant and competitive young man who joined the German Navy in 1922. From the beginning he was not particularly liked, but he was admired for his devotion to duty and professional skills.[14] By those that admired him he was known as the "blonde Siegfried", by others, because of his bleating loud laughter, "Ziege" – the nanny goat. Heydrich, after his "disgrace",[15] joined the SS at the age of only 27.

He made the SD an effective arm of the SS and himself completely indispensable to Himmler. However, he had nothing but contempt for ideological Nazis or any form of idealism. He was, in simple terms, out to grab as much power as possible for himself whatever the cost to Germany or to the people who stood in his way. The men he selected for the SD and Gestapo, such as the communist-admiring Heinrich Müller or the charming but ruthless Walter Schellenberg, were not Nazi idealists. They were German technocrats like himself, out to expand their power and influence. Men who would have served any regime so long as it served their interests to do so.

The Colonel: Reinhard Gehlen

Both Canaris and Heydrich were spymasters, but they were not the most efficient or the most successful that Nazi Germany possessed. Canaris was too obsessed with trying to frustrate Hitler's rampage across the Continent. He was too involved in machinations, plots and the tortured politics of the Third Reich and the Abwehr to be a truly effective, full-time spymaster. Heydrich suffered from the same diversion of effort, and his energy went into grandiose schemes such as planning the extermination of the Jews or plotting aggression against Germany's neighbours. In fact the achievements of Canaris and Heydrich pale by comparison with those of Reinhard Gehlen: the one truly great German spymaster in the tradition of Colonel Nicolai of the ND. Gehlen was not involved, like Heydrich, in crimes and dirty tricks, and unlike Canaris he served Hitler to the bitter end, though with declining enthusiasm as the war progressed. Gehlen was devoted to spying and completely absorbed by his task, even after the German defeat.[16]

Gehlen was born in 1902 in the Prussian enclave of Erfurt, inside Thuringia; the son of an upper middle-class Prussian family whose father, Benno Gehlen, came from a military background. The family motto, "Never Give Up", was quite apt given Reinhard's future career as the head of the Fremde Heere Ost (FHO). Gehlen was a dyed-in-the-wool Prussian military conservative, devoted to upholding the existing Imperial German order.

His father was a war veteran who won an Iron Cross on the Western Front and ended World War I a major. Benno Gehlen avoided post-war unemployment by moving to Breslau, the capital of Silesia, and joining a publishing business. In Breslau, Reinhard did very well at school, shining at his special interests, mathematics and statistics.

Gehlen joined the Reichswehr (the armed forces of the Weimar Republic) in 1920, and was stationed in his adopted home province of Silesia, which seemed constantly threatened by the Poles. Gehlen was used to guide German spies across the frontier into Poland, but he was not impressed with the freebooters and hardened mercenaries who joined the Freikorps, a collection of paramilitary units that were involved in revolution and border clashes from 1918–23. Nor was he impressed by the loutish Bavarian Brownshirts of the NSDAP. It was the communists of the KPD who he viewed as the most serious threat to Germany's future. Gehlen, although a fanatical opponent of the communists both at home and abroad, had a grudging admiration for the NKVD and was fascinated with the USSR. He used his spare time to become a self-taught expert on communism, the *Comintern* and the USSR. In 1930 he married into the Silesian nobility when he wed Herta von Seydlitz-Kurzbach whose family had an estate, Zukowken, near Glogau in Lower Silesia.[17] This marriage into a famous Prussian military family opened doors, and Gehlen quickly joined the General Staff (OKH). Gehlen and his family were enthusiastic about Hitler's rise to power, but their initial euphoria soon faded as the harsh reality of the National Socialist regime became apparent.

Gehlen was an effective technocrat, cold and calculating. He was brilliant at playing the obedient servant while in fact manipulating situations to impose his own views and ideas on those of his own superiors. He was also good at camouflaging his manipulation, like Schellenberg and Heydrich, but without their gangster methods. In April 1942 Gehlen would take over as head of army intelligence on the Eastern Front and completely reorganize that service, turning it into one of USSR's most formidable opponents (see Chapter 7).

Chapter 4

Easy Victories

"I'll cook them a stew they'll choke on!"
Adolf Hitler (31 March 1939) upon hearing about Chamberlain's guarantee to Poland and Romania.

A NEGLECTED ASPECT OF GERMANY'S BLITZKRIEG CAMPAIGNS in 1939 and 1940 is the role of the Abwehr and the SD in assisting the armed forces to invade and conquer with such speed and with relatively low casualty rates. This was especially true of the Netherlands: a country with a large conscript army, several lines of fortress defences, and a series of major water obstacles to impede an attacker. The country was conquered in only four days, and much of the credit for this outcome has to go to the work of the intelligence services.

Poland had been Germany's main espionage target before 1939,[1] but with Hitler's determination to wage a war of conquest came entirely new demands on the SD and the Abwehr. In August 1939 the Abwehr's secret commando troops, the Brandenburgers, made preparations for a campaign of subversion. They were to begin operation "Case White" against the Polish frontier, dressed both in German uniforms and disguised as Polish troops. Case White was designed to ease the passage of troops and tanks of the Wehrmacht into Poland past the frontier defences. Originally the order to invade Poland had set a start date of 25 August 1939, but then Hitler, for reasons of political expediency, decided to postpone it so as to seem reasonable in the "negotiations" he was conducting with the

Western Allies and the Poles. By this time the Brandenburgers and the SD units were observing absolute radio silence and had taken up positions along the vast Polish frontier. They were difficult to contact and in some cases impossible to reach. Hitler's order to halt the invasion therefore came too late. The Brandenburgers went into action, and around the strategic railway at the Jablunka Pass on the Polish-Slovak border, engaged in several hours of fighting with Polish frontier troops. At the same time Heydrich's SS group, disguised as Poles, staged a mock attack on the German customs post at Hochlinden.

Hitler had needed border incidents that could be blamed on the Poles so he could justify his aggression against a peaceful neighbour. To this end he had asked Canaris to use his Brandenburgers, suitably attired in Polish uniforms, to stage a fake attack on the German radio station at Gleiwitz, just across the frontier. Canaris was horrified at the idea and refused to use his men for such a scheme. It was one thing to stage attacks on the enemy by subterfuge, quite another to stage an "incident" to give Hitler the justification to stage an invasion.

As Canaris had refused the job Hitler turned to the SS and Heydrich, who readily agreed to take it on. But even some of the SD men had doubts about the feasibility and legality of such an operation. Walter Schellenberg advised his colleague, Mellhorn, not to take on the task. Mellhorn did as he was advised and ended up being fired from his post by Heydrich. Instead it was his assassin, Alfred Naujocks, who got

LEFT: *A German horse-drawn column enters the conquered city of Warsaw in 1939 after the short Polish campaign. The PIS continued the fight in exile.*

ABOVE: *Canaris adopted many exotic disguises during his frequent journeys across Europe. He is shown here wearing the peaked cap of a senior Italian Air Force officer.*

the unpleasant task of dealing with Gleiwitz. Naujocks was called into Heydrich's office on 10 August 1939.

A Distasteful Venture

Though he had wanted the Abwehr to play no part in the attack, on 17 August Canaris agreed to supply the SD with "150 Polish uniforms and accessories for Upper Silesia", as Franz Halder, General Chief of Staff of OKH, noted in his diary. Canaris had

consented to supply the uniforms with great reluctance, and did so only on the express orders of his nominal superior Field Marshal Keitel. Naujocks had already arrived at Gleiwitz two weeks before the attack was due to be staged. Heinrich Müller, head of the Gestapo, met Naujocks in Oppeln, telling him that the "canned goods" (some 12–13 Polish-speaking KZ[2] prisoners) would be delivered to Naujocks before the attack to add some veracity to the incident. Naujocks was also instructed to seize and hold the radio station long enough for one of the prisoners or one of the SS officers in charge to make a speech in Polish denouncing Germany. At 12:00 hours on 31 August, Heydrich phoned Naujocks with orders to stage the attack that same evening, at 20:00 hours. The attack came at the appointed hour with SS troops in Polish uniforms, one of whom made a three-minute speech over the airwaves. The KZ prisoners were shot, except one who was left as living evidence of the "attack", while the SS men shot off a few rounds and then supposedly fled in the direction of the Polish border. The "canned goods"operation had been completed to perfection. At the German Foreign Office, the Auswärtige Amt (AA), Ribbentrop and Permanent Secretary Ernst von Weizsäcker used the Gleiwitz attack as justification for the invasion of Poland, and as the panzers rolled across the border, Hitler used it in his infamous Reichstag speech of 2 September 1939 to defend his aggression. No-one, however, except the Germans were fooled by this clumsily staged piece of nonsense.[3] Foreign observers immediately denounced the attack as a German provocation, stage-managed for Hitler's benefit. At 04:30 hours on 1 September German tanks, troops and horse-drawn artillery crossed the Polish frontier. An hour later German radio reported 14 similar border incidents to prove to the unenthusiastic and sceptical German nation that the war against Poland was a just and defensive one.

For political reasons Canaris and his conservative allies were generally pleased at the news of the Polish invasion, since it was believed that war meant the beginning of the end for the Nazis. However, the intervention of the Western European powers would put Germany in real danger. Canaris knew that Hitler's hope of Britain staying out of the Polish

ABOVE: *The Germans thought Poland would be walkover. But the terrain, poor roads and numerous river obstacles (as seen above) made the campaign harder than anticipated.*

conflagration was forlorn, and when Hans Gisevius, the anti-Nazi vice-consul in Zurich, met Hans Oster, Canaris' chief assistant, in one of the dimly lit corridors in Tirpitz Ufer, the Abwehr officer muttered to him that the British declaration of war (on 3 September) meant the end of Germany. The Abwehr knew before anyone else in Germany that Britain had decided to declare war, since its interception department had read the signal from the Foreign Office in London to Ambassador Sir Neville Henderson in Berlin.

Canaris called his senior staff to a meeting in his office to give them notice of this new threat from the west. He told them that the SIS was a most dangerous foe but that it was vulnerable, since it paid its agents badly, frequently betrayed them, and that their ciphers could be broken. The admiral pointed out to his men that if Germany lost the war it would be a disaster, but if Hitler won it, that too would be just as bad. Canaris summed up the Abwehr's position: while it waged a war against Germany's external intelligence foes, it

Canaris hoped that the invasion of Poland would be the beginning of the end for Hitler

would also try to curb the excesses of Hitler and his Nazi cohorts.

During the Polish campaign Canaris was deeply disturbed and disgusted by the actions of the SS, and he ordered the Abwehr to monitor their crimes for eventual prosecution after the war. On 12 September he told an unsympathetic Keitel about the SS Einsatzkommando's (SS Special Action Groups') barbarous operations in Poland. Their crimes, he told the field marshal, would eventually be paid for by Germany, since the Wehrmacht could not put a stop to them. Canaris found no sympathy or support for his views. When General Johannes Blaskowitz, commander of the Fourteenth Army in central Poland, protested about the murder squads of the SS Einsatzkommando, Hitler promptly fired him. Canaris won one minor victory, however: he had the satisfaction of preventing von Woyrsch's Einsatz-gruppe from operating in the German Fourteenth Army's area.

The Polish Network Survives

If the Germans believed that with the invasion they would crush the Polish PIS[4] then they were sadly mistaken. Bureau Zychon had been evacuated safely to Paris taking its expertise, broken codes and a copy of the German Enigma encoding machine with it. The Germans did have one stroke of good fortune, though. An intelligence officer who discovered a Polish bunker outside Warsaw chose to investigate. His curiosity was rewarded since, among all the rubbish inside, he found part of the PIS archives. The most important information had been removed but the identities of some agents were revealed. This was one of the very few errors that an otherwise superbly professional service committed. What the archive also showed was the extent and potential influence of the PIS network inside Germany itself.

The SD soon had proof that the PIS was still a formidable foe. The Dortmund area of Westphalia, in the industrial Ruhr, had 400 manufacturing plants and a population of 3,500,000, but had only a small SD office consisting of five agents, a handful of assistants and a few secretaries.[5] That was not much to carry out counter-intelligence, which was the SD's main duty, considering that the Ruhr contained 200,000 Polish workers. Walter Schellenberg was sent from Berlin to put some energy into the SD effort in Westphalia, and he immediately did so. In one factory, producing anti-tank guns, Schellenberg found a likely suspect. He was of Polish origin, highly intelligent, a superintendent married with three children who had lived in Germany for 18 years without a hint of misconduct. But he was now an enemy alien and therefore suspect, and Schellenberg had him closely watched. When seven blueprints went missing the SD surrounded the superintendent's home, covering every possible escape route. Two other men had been seen entering the house and when the SD, with drawn pistols, burst into the flat they found the three men lying on the floor studying the blueprints. The superintendent had worked for the PIS since 1928. One of the men was his brother, the other was a PIS officer whose cover was as a salesman for a bogus oil and grease firm. During the years of the spy ring's existence, literally tons of material had been shipped back to Poland. The three chief defendants, including the superintendent, were sentenced to death. Schellenberg admired the courage and calm of the men. In the face of execution the superintendent told Schellenberg: "Today Germany is triumphant – but in the end, who knows?"[6]

The Abwehr in Scandinavia, 1933–40

The Scandinavian states (Denmark, Norway, Sweden, Iceland and Finland) had managed to stay out of World War I relatively unscathed, although in Finland a bloody civil war was fought in 1918 between socialists and communists (the Whites and Reds).[7] The region was of enormous interest to Germany for several reasons. Swedish ore from the mines of Gällivare and Kiruna, in Swedish Lapland, supplied most of Germany's iron and without this source Germany would be unable to produce arms. Sweden was also an important supplier of copper and ball bearings.

The iron ore was transported during the summer from Swedish ports in the Baltic, but during the winter these vital ore carriers depended on routes through Norwegian waters, using the ice-free port of Narvik in northern Norway and the Norwegian leads (ice-free channels) to transport the ore to Hamburg and Bremen. This made Norway vitally important in keeping Germany supplied all year round. In addition the long, ice-free Norwegian coastline, with its fjords and islands, could be put to good use by the Kriegsmarine. Norway was therefore a potential base for the Germans in any future naval and air war conducted against Britain. To launch an attack on Norway, Denmark would be needed to secure entry into the Baltic and as a staging post for troops and supplies. Finally, Finland was an important ally should relations with Stalin sour, and would serve to divert Soviet troops that could otherwise be used against Germany. For all these reasons, but mainly for Norway's ports and Sweden's iron ore, Germany took a very keen interest in the region.[8] Even Iceland was of interest.

Indeed, in 1938 when Peter Tennant, the British press attaché in Stockholm and a future representative of the Special Operations Executive (SOE) in Sweden, was on holiday in Iceland, he was surprised and dismayed to find in a country so close to Scotland and the North Atlantic sea lanes two German expeditions in residence. One of these was supposedly there to study, on behalf of Alfred Rosenberg the Nazi Party's chief ideologist, the Nordic culture of this "pure" Germanic race, while the other was surveying the island on the pretext of studying the volcanic rocks. Tennant was sure both were there to spy and find out where airfields, naval bases and other military installations, such as submarine pens, could be located.

Meanwhile, intelligence operations were under way in Norway. Hitler had visited the country in 1934

BELOW: *Cranes loading railway cars with iron ore from the mines of Kiruna in northern Sweden in 1940. These mines were of immense value to the German war effort.*

on board the battleship *Deutschland*, and had been mesmerized by the stupendous landscape and, of course, the coastline which could serve the Führer's expanding navy. It was the navy's interest in Norway that prompted the Abwehr I Marine division to expand its coverage in Scandinavia through the German Consulates in Bergen, Stavanger, Oslo, Christiansand, Skagen and Gothenburg. In September, naval Captain Mark Nolde was appointed German Consul in Trondheim. Nolde proved his worth to the Abwehr with his good contacts, while he also found out about Allied plans to invade Norway themselves. The head of KO Norwegen (the Abwehr station in neutral Norway) was the charismatic, unconventional and energetic Major Berthold Benecke. He was born in Hanover in 1889, and it was while working for the local Ast (Abwehr station) in Hanover that Benecke took the cover of Nordic representative for Ruhrstal A.G. Wittens Ltd. He

conducted an extensive tour of Scandinavia in 1937, including the Norwegian iron ore mines in South Varanger. His work earned him the praise of Canaris himself.

Benecke, disguised as "Dr. Altvater", returned as head of KO Norwegen on 1 December 1938, with radio operator Erich Opitz in tow as his assistant. Benecke, who liked the good things in life, rented a suite in Oslo's Grand Hotel and a flat in Bärum, one of the better parts of the Norwegian capital. Among the agents that Benecke recruited was Tor Glad,

better known as Agent "Jeff",[9] who was used by Benecke to find out which Norwegians in southwestern Norway and the Trondheim region were pro-Allied. Another agent was Eilif Hammerø, the leader of NNSP, the Norwegian Nazi Party,[10] who undertook a photographic tour of Norwegian coastal defences accompanied by Wolfgang Bödtker. Their information was sent by Opitz in radio messages which were picked up and reported to the Norwegian Secret Police (Sipo) by Norwegian radio amateurs. Despite this Opitz and Benecke were not served with expulsion orders until 4 April 1940, only five days before the Germans invaded.

The Norwegian Sipo kept a very close eye on a number of foreign nationals, including Lieutenant-Colonel Hermann Kempf,[11] a German "shipping

(via Switzerland) that élite Alpine troops, the legendary *Chasseurs Alpins*, had been moved from their encampment at Metz (where they were supporting the Maginot Line) to Britain. To Canaris this meant only one thing: the Anglo-French Allies aimed to move against Scandinavia. He believed they would use the excuse of aiding Finland against Stalin, to march from Narvik and seize control of the Swedish ore fields. This would cripple Germany's arms production and might lose her the war despite the conquest of Poland. The Naval High Command (Oberkommando der Marine – OKM) in Berlin agreed with the Abwehr analysis of the threat, and advanced plans for an invasion of Scandinavia.

Abwehr Moves on Denmark

At the end of February, an officer at the Hamburg Ast was called to the Brandenburger section (Commando zbV 31) on the top floor of the Tirpitz Ufer to report for "top secret duty". The intelligence officer (AO) was met there by a member of the General Staff and told he was being sent on a covert mission to Denmark. He was told about the Abwehr report from Metz that had triggered his mission, and that he had less than one month to make a thorough report on Denmark's defences. The Abwehr had traditionally used its presence in Denmark merely as a passive conduit for agents in other parts of Scandinavia. Denmark was not viewed as a military target in itself, and the German General Staff believed its tiny army, weak socialist government, flat geography and peaceful population would pose few problems for them if they chose to invade the country.

With the unnamed AO's arrival all this changed, and the V-men (undercover German agents) would for once have to prove their worth and actually do some active and uncomfortable field work. The V-men were sent to every corner of Denmark, especially Jutland and Zealand, to spy out defences. They reported back to the AO, stating whether the Danes had mined roads, obvious approaches and strong points on the Danish side of the German frontier. Danish military intelligence and the small security section of the Danish Police were totally unaware of this undercover reconnaissance work being carried out right under their noses. The agents

agent", together with Regierungsrat Pohl (Abwehr Major Erick Pruck) and Oberregierungsrat Berg (Korvettenkapitän Hans Meisner) both of whom were accredited to the German Legation.

The Abwehr I Marine division was to prove very efficient and controlled a coastal network to spy on Allied shipping. So accurate and fast was the intelligence that this section provided, that the Luftwaffe's X Air Corps could pinpoint and attack convoys with deadly precision. There was such a shortage of U-boats that it was the Luftwaffe that had to sink Allied shipping. During the winter of 1939–40, over 150,000 tonnes (152,400 tons) were sunk due to these agents' reports. During the second half of January 1940, the resident Abwehr agent in the French city of Metz reported to the Hamburg Ast

ABOVE: *The élite French* Chasseurs Alpins *disembarking in a characteristically flamboyant fashion during their landing near Narvik in northern Norway in April 1940. They fought well during the Norwegian campaign.*

all returned to Copenhagen safely. No-one had been aware of their work or even presence in such sensitive areas. They reported that taking Denmark would be, from a military point of view, simply a matter of marching in and taking over. The AO decided to attach an intelligence officer to each of the invading columns that would take Jutland. These columns would be spearheaded by Abwehr officers, both in disguise and in uniform, to pave the way for the invasion. The Germans were confident the invasion and peaceful occupation of Denmark would be a repeat of Operation Otto, the takeover of Austria in 1938.

The Norwegian Sipo may have been observant about what the German spies were up to, but it missed one crucial German visitor. It did not spot

that a certain "Oberregierungsrat Fuchs" had taken a suite at the Grand Hotel in Oslo on 31 March 1940. "Fuchs" was none other than Canaris on one of his fact-finding trips. The admiral hoped that he could persuade Hitler that invading Norway would only extend Germany's military resources needlessly. He also wanted to speak with "La Roche", Abwehr Major Walter de Laporte, who had two major agents in Norway. One was the former defence minister and leader of the right-wing nationalist NS Party, Vidkun Quisling, and the other was Dr. Hermann H. Aall. Both were valuable agents with contacts and friends that could prove useful. On Hitler's express order, a senior Abwehr officer called Piekenbrock summoned Quisling to Denmark for a top-secret meeting at the Hotel d'An'laterre in Copenhagen on 3 April. Quisling told the Abwehr officer more or less what he already knew, but he included three vital pieces of new intelligence. The Norwegian forts at Horten and Dröbak, that guarded the entrance to the Oslo fjord, would not fire without express permission from higher authority. Furthermore, the Norwegians had not had the forethought to place mines in the Oslo fjord, and none of the Norwegian airfields were properly defended. These useful pieces of intelligence greatly facilitated the plans for Operation Weser, the German invasion of Norway and Denmark.

Meanwhile, the diplomatic staff from the legation in Oslo also began making invasion preparations. The air attaché, Eberhard Spiller, and his naval counterpart, Richard Schreiber, were caught taking photos of British ships in the harbour of Ålesund. The Norwegian Sipo had had both men watched for a considerable length of time. They were caught red-handed and the film, despite their loud protests that they were diplomats, was confiscated. Both men were released, but others were not so lucky. Among the agents working for Admiral Steffens in Stockholm Abwehr M, and for Hermann Kempf (Oslo KO), was agent "Fidelio", Karl Muller,[12] a German iron ore inspector in Narvik who worked closely with the German Consul in Narvik, Fritz Wussow. Muller was picked up by the Norwegian Ovpo[13] (Surveillance Police) on 23 January 1940, and an inspection of his papers revealed that he had been in Norway since April 1939. Wussow was lucky not to be swept into the net. Another German diplomat, the German Vice Consul in Kirkenes, Korvettenkapitän Otto Beutler, stayed in a local hotel where he had set up a transmitter and conspicuous aerial sticking out of a window. The Ovpo had kept Beutler and his suspicious radio set under observation, and on 20 April, a week after the invasion, he was arrested and kept in custody.

Invasion (9 April–10 June 1940)

It was no coincidence that the Abwehr KO in Oslo was housed in a large flat at 7 Klingenbergsgaten with an excellent view of the harbour. The socialist government of Prime Minister Johan Nygaardsvold was blind to every sign that there was a German invasion on the way, while the Norwegian foreign minister, Halvdan Koht, who combined an unfortunate capacity for limitless gullibility with pacifism, believed the rumours of an invasion were deliberate propaganda on the part of the British to sour relations with Germany.

Despite confusion at the highest levels of government, there were some in Norway who acted with decision during the early hours of the invasion. During the morning of 9 April the commandant of Oscarsborg at the mouth of the Oslo fjord, ordered his guns and torpedoes to fire at an unidentified ship. That ship was the German battleship *Blücher* which sank with nearly all hands, including the administrative staff that was to run occupied Norway. Meanwhile, the Speaker of the Norwegian Parliament organized the evacuation of the government, parliament and the royal family out of Oslo.

Averting Potential Disasters

On 9 April, the same day that the Germans began the invasion of Norway, they occupied Denmark without any serious resistance. Norway, however, which was supposed to collapse the same way, proved a harder nut to crack. To begin with German plans were upset because the Wehrmacht radio sets and the crews to man them had gone down with the *Blücher*. The situation was retrieved by the fast work of Abwehr agent Hermann Kempf, who set up his radio on the moored steamer SS *Vidar,* and was able to send Hamburg Ast over 250 messages during the first day of the invasion. This intervention, and it was not the last by the Abwehr, was crucial in keeping Berlin informed of events on the ground.

Having escaped Oslo, the Norwegian Government retreated north to the town of Lillehammer. The Wehrmacht wanted to land commando troops on the ice of Lake Mjösa south of the town and from there capture Lillehammer, cutting off the Norwegian leadership from escape and forcing a nationwide surrender. Major Benecke, head the Abwehr KO in Norway, was sceptical about the feasibility of the plan and sent one of his agents to Lake Mjösa. The agent found that the ice was too thin, and Benecke managed to avert a total disaster. The major felt, as did many Germans, that the Norwegians would be willing to talk and capitulate given the right emissary. Benecke therefore sent his agent Christian Preuthen for talks with King Håkon VII. Preuthen was sent to get in touch via the king's physician,

LEFT: *The Brandenburgers crossing a lake behind enemy lines on the Finnish sector of the Eastern Front, with the aim of cutting the Soviet-controlled Murmansk railway.*

Professor Slavesen. Nothing came of this approach, but Preuthen was able to find out about the political intrigues and public mood in Lillehammer. Benecke also sent his agents to Telemarken, where they were almost shot as Allied agents by a roving and trigger-happy German patrol.

Benecke was active on all fronts. He sent Emmerich Neumayer,[14] disguised as a field pastor, into Sweden to spy out whether this neutral state was making any preparations to assist the Norwegians. Neumayer went north by rail to Narvik, where German élite mountain troops under General Dietl were fighting. He later reported that the Swedes were too paralyzed by fear to do anything to support the Norwegians.

He reported that the Swedes were too paralyzed by fear to do anything

The Abwehr Agent in Ballet Shoes

The star of Benecke's network was a Russian ballerina, Marina Goubinina, born to lower Russian nobility in 1902, and whose family had been deported and put to death in one of Lenin's Siberian death camps in 1918. Marina, combining brains, looks, charm, courage and a good portion of luck,[15] managed to survive in the new socialist Russian state. She became an established ballerina, set up her own ballet ensemble in Leningrad (St. Petersburg), and in 1931 met and married a Norwegian businessman, Einar Lie. What her new husband did not know was that Goubinina was a long-serving agent of the NKVD. Ordered to replace the NKVD resident in Oslo, Rudolf Abel, Goubinina got herself and her husband expelled from Russia so that she could go to Norway. Goubinina set up a ballet company in Oslo as a cover so that she could make regular trips to Italy and Germany. In 1938 she met Benecke, and from the beginning it was a case of mutual attraction.

Goubinina reported directly to the Soviet Ambassador in Stockholm, Madame Kollontay, and returned to Leningrad for new instructions in August 1939. A month later Goubinina, with the NKVD's blessings and with express orders to fulfil her new "duties", was recruited by the Abwehr. She was to prove Benecke's star agent, but he never knew that the Russian ballerina was a double agent working for the NKVD. Goubinina was sent with Christian Preuthen on the aborted mission to negotiate with the Norwegian king. Having failed to parley with the stubborn monarch, Goubinina was given another task. She was sent to Narvik and General Dietl's HQ at Bjønefell via Sweden, and there she donned the disguise of a Red Cross nurse. She infiltrated the Allied HQ in Bjerkvik and from there she directed a Stuka attack which almost killed the Allied commanders in Narvik, Norwegian General Otto Ruge and French General Béthouart. On 20 May 1940, Goubinina was back in Sweden where she gained access to the Norwegian legation in Stockholm. During a party there she overheard a conversation between the Norwegian ambassador and military attaché about the poor situation on the Norwegian side of the Narvik Front. She took the first train north and was back at Dietl's HQ by 24 May, where her report persuaded Dietl to continue fighting rather than retreating into Sweden where his troops would have been interned for the duration of the war. This was quite a coup for Benecke and earned him great praise in Berlin.

Benecke's Downfall

Despite the successful work of his field agents, Benecke's career was to be ruined by his meddling in the murky waters of Norwegian politics. Benecke hated the nationalist leader Quisling and viewed him, with some justification, as a crooked Nazi traitor and a liability to German efforts to establish a collaborationist regime acceptable to most Norwegians. Benecke obtained material via Goubinina that showed that as early as 1923 Soviet state security (then known as OGPU), had suspected Quisling of being in the pay of the British SIS. Attempts to discredit Quisling were to prove the

Abwehr chief's undoing because the Norwegian's powerful German sponsors, Grand Admiral Raeder and Alfred Rosenberg, found out about Benecke's intrigues. Benecke was forced to leave Norway in June 1940, but not before he prevailed upon Canaris to transfer Goubinina to Spain where she remained until her death in 1976.

The conquest of Scandinavia, completed with Norway's capitulation on 10 June, was a major success for the Abwehr. But even greater laurels lay ahead in the West against the Low Countries and France. No campaign established the reputation of the German intelligence services for efficiency as that of the Western campaign through the Netherlands and Belgium in May 1940. Germany's enemies, above all Britain, would come to believe that the Abwehr, and even more so the SD, had agents everywhere.

It was through the Ausland Organization of expatriate nationalists that the German intelligence services established lasting and valuable contacts with the Flemish nationalists in Belgium. This group opposed the French-dominated Belgian Government and royal court but were not exactly pro-German They were even less sympathetic to the Nazis during the 1930s. However, the Flemish nationalists could be trusted to disrupt the Belgian armed forces during the May 1940 campaign.

During the period of the "phoney war" the Germans were investigating ways of invading neutral Holland and Belgium as part of a general offensive in the West. The key to outflanking the Dutch river defences was to seize the bridges across the Maas and Rhine rivers intact before the defenders could blow them up. The idea of tricking the Dutch with disguised German troops was

Gerken's two collaborators denied all knowledge of the purchases of uniforms, but the police searching the premises found several trunks filled with uniforms addressed to Richard Gerken. They told the men that they knew that Gerken was an Abwehr agent working in the Netherlands, and both father and son broke down and confessed their complicity in the plot. Despite this success it seems that the Dutch did not make the best use of this intelligence, since the Germans took defending troops by surprise by disguising themselves in Dutch uniforms on 10 May when their invasion began.

This campaign of infiltration was to begin badly, however. At Venlo the Dutch destroyed a German armoured train with 10 German agents on board, though the railway bridge at Gennep was captured intact. A troop train passed the bridge safely but the Dutch managed to blow up the bridge at Zeeland. At Nijmegen the road and railway bridges were blown up right in front of the infuriated Germans. Nevertheless, on other sectors of the front the Germans broke through and moved deep inside Dutch and Belgian territory with consummate ease. On 15 May after both determined and stubborn resistance, the Dutch were forced to capitulate to the invaders: Belgium surrendered on 28 May.[16]

France: The FHW's Finest Hour

France had both an inflated reputation for military power and for superb intelligence services, neither of which was, in the light of later events, justified. The German armed forces, as well as the Abwehr and other intelligence agencies, also had an exaggerated respect and fear of the French. The task of defeating the French in the field of intelligence was the responsibility of Foreign Armies West (Fremde Heere West – FHW), under the leadership of General Ulrich Liss and his subordinates, Major von Xylander and Colonel Count von Rönne (a committed anti-Nazi and later head of the FHW during 1943–44).[17]

Hitler's. Why not infiltrate the Dutch defences with German troops wearing Dutch uniforms? Abwehr agent Richard Gerken was despatched to the Netherlands to buy the uniforms. Gerken went to the small town of Dennekamp where he knew of an ardent Dutch Nazi who might help him, and the Dutchman was more than willing to assist.

Gerken, the Dutch Nazi and his 20-year-old son travelled to Amsterdam where they made contact with two other Nazis. Together they went to a clothes store run by a Dutch Jew, Heer Blum, and requested that they needed 150 Dutch Army uniforms for an opera performance in Osnabrück of "The Count of Luxembourg". Blum was not convinced and so, deeply suspicious, made a note of the car's registration number and phoned the Dutch Police. On 2 November 1939 the police raided the Nazi's home in Dennekamp.

Liss correctly judged that the French were poorly led and even more poorly equipped. Before war broke out, an accurate assessment of the French armed forces had been provided by the Abwehr agent "Frogé", who worked in the French Army Commissariat Office. Frogé showed that the French reserves were poorly equipped, poorly disciplined and lacked motivation. Furthermore, he reported that the French arms industry was not only slow in delivering arms but also in producing them. Frogé was eventually caught by French counter-intelligence but not before he had provided the Abwehr with useful intelligence of every kind.

Fighting a Paper Tiger

If Liss could conclude that the French Army and Air Force would not pose too many problems for the German panzer forces, then what about the fabled Maginot Line which shielded France's eastern frontier? Liss saw it as his main task to get as much intelligence on this vaunted defence work as possible. The Czechs had been given access to the line during the alliance with France in 1935–38, and a great deal of information about it was provided to the Germans when the archives of Czech military intelligence were captured in Prague in April 1939. The FHW made a detailed model of each fort in the Maginot Line, and then proceeded to give German officers a "tour" to familiarize them with the layout.

When war broke out Liss did not have a single agent inside France, and had no information on the British forces being deployed on the Continent. He had to rely on general assessments of where French units were deployed. But the FHW broke the French Army codes and gradually built up an accurate picture of the French order of battle. Intelligence soon revealed a picture of how weak the French Ninth Army in the Ardennes was. When Liss showed the map with French deployments on it to the OKH chief, General Halder, the general immediately spotted this weakness: "Hier ist die schwache Stelle", Halder

LEFT: *Guderian and his HQ staff using the famous Enigma machine. The Enigma was a mechanical masterpiece but its codes were cracked by the Allies.*

said pointing at the Ninth Army sector, "Hier müssen wir durch". (Here is the weak point. Here we must punch through).

Liss' knowledge was far from complete, though. He did not know the exact location of the French reserves or their strength, nor could he tell the OKH whether the French could launch a strong counter-attack from the south against the advancing panzer columns. Liss' hunch was that the French would be unable to react with any great force or speed. This view was reinforced by reports from Abwehr agents in the field: French troops manning the Maginot Line had low mobility. They could not, therefore, be switched to a more exposed sector with ease. This was doubly unfortunate since Liss believed the French had placed their best troops in the Maginot Line. Superb aerial photographs, taken in January 1940, revealed that the Ninth Army had not been reinforced and that the French had not used the time granted them to improve their border defences in the Ardennes sector. It was still Halder's "weak spot" and therefore suitable for a large-scale offensive.

Placing the Final Pieces of the Jigsaw.

New intelligence arriving in March 1940 revealed the whereabouts of the French reserves and these were, fortunately for the Germans, evenly spread behind the French lines. The Allies, to judge from radio monitoring and decoded messages, were still completely in the dark concerning German intentions. During early 1940 German intelligence on the Allies improved greatly due to a flow of decoded radio messages, and by end of April Liss had completed the French and British orders of battle. Liss underestimated neither Allied power nor overestimated it; he got the estimates just right, which is most unusual in a wartime situation.

France was defeated in a swift and brilliantly conducted German military operation of only seven weeks, from 12 May to 25 June. British Prime Minister Winston Churchill could not believe that the "Austrian corporal" had broken France in a mere few weeks when the Kaiser had failed during four long, bloody years. Much of the credit for defeating France went to the FHW and Liss. This was their finest hour; they were not have such a golden moment again.

Chapter 5

The Island Fortress

"Ah, Schellenberg, when you've been as long in this business as you and I one starts to see pink elephants everywhere!"[1]

Abwehr Colonel Helferich to W. Schellenberg (1943)

THE GERMANS HAD A STRANGE LOVE-HATE RELATIONSHIP with their British "cousins". They respected Britain as a fellow "Germanic" power. Indeed, had not the Saxons come from northern Germany? The Germans admired the British for their style, wealth, polished manners, colonial empire, and they were in awe of the British Secret Intelligence Service (SIS). Canaris saw the SIS as the intelligence organization that his Abwehr should imitate, while Heydrich had an almost schoolboyish admiration for British spies, especially the founder of the SIS, the mysterious Mansfield Cumming, the spymaster also known as "C". Like Cumming, Heydrich wrote his signature in green ink, but such exaggerated and immoderate admiration was quickly transformed the moment that Britain dared to stand in the way of Germany.

On the British side, during the late 1930s, the government of Neville Chamberlain hoped that a group of German conservative generals would take action to put a stop to Hitler's madness and move to overthrow the Austrian "guttersnipe". For their part, Hitler and many other Germans were sure

that Britain would come to her senses and make a compromise peace once Poland had been crushed. After all, wasn't it fair that in return for a free hand to run her empire Britain allowed Germany the same courtesy in Europe?

Such views were indicative of the fact that neither side understood the psyche of the other particularly well. No German officer, however strongly opposed to Hitler's rule, would take lightly the prospect of committing treason against the state by plotting the overthrow of the country's Chancellor and Führer, while the British were at their most intransigent and stubborn, even fanatical, when their collective backs were up against the wall. During 1940 the British will to resist Hitler grew and became rock-solid, and there was popular support for a war to the finish, though not all agreed with the "fight to the last man" attitude, embodied by Winston Churchill. But this did not mean there existed a powerful peace party in Britain or that such a political group was willing to negotiate in a serious manner with Hitler.[2]

In late 1939, the eagerness of the British to recruit Germans willing to mount a coup against the Nazis would lead to a major intelligence debacle for the SIS in the Netherlands. Holland was Britain's intelligence bridgehead on the continent for good reason. It was still a neutral country and within easy

LEFT: *Aerial view of 1940s London, the centre of the British Empire and the seat of the British Government. German attempts to infiltrate Britain during the war were poorly conceived and all came to naught.*

reach of Britain. It had good communications, the population was generally Anglophile, and most importantly of all it was very close to Germany. The drawback was that the Germans also had a strong presence in the country. In The Hague (*Den Haag*), a Dutch agent of the local SIS station was bribed by the Abwehr into becoming a double agent, and supplied his new masters with detailed insights into the SIS station's work. Another Dutch double agent, SD Agent F–479, posed as a German double agent and convinced the local SIS chief, Major Richard Stevens, and his deputy, Captain Sigismund Payne Best, that he was in touch with just the kind of German military opposition group the British had been hoping to contact. The agent was in fact in touch with the SD and Walter Schellenberg. Schellenberg and a colleague posed as members of the alleged group, and did their work so well that Best and Stevens were convinced that they had found what they were looking for. The British agents set up a meeting to take place at Venlo, just inside the Dutch frontier, and went so far as to offer Schellenberg the chance to escape to London. The daring young SD commander wanted to take them up on their offer and make contact with the SIS in London, but both Heydrich and Himmler were wary. They ordered Schellenberg to break off his plans for the trip to London and instead kidnap the two senior SIS officers. Schellenberg protested, but to no avail.

The plan the Germans drew up was simple. Best and Stevens would be lured to a meeting at the border town of Venlo, where a squad of 12 SS men handpicked by Heydrich would crash through the border barrier and grab them.

Abduction in Holland

On the afternoon of 9 November 1939 Schellenberg entered a Venlo cafe just across the

BELOW: The hotel in Venlo on the Dutch side of the Dutch-German frontier where, in November 1939, SIS officers Best and Payne were seized and taken back to Germany.

border, where he waited nervously drinking coffee for over an hour and a half. The two SIS officers were not taking any chances, and the heavy presence of Dutch border police and frontier guards only made Schellenberg more nervous. Finally Best and Stevens' Buick appeared and drove around the cafe at high speed, finally coming to a crashing halt outside the cafe's back entrance. Schellenberg was just making his way out to meet them when there was an almighty crash as an SS truck smashed through the Dutch border barrier. The Dutch frontier guards were thrown into confusion and failed to stop the determined SS intruders.

Best was at the wheel of the car but it was a Dutch intelligence officer, Lieutenant Coppens, who was accompanying the two SIS men, who jumped out. He brandished a heavy service revolver at Schellenberg, who was unarmed, and was about to shoot him when the SS truck careered around the corner of the cafe. Coppens shot at the truck but the SS man driving it got out unharmed and shot Coppens, who fell to the ground. As Schellenberg fled back to his own car an SS man was about to shoot him, as he looked something like Best, but this time it was the SS squad leader who intervened. Outnumbered and outgunned, Stevens and Best were dragged out of their car, bundled into the truck, and driven across the border at high speed. They were then taken to Berlin for a thorough "debriefing". Their intelligence provided the SD and the Gestapo with a wealth of detailed and highly damaging intelligence about the structure and divisions within the Secret Intelligence Service; its offices, departments and staff in London, as well as overseas. The SS squad which snatched the two officers was thanked by Hitler personally in the Chancellery, and awarded Iron Crosses for their heroic exploits. Venlo was a major propaganda coup for the Germans and a major setback to the SIS. With the capture of Best and Stevens the whole of the SIS network in Europe, which was run directly and indirectly from the Netherlands, was compromised. It also had a serious effect on SIS morale. Having burnt their fingers badly, the SIS would be wary of any future contacts with the German opposition.

ABOVE: *Walter Schellenberg. Born in the Saarland, Schellenberg was known for his charm and easy going character as a Halbfranzose (half-French). It was not meant as a compliment, but implied shiftiness and unreliability.*

Throughout 1940–41, the darkest days of the war for Britain, the USA, though still ostensibly neutral, gave friendship and indirect material support that was a beacon of hope. However, not all Americans were enamoured with this flourishing de facto alliance with the British.

Traitors in the US Embassy

In Paris, US Ambassador William Bullitt predicted in early 1940 that France would fall, Britain would follow suit and Oswald Mosley, the leader of the BUF,[3] would replace Chamberlain as prime minister and make a reasonable peace with the Germans. Bullitt's fellow ambassador in London, Joseph Kennedy, was just as defeatist. President Roosevelt, usually a shrewd judge of character and good at choosing the right men, picked disastrously when he appointed Kennedy. The British were not pleased to have an outspokenly

Anglophobic Irish-American, with a shady past from the bootlegging era and some very unsavoury views, as the US Ambassador. Kennedy predicted Britain's imminent destruction, and took the view that it was a fate well-deserved. His reports were riddled with inaccuracies, falsehoods and as much defeatist gossip as he could cram into them. Churchill avoided Kennedy, as did most members of the British Government. To avoid having to communicate through his ambassador, President Roosevelt sent his own representatives to Churchill and had a direct telephone line installed to London. Kennedy ended up creating so much suspicion that his phones were bugged and his mail was opened by MI5. In some respects he merited the same treatment as a suspected spy, and in a way he was an agent of sorts; an agent of bad influence.

Vigilant officers of MI5 had kept Del Monte under surveillance for a long time

Del Monte and the Right Club
But Joseph Kennedy was not the real traitor in the US Embassy in London. That turned out to be Tyler Kent, a junior clerk in the embassy communications HQ. Dissatisfaction is the first danger sign in a traitor, and Kent was an educated and well-connected member of the East Coast élite down on his luck and dissatisfied with his lowly position in the embassy. He also had access to the communications that passed between the president and the prime minister. Kent did not like what he read, since like many Americans he opposed US entry into the war. He began to copy documents and hide them in a brown leather bag in his apartment. Then, in early 1940, Kent met and befriended Anna Wolkoff, a member of the pro-fascist Right Club, who had close links with Captain Ramsay, the club's founder and renegade Tory Member of Parliament. Kent showed the documents to Ramsay and Wolkoff, who had the documents photographed. Wolkoff then passed the photos on to the Italian military attaché in London,[4] Don Francesco Maringliano, Duke of Del Monte, who in turn passed the information on to Rome for further transfer to Berlin.

MI5 officers had kept Del Monte and other guests of the Right Club under surveillance for a long time. They knew Del Monte knew Wolkoff and that the Italian was a suspiciously frequent visitor to her parents' cafe in London, the Russian Tea Room, where Kent also met her for clandestine transfers of documents. Having seen, heard and collected enough evidence, MI5 decided to act. Early on the morning of 20 May 1940 MI5 officers, accompanied by a security officer from the US Embassy, raided Kent's flat at 47 Gloucester Place in central London. After breaking down the door (Kent at first refused to let them in when they knocked), the MI5 officers presented Kent with a search warrant and found almost 2000 embassy documents spread around the flat, including the Roosevelt-Churchill correspondence. When Ambassador Kennedy was told of Kent's activities he fired the errant clerk immediately so that the British could haul him before a criminal court. Kent was found guilty and sentenced to seven years in prison for spying.

The Swedes and the Anglo-German Peace
Sweden has a long and unpleasant history of "peace at any price", and its fear of war has often been fronted by an ideological veneer of pacifism. By mid-1940 the "pragmatic minded" Swedes could not understand why the British would not accept that they had been beaten by Germany. In June a most interesting conversation took place at the Foreign Office in Whitehall between Björn Prytz, the Swedish Ambassador, and "Rab" Butler, the British Parliamentary Under-Secretary of State for Foreign Affairs. While Butler made it quite clear that Britain would fight on, he also mentioned that no stone would be left unturned if a reasonable peace could be reached with Germany. This attitude should not be misconstrued in Stockholm, Butler stressed. The possibility of a negotiated peace still existed, but Britain would not accept "peace at any price". It was later suggested to the ambassador by some Members of Parliament that these negotiations would begin on 28 June, once Churchill had been replaced as prime minister by Lord Halifax, the

foreign secretary. Churchill intervened to put a stop to these peace moves. In 1941 Halifax was shipped off to the USA as British Ambassador, while Butler spent the rest of the war as Minister of Education, where his alleged defeatism would not undermine the war effort.

Efforts by the Swedes to broker a peace took another tack later the same summer. Between 26–28 July 1940, Göring called in his old Swedish crony and "peace emissary", Birger Dahlerus, for consultations. Göring hoped that Dahlerus could establish a conduit for talks with London through the Swedish king, Gustavus V. The Swedish King was a Germanophile and acceded to Göring's suggestion, writing a letter to King George VI appealing for peace before Europe was destroyed. Suspicious of Sweden's pro-German leanings, neither the king nor Churchill were particularly pleased with this uncalled for and uninvited gesture. The British reply was both frigid and clear on one point: under no circumstances would there be any peace negotiations with Hitler.

The Germans could not accept that the British, under Churchill's intransigent leadership, really meant business. In response to an off-the-cuff

ABOVE: His Excellency the American Ambassador to the Court of St. James, Joseph Kennedy, wearing his characteristic glasses, with staff at the US Embassy.

remark by the British envoy in Stockholm, Sir Victor Mallet, that the British Government was interested in secret peace negotiations, the Germans hatched another plan. Following Mallet's remarks, a special peace envoy, Dr. Ludwig Weissauer, arrived in Stockholm from Berlin and the Swedes assumed he had been sent by Ribbentrop. In fact Weissauer was an agent of the SD.

Secret Negotiations

Weissauer went to see a Swedish contact, Birger Ekeberg, and suggested he act as a go-between to set up a clandestine meeting between Weissauer and Mallet to explore the chances for peace. Ekeberg saw Mallet on 5 September 1940 and broached the German invitation which the British envoy declined, but said he would contact London for instructions. Ekeberg emerged from this meeting with the firm opinion that the British Cabinet was deeply divided between a peace faction in favour of talks with Germany and the Churchill group, which wanted nothing to do with such talks. When Mallet's report arrived in London the Weissauer approach was treated, quite rightly, with the deepest and most hostile suspicion. On 19 September 1940 Churchill's secretary, Colville, noted in his diary that there had been more peace feelers from the enemy and not just from Stockholm. They had all had been rejected, as was the Weissauer-Ekeberg channel. The British Government, divided or not, believed this peace overture was only designed to sow discord in the Cabinet's ranks. Mallet informed Ekeberg that there would be no meeting with Weissauer and that further overtures were not welcome. Nevertheless, Weissauer returned to Berlin and waited for a signal from London to return to Stockholm to begin peace talks. The signal from London never came.

Hitler admitted to being a land animal with an abiding fear of the seas. After the British Army had been pushed out of France in early June, the question remained how the war could be taken to Britain while the Royal Navy controlled the seas, and in particular the narrow, but dangerous, stretch of water of the English Channel.

Himmelfahrtskommando: Operation Lena

Canaris realized that the British would fight on and that Hitler would have to plan an invasion. Hitler, however, only came around to planning the operation in July. He was too busy savouring the sweet aftermath of his victory over France. When he finally revealed his invasion plan, "Sea Lion", the plan left his senior military commanders quite cold. The German Navy complained that it had lost many of its ships during the invasion and occupation of Norway, while the army pointed out that its invasion force travelling across the Channel in barges needed both air and sea protection from a British attack. The two senior services then looked sternly at Göring's Luftwaffe and demanded that the German Air Force gain absolute air superiority over the skies of southern England before Sea Lion was launched. Göring agreed to the task very reluctantly. Göring's problem was that unlike the Royal Air Force (RAF), the Luftwaffe was not suited to wage a battle on its own. It had won its campaigns in Europe fighting in close cooperation with the

ABOVE: *King Gustavus V of Sweden was not a neutral or reliable conduit for peace with the British, given his natural inclination to support Germany. This made him a very unpopular figure with the British.*

other arms, particularly the army, and was not equipped to sustain a strategic air campaign.

Senior commanders were not the only ones to have reservations about the invasion plan. Hitler did not underestimate his foe and he rued the lack of accurate intelligence. Hitler lamented: "We are divided from England by a ditch 37km (23 miles) wide and we are not even able to get to know what is happening there!"[5]

On 2 July 1940, Canaris, Piekenbrock and Lahousen attended the OKW conference that outlined the plan of Operation Sea Lion. Given that OKW was planning an invasion with virtually no information about British defence preparations, it was obvious that Hitler and Field Marshal Keitel, the Abwehr's nominal bosses, expected some kind of miracle from their military intelligence service. Canaris could not conjure up agents overnight, and he viewed the whole undertaking as madness. The admiral pondered how many agents would be needed to deliver the kind of intelligence desired, and where he was going to find enough agents willing to go on what would most likely be a suicide mission.

The Calibre of Recruits

The recruits came from the strangest of sources. None were stranger or more exotic than Vera Chalburg.[6] She is believed to have been a Russian Jewess born in Kiev in 1914 whose brother, blonde and blue eyed, joined the Danish Palace Guard and died fighting alongside the SS on the Eastern Front. There were many people of Jewish ancestry in the German armed forces, and the SD and Abwehr took the same attitude to their recruitment: employing Jews for secret work when it suited their purposes to do so.

According to one Abwehr agent, Jörgen Börresen, Vera first turned up in Paris where she began working for the NKVD, while also maintaining close contacts with the SIS station head, Commander Dunderdale. She ended up supposedly working for the Abwehr when she became the lover of Hilmar Dierks, the head of the Abwehr's marine intelligence section.

The Abwehr's preparation for Sea Lion, which included both infiltration and sabotage, was codenamed Operation Lena, and was organized by the Hamburg Ast under Captain Herbert Wichmann. The plan was so secret that the Abwehr needed another layer of security to cover its tracks. The service had acquired the firm of Stegemann Ltd., which had offices in the centre of the busy port city. In charge of this elaborate cover operation was the head of the Economics Section of the Hamburg Ast, Captain Dr. Praetorius. To parachute its agents into England the Abwehr had set up a special squadron under Luftwaffe Captain

ABOVE: Prime Minister Winston Churchill (left) strolling through Whitehall in London accompanied by his secretary and loyal right-hand man, the diligent and tough-minded Brendan Bracken.

Gartenfeld, the imaginatively titled "Gartenfeld Squadron". Actual command was in the incapable hands of Abwehr man Nikolaus Ritter, who had only the most theoretical experience of intelligence work.

One of Ritter's more unrealistic schemes was to spy on the British political establishment by financing a brothel in the Mayfair district of London, known as the Green House, run by a Mrs Erikson from Grimsby and a rather dubious Italian who called herself the Countess Montabelli de Condo. The idea, borrowed from Heydrich's infamous SD brothel, Salon Kitty, in Berlin, was that clients would engage in unguarded pillow talk that could provide useful intelligence.[7] Though Ritter believed that the Abwehr had already infiltrated The Green House, the brothel was in fact run by MI5 who also employed the Countess and Mrs Erikson as double agents. Unaware of his mistake, Ritter used the The Green House as a cover for Vera, who was sent to London posing as Mrs Erikson's Norwegian niece, "Miss May Eriksen."[8] Two agents were found to accompany Vera on her mission. They were the Swiss, Werner Walti, and a Belgian, Karl Druegge.

Amateurish Agents

The three Abwehr spies got off to a poor start. On 26 September 1940, they made a failed attempt to land on the Scottish coast by seaplane and were forced to return to their base in Norway. Finally, on 30 September, they made it, landing on an isolated stretch of coast east of Inverness. While Walti made his way to Glasgow on his own, Vera and Druegge found their way to Portgordon train station. Their unexpected arrival with suitcases and soaking-wet shoes aroused the suspicions of the station master, who told his colleagues to keep an eye on the pair while he phoned the local policeman, John Grieve, who arrived promptly. Grieve noticed the same things about the pair and more besides. They had no entry or immigration stamps in their passports, Druegge spoke no English and all their papers were filled out in a foreign-looking script. Police Inspector John Simpson arrived soon afterwards to carry out a search and interrogation. Druegge was not only found to be carrying a torch made in Bohemia but in his wallet was £327 in sterling, a year's wages in 1940. Both Druegge and Vera were promptly arrested as German spies. During their trial held *in camera* (meaning it was a closed or secret

In desperation, the Abwehr sent several agents to Britain who spoke no English!

session) Vera testified against Druegge, which resulted in the Belgian's death sentence.

Walti, meanwhile, had got as far as Edinburgh where he deposited his suitcase, though not without arousing the attendant's suspicion. The attendant phoned Special Branch which sent Chief Constable Merriless, disguised as a porter, to keep an eye on the luggage desk. It wasn't too long before Walti reappeared, walking past left luggage several times before he finally approached and in a foreign accent asked for his suitcase. Merriless made his move, and in the ensuing struggle managed to overpower Walti before the Swiss had a chance to pull out his Luger pistol. Walti shared Druegge's fate at the hands of the British hangman.

Another of the Operation Lena agents, Karl Richter, a red-haired extrovert and enthusiastic piano player, also shared that fate. Richter was parachuted into England in 1941, and after his capture claimed repeatedly that he was innocent; a pretence he maintained right up until the moment he was brought to the scaffold. Vera, by contrast, survived the war. After she had told her full story at the MI5 interrogation centre known as Camp 020 on Ham Common outside London, she stayed in Britain and eventually married a man in the British armed forces.

Agents Jeff and Mutt

Tor Glad and John Moe were recruited in Norway by the Oslo Ast to spy on Britain. Glad was chosen because he appeared to be a loyal Nazi, while Moe was half English and spoke the language fluently. After one failed attempt they were landed off the coast east of the Moray Firth in Scotland, near the tiny hamlet of Crovie, at dawn on 7 April 1941. Their luck then quickly ran out. They had two British-made bicycles with them, and were stopped two hours later on the road by a police patrol car. They made no attempt to hide their purpose. Glad handed over his gun to the policemen while Moe showed them a transmitter hidden in his suitcase.

The following day the two men were taken down to London by the Aberdeen police, and handed over to MI5 for interrogation at Camp 020. It was there that Colonel Stephens, the camp's ruthless commandant, and his colleagues decided whether a spy was to be handed over for trial and probable execution or whether he would be allowed to collaborate with MI5 against the Abwehr. Moe's and Glad's lives hung by a thread. During their interrogation Moe pointed out that they had surrendered voluntarily. He also maintained that he was a British citizen and that the Norwegian Foreign Minister (in exile), Tryggve Lie, could vouch for his good character. Stephens was convinced and the pair were let out of the camp to begin work as double agents under MI5 supervision.

They were set up in a flat in north London (33 Crespigny Road) under the codenames of Jeff and Mutt (Moe and Glad respectively), from where they were to transmit bogus messages to the Abwehr in Hamburg. Soon afterwards Glad was shipped off to an internment camp for enemy agents on the Isle of Man after breaking his curfew to go on a drinking session with his MI5 minder, Phil Rea. It was not so much that Glad broke the curfew, but that he had managed to get Rea drunk while showing a little too much interest in Rea's previous operations overseas with the SIS. Either way MI5 was not taking chances. Glad's later contact with an Abwehr agent in Dartmoor prison (Camp 010) confirmed that he was probably a genuine Abwehr plant who had worked his way into Moe's confidence.

While Glad fell under suspicion, Mutt went to work for MI5 transmitting false reports to the Abwehr under the codename Agent Ja. He began by sending bogus reports of sabotage raids. These proved so believable that when the Abwehr asked for information about future British intentions, Mutt invented, after an imaginary inspection tour of Scotland, a story that the British had gathered a large invasion fleet aimed at Norway. This piece of deception contributed to the German failure to detect Operation Torch, the Allied landings in North Africa in November 1942. In February 1943, the British

launched Operation Oatmeal to fool the Abwehr into resupplying Mutt with money, a new transmitter and other supplies. It was a clever plan, but it came with a nasty surprise. The supply canisters the German aircraft dropped were found to be full of British equipment that had been previously dropped to the Dutch and French resistance movements. A year later, in 1944, Moe (Mutt) ended his career as a double agent and joined the regular British Army. He spent the years 1945–46 putting his language skills to good use interrogating German prisoners of war and former Nazi agents.

Eddie Chapman's Amazing Wartime Career

During the spring of 1940 London was hit by a wave of safe breakings that involved the use gelignite explosive. Soon the burglaries were dubbed the work of the "gelignite artiste". The man responsible was a

RIGHT: The target of aerial bombing and resistance sabotage: German invasion barges being massed in French Channel ports for the invasion of Britain in 1940.

ABOVE: The most famous, or infamous, brothel in Berlin: the SD-run "Salon Kitty", created and frequented by Heydrich himself. The intelligence gathered in the salon was mostly of limited use.

28-year-old called Eddie Chapman. In late June 1940, Chapman was cooling his heels in a prison cell on the island of Jersey (his criminal activities were not restricted to the mainland) when the Germans invaded this tiny speck of British soil off the coast of France. The Germans soon recognized that a man with Eddie's talents could be useful to the Abwehr and its campaign of sabotage during Operation Lena. Around Christmas 1940 Eddie, or "Fritz" as he was dubbed, was brought to the Hotel Lutetia in Paris, the headquarters of the Abwehr in France. He was then sent for a year-long sabotage and agent-training course at Nantes.

On 18 December 1942 Eddie was dropped in bad weather over East Anglia, and despite zero visibility made a safe landing. A month later gelignite was found to have been stolen from a quarry in Kent. Shortly afterwards the de

Havilland aircraft plant at Hatfield in Hertfordshire mysteriously went up in flames. Eddie's controller, Dr. Graumann, was delighted that his confidence in Eddie had not been misplaced. Chapman made his way back to Paris via Lisbon, and when he arrived he celebrated his exploits with his new Abwehr employers. He explained to them that some of his friends from the old days in the safe-cracking business helped him with Hatfield.

Unfortunately for the Abwehr, this was a complete tissue of lies, fabricated by Eddie and his MI5 controllers, who had given him the appropriate codename of "Zigzag". Eddie had stolen the explosive from a quarry in Sevenoaks, but he had gained entry to the de Havilland plant with the help of MI5. It was Eddie's MI5 controller, Major Jasper Maskelyne – an expert in deception – who had blown off part of the roof of the de Havilland factory, planted smoke bombs, blackened the adjoining area and spread debris around. All to fool German aerial reconnaissance into believing that the de Havilland plant was out of action and that aircraft production would be interrupted. The Abwehr accepted Eddie's version of events, and the next time the former safe-cracker popped up was in Oslo in May 1944, sporting an Iron Cross and living the good life on board a yacht. By World War II standards he was an exceptionally lucky man.

Agent "Tricycle": Double Agent Extraordinaire

Agent Tricycle was the British codename of Dusko Popov, a Serb whose family was rich by the standards of 1930s Yugoslavia. This enabled Popov to receive an education in Germany, at Heidelberg University, where he met and befriended Johann Jebsen, the supposed son of a wealthy Danish-German family of shipowners and traders. Jebsen (if that was his true identity) also worked for the Abwehr and recruited Popov into the service during the summer of 1940.[9] Popov's first meeting with his Abwehr controllers took place in Lisbon later the same year when he met the local station chief, Major Ludovico von Karsthoff. Karsthoff then introduced Popov to the head of Abwehr III (counter-intelligence), Captain Kramer. Kramer did a thorough job of exposing double agents and Popov was highly suspect in his eyes.

When he returned to his hotel one evening, an attractive brunette woman kept giving Popov the eye. Popov was shrewd and understood the girl had been sent to check him out. The following day Karsthoff could tell Popov exactly what had been said between the two the previous evening, and Popov admitted to knowing, and feeding the woman a load of rubbish. After this test he was accepted into the fold of the Abwehr and his training could begin. Karsthoff was in charge. Popov was taught how to operate a Leica camera, the use of codes and the correct method of sending reports. At the end of training his controllers gave Popov the unimaginative codename "Ivan 1".

Popov entered Britain on 20 December, after taking a 10-hour flight from Lisbon to Bristol with the Dutch airline KLM (which still operated between neutral and Allied countries). After landing he was not met by an Abwehr contact but was driven to London by Jock Horsfall of MI5's A Division. Popov was dropped off at the Savoy Hotel where he met and dined with Colonel "Tar" Robertson, head of MI5's Section B1. Section B1 was in charge of the double agents that the SIS were using to subvert the Abwehr's intelligence system. After four days of intense questioning by B1 officers, Popov was

BELOW: A Heinkel He III aircraft being painted black for its deployment as a transport plane for the Abwehr to drop agents in Britain.

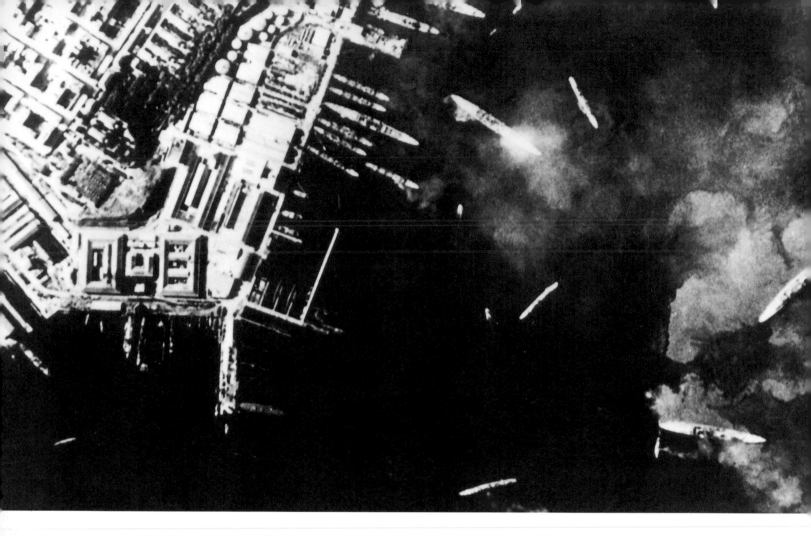

ABOVE: *The aftermath of the brilliantly executed British torpedo attack on the Italian fleet at anchor in the shallow bay of Taranto in 1940. The Japanese subsequently studied the raid in preparation for the Pearl Harbor attack.*

accepted into the SIS as agent "Scout". The new agent also had the privilege of meeting Stewart Menzies, the SIS chief, and of being invited to weekend parties to meet the great and the good of the British intelligence community. The Abwehr, of course, knew nothing of any of this.

Popov's controller was Bill Luke and as a cover an import/export company called Tarlair Ltd. was set up, ostensibly to trade with Spain and Portugal. Once his cover was established, Popov flew back to Lisbon where Karsthoff suggested that he set up a ring of agents for the Lisbon Ast. MI5 readily agreed.

The network Popov and MI5 established included Dickie Metcalfe; a businessman with good contacts, who, because he was quite rotund was given the codenamed "Balloon". There was also Friedel Gärtner, who had worked for Max Knight (a senior MI5 officer involved in the XX – Double Cross – scheme) in keeping an eye on Germans and Nazi sympathizers in Britain before

the war, particularly as a guest at the Ausland Organization's offices in Eastbourne Terrace. Gärtner was given the codename "Gelatine" and fed the Lisbon Ast with political intelligence. Popov's brother, Dr. Ivo Popov, also joined his brother's network as "Dreadnought", where his role was to keep the SIS informed about Abwehr operations being planned against the British Isles. Meanwhile, Popov was given a new mission name: "Tricycle".

In March 1941, Karsthoff met Popov in Lisbon and gave him a new mission designed to help Germany's ally, Imperial Japan. During a visit to Berlin, Japanese Ambassador Yoshiro Matsuoka had wanted the Germans to take a Japanese naval and naval aviation delegation to Taranto in Italy. It was there in November 1940 that a Royal Navy force under Admiral Cunningham had sent two squadrons of torpedo bombers to sink a good section of the Italian Navy. The Germans obliged the Japanese and persuaded the Italians to agree to the delegation. At Taranto the Japanese officers studied every detail of the bay, including its defences, and interviewed Italian officers who had experienced the British attack. Clearly the

Japanese wanted to learn how much could be achieved by a surprise air raid on a fleet at anchor.

In light of the Japanese Navy's sudden interest in Taranto, Karsthoff wanted Popov to travel to the USA, set up a network of agents there and spy out the US naval base at Pearl Harbor on the island of Oahu in Hawaii. Popov flew to New York in August 1941. He was met by agents of the FBI and driven to Manhattan where he had a disastrous meeting with Director J. Edgar Hoover, who took an instant dislike to him. Popov tried to warn the bigoted and narrow-minded American intelligence chief that the Japanese were using the Abwehr to spy out Pearl Harbor, and that they had taken a most keen and unhealthy interest in the British attack against the Italian Navy at Taranto. But Hoover wasn't interested in what Popov, a Nazi spy and "Balkan playboy", had to say. Popov stayed in New York womanizing, dining and boozing for the next year, and only returned to Lisbon in October 1942. He blamed his failure to create a spy network in

ABOVE: Dusko Popov, alias agent Tricycle or Ivan, the most famous and fascinating double agent of World War II. This photograph was taken after the war.

BELOW: Agent Zigzag (Fritz) had as his aim the disruption of production at the British Mosquito factory at Hatfield. Here, female employees work on the assembly line.

and fur-lined overalls. He was issued with Benzadrine tablets to keep him awake, a cyanide capsule to prevent being captured alive by MI5, a fake ID card, and £400 in sterling in his English patent leather wallet. He left Orly airport, near Paris, during the night of 6/7 September in an Abwehr plane, and was flown across the Isle of Wight heading for London.

The aircraft was quickly discovered. MI5 was on the alert, and radar tracked the lone plane as it progressed across the night skies over England. Schmidt, like Caroli, was picked up by a police patrol soon after landing and handed over to MI5. Schmidt, after some initial resistance, was turned into double-cross agent "Tate". "Tate" became invaluable to his British masters. He created massive fortifications and defences on the south coast where none really existed, and closed off 57,600 square kilometres (36,000 square miles) of water to U-boat operations by inventing a non-existent minefield off Britain's shores. He exaggerated, wildly, the size of the RAF, its capabilities and the state of British military aircraft production.

Wulf Schmidt, Agent 3725, continued to send reports until the very end of the war

A Successful British Operation
These claims left the Fremde Heere West (FHW) deeply suspicious of Agent 3725's facts and figures. The ever-unreliable Ritter was, of course, on hand to verify that Schmidt was a top agent and that his intelligence, at least to the Abwehr, was invaluable. Encouraged by success, Agent 3725 sent a request to the Hamburg Ast for more money and lots of it. Ritter, who believed that spying was really only about money, obliged, and asked the Japanese for their help in the transaction.

Before December 1941, Japan had not yet entered the war and still had a diplomatic presence in London. Schmidt was told to get on the No. 11 bus at Victoria Station. When he saw the Japanese courier, the assistant naval attaché Mitinori Yosii, he asked if there was anything new in the copy of *The Times* Yosii was carrying. Yosii replied:

"Nothing special, but you can have the paper if you like. I have read it." But it was only at the fifth stop that the Japanese agent handed over the folded newspaper that contained £20,000 in cash. MI5 was delighted with this since it proved that Schmidt still had the confidence of both Ritter and the Abwehr.

Schmidt continued to send reports until the very end of the war. After 1945 he was given a new identity and life by the SIS. He lived and worked in London to the end of his life. Schmidt played an important part in saving Britain from an invasion in late 1940 and early 1941. But he was only one of a huge number of double agents that sunk Abwehr espionage in Britain. Of the reputed 137 agents working for the Abwehr and SD, very few escaped the grasp of MI5. With the assistance of watchful train guards, policemen and a suspicious general public, the British security services had remarkable success in sabotaging the enemy's operations throughout the British Isles.

Germany's Best Agent
One of Germany's more successful agents went by the codename of "Ostro". Ostro had been an Abwehr agent since the early 1930s, running a worldwide network of spies from his headquarters in Lisbon. He had been spying in Eastern Europe since 1933 and Piekenbrock claimed that he was the Abwehr's best agent, remaining hidden and in full operation throughout the war years. He supplied the Abwehr with Polish operational plans prior to the invasion in September 1939, provided the Germans with Romanian oil production figures, and with vital data on the French and Belgian arms industries. He and his Scandinavian wife were spying in Denmark prior to the invasion of that country when they were arrested, but the Danes agreed to exchange the pair for four of their agents in Germany.

In 1940 Ostro moved to Lisbon where he set up an international trading company with a Belgian and Austrian émigré as partners. Ostro, who was both charming and a generous friend, gained

Right: A member of the Dutch resistance receiving instructions by radio from Britain. It was such transmissions by radio that could alert the German occupiers to this operator's existence.

access to most secrets in the Portuguese capital. But his equally charming and beautiful blonde wife was an even greater asset in getting intelligence from unsuspecting men. In Lisbon not much escaped this pair of master spies. Among his many achievements, Ostro recruited men to break into the British Embassy's safes, thereby acquiring the notebooks of British Ambassador Sir Ronald Campbell and his air attaché, Air Commodore Fullard, thus jeopardizing the outcome of Operation Torch.

What General Reinhard Gehlen, head of the Fremde Heere Ost (FHO), was to the ranks of the German spy masters so Ostro was to the unhallowed list of German spies. Ostro's real name was Paul Fidrmuc, born in Czechoslovakia in 1898. He served in the Austro-Hungarian Army and was recruited by the Abwehr in the late 1920s or early 1930s, though specific dates are unclear. Like Gehlen, he was a born survivor and flourished in the chaos of the inter-war years. Through his knowledge of Eastern European affairs he ended up in General Franco's Spain, where he served the Spanish intelligence services as loyally and competently as he had served the Abwehr.

Operations in the Netherlands

In intelligence terms Britain was to the Abwehr what the Bermuda Triangle was to shipping: agents sent in never came out.

The Abwehr, however, had its own deadly black hole waiting for its enemy, the British Special Operations Executive (SOE),[12] and that was the Netherlands. That country had been, as noted before, the scene of one of Britain's greatest intelligence debacles, and the German success was mainly due to uniquely harmonious and successful cooperation between the Abwehr and the SD.

After the fall of Holland in May 1940, the Dutch intelligence services in exile, based in London, had tried and failed to infiltrate themselves back into their country. The SOE should have taken heed of the Dutch failures. By mid-summer 1940, Dutch Police Chief F. van't Sant had rebuilt the CI (*Centrale Inlichtingendienst*)[13] with the help of the SIS in London. His first agent, naval Lieutenant Lodo van Hamel, was dropped into Leyden on 28 August 1940. Hamel helped to organize the Dutch resistance group, *Orde Dienst* (OD), which spread across Holland during the latter part of 1940. Hamel, OD representative Baas Becking and two others made their way to the small village at the Zuider Zee where a British flying boat was due to

ABOVE: *The Tower of London, where several German spies were executed during World War I. In World War II German spies were not shot but were executed by hanging, the fate of common criminals.*

pick them up. Unfortunately for them the village contained an SD informer, who reported their presence. They were arrested and brought to The Hague for questioning by the SD. Becking and the others were released but watched. Hamel admitted to being in the service of the Dutch Government and he was shot, as a spy, in June 1941. The Dutch had not been at war for almost 150 years. They had no experience whatsoever of resistance and proved inept at this sort of business. The OD and its operatives were easily therefore rounded up and shot by the Gestapo.

Giskes Arrives in Holland

In early 1941 Hitler's policy of leniency in the Netherlands ended and Himmler sent SS-Gruppenführer Hans Rauter to beat the Dutch into obedience. Rauter was an unpleasant individual. During his time in Holland he succeeded in deporting 100,000 of the 140,000 Jews in the Netherlands (the highest percentage on the western rim of Europe). The resistance tried, but failed, to assassinate him. It was an operation that was to have tragic consequences. For example, one hundred and sixteen men were

immediately rounded up and transported to the scene of the ambush, where they were all shot dead, their bodies being buried in a mass grave in Heidehof Cemetery in the village of Ugchelen. In Gestapo prisons all over Holland, prisoners were taken out and shot in reprisal for the ambush. In all, a total of 263 were shot in reprisal for the assassination attempt.

In Holland the police apparatus was under Rauter's control; for most of the time it was headed by Dr. Wilhelm Harster, and attached to it was a branch office of IV B 4, Adolf Eichmann's section in the Reichssicherheitshauptamt (Reich Security Main Office; RSHA). On Seyss-Inquart's instructions, Dr. Hans Bohmcker, his representative in Amsterdam, was also in charge of Jewish affairs in the city.

The powers of the Gestapo and SS increased under Rauter's direction, which prompted Canaris to act before it was too late. He ordered Major Hermann Giskes from the Paris Ast to Holland to retain the Abwehr's influence against the expansionist SS. Giskes was a truly professional counter-intelligence specialist and joined Abwehr III under Colonel Bentivegni's command.

Giskes was a tall, sturdy, balding man in his late forties, but he was cultured, keenly intelligent and had a good sense of humour which helped him to get along with people, including those he disliked. The latter group included the head of the Dutch SD, Joseph Schreieder, whom Giskes described as a short, flabby unpleasant man with rat-like eyes. It says something for Giskes' sturdy character that he could lay aside his personal feelings for the SD boss in the interest of professional results. On a tip-off from the Dutch harbour police, which was riddled with SD agents, the SS, using both troops and motor launches, captured four senior OD officials trying to leave the coast for England during the night of 2 April 1941. They were tortured by the Gestapo and then brought to Berlin to be executed. The SD's reputation soared at the expense of the Abwehr. Schreieder, by using the resources of the Funkabwehr (Radio Security Service), caught the Dutch SOE agent Hans Zomer and captured his transmitter. SD Sergeant Ernst May, who was both resourceful and intelligent, sat down to break the codes and the British security checks. But despite Gestapo torture, Zomer refused to collaborate with the SD in sending false messages to London.

A Happy Hunting Ground

Giskes had a lucky break when one of his agents proposed that he meet M.A.G. Ridderhof, a well known gangster figure in the Amsterdam underworld. Giskes was keen to score a success to re-establish the Abwehr's credentials in Holland and he agreed to drop all charges against Ridderhof, who became Abwehr agent F2087 or "George". Ridderhof penetrated both an OD group and the SOE network run by Thijs Thaconis. The Funkabwehr had established that the Thaconis network transmitter was located on Fahrenheitstraat in The Hague. They kept the flat under observation, and on the evening of 6 March 1942 the apartment was raided by three truckloads of troops and police. Two Dutch SOE men were captured, and another raid in Arnhem netted Thaconis himself. He refused to collaborate and when his Gestapo guard began to hit him Thaconis did what most prisoners did not do: he beat the Gestapo man senseless. It did him no good, though: Thaconis was shot in Mauthausen concentration camp (located near Linz in Austria) in 1944.

One of the other captured men, Hubertus Lauwers, agreed to turn but his messages were not important and he made continuous efforts to alert the SOE Section L (Low Countries) to the fact that he was controlled by the enemy, but to no avail. The SOE continued to send back details of drops of agents and arms. During night of 27 March 1942, SOE agent Lieutenant Arnold Baatsen was dropped at Assen and greeted by Abwehr men posing as members of the OD. Escorted by Ridderhof to a waiting car, he was arrested by Giskes. When George Dessing (an SIS agent) was captured he managed to escape back to London, but he was not believed when he claimed the Abwehr and SD controlled most of the SOE agents in the Netherlands.

The Abwehr and SD in Holland

As with the Double Cross system which created the illusion of a large network of agents, the same illusion was created by Giskes in the Netherlands. By June 1942 he controlled six radio sets feeding London completely false information. Thus Giskes sabotaged two major SOE operations, "Holland" and "Roundup", which ensured that the Netherlands was quiet compared to France. At the same time the Germans captured tons of materiel, including 75 radios and 3000 Bren guns that they used to equip their agents. By November 1942 – with a huge staff at his headquarters in Scheveningen outside The Hague – Giskes controlled 14 radio sets. Using his agents Ridderhof (Agent F2087) and Richard Christian, Giskes penetrated the Belgian resistance, the SOE and the Prosper network that helped Allied POWs escape back to Britain.

By the winter of 1942, Giskes believed that it was only a matter of time before London realized what had happened to their agents. In the spring of 1943 Giskes sent a suitably sarcastic last fanfare to London: "You are trying to make business in the Netherlands without our assistance. We think this rather unfair in view of our long and successful cooperation as your sole agents. But never mind, whenever you come to pay a visit to the Continent you may be assured that you will be received with the same care and results as were all those you sent to us before. So long." For Giskes, his operations had been a great success.

Chapter 6

The Neutral Battleground

"To be neutral is to be damned by all sides in a war"

Anon.

IN MOST ACCOUNTS OF WORLD WAR II THE NEUTRALS ARE often only mentioned in passing. The secret war, by contrast, fought many of its major battles on neutral soil. Whether the neutrals really were "neutral" is open to debate, since many favoured Germany during the first half of the war, until fortunes changed in mid-1943 after which they collaborated, more or less openly, with the Allies. Only Spain, under General Franco, proved to be loyal in its commitment to Germany. In the secret war Franco's support for his old friend Canaris proved invaluable to German intelligence.

Switzerland was the only neutral state in World War II that had a consistent policy of principled and established neutrality, a status that was internationally recognized and accepted by the belligerents. It was also the most vulnerable to German influence and pressure in that the most economically influential language group in the country were the German speakers.[1] Though Switzerland was a small country of 40,000 square kilometres (25,000 square miles) with 4.2 million inhabitants, its location at the very heart of Central Europe made it an important neutral in the war. It could affect Germany's communications with Italy, it was a listening post for the Allies on the German-controlled Continent of Europe, and it also served as a meeting ground for the warring sides. Without this neutral "island" in the centre of the Continent, the

LEFT: *Ankara, scene of many espionage duels between the Germans and Allies during World War II. The SD's greatest coup was recruiting Agent Cicero in 1943.*

espionage war would have been severely hampered in its scope. As the American military attaché in Berne, the Swiss federal capital, remarked, Switzerland was the whispering gallery of Europe and the best intelligence could be collected there if one looked hard enough.

The Germans and Austrians had a difficult and complex relationship with Switzerland. In 1937 Hitler told Edmund Schulthess, a member of the Swiss ruling Council, that he would respect the country's neutrality come what may. In his talks with Mussolini, in June 1941, the Führer was far more candid: the Swiss were the enemies of Germany, a small, miserable nation with an equally miserable political system. When Mussolini asked Ribbentrop what the future of the small nation was, the Foreign Minister only smiled cruelly and told him that Switzerland's future depended upon Hitler's "goodwill". The implication was that at some time in the future Switzerland was to be conquered and incorporated into the Reich as a province. There were many aspects of Swiss society the Nazis despised. The Swiss believed in democracy, federalism, independence, cooperation between the language groups, and were avid conservative Christians. They also believed in a free press and had 400 newspapers, most of them anti-Nazi. All this made the Nazis hate the Swiss and most Swiss, in turn, reciprocated. It was not a country of political extremes. Only 40,000 Swiss were communists or Nazis, and democratic-capitalist Switzerland had no official diplomatic relations with the Soviet Union.

As far as international diplomacy, indeed international interaction went, Switzerland preferred to stay out of the limelight.

German Subversion

As had been the case in Czechoslovakia, another small Central European democracy with a large German-speaking minority, the Nazis practised large-scale subversion in Switzerland; the only neutral state in which they attempted this after the outbreak of war. What Hitler did not understand, or chose not to take into account, was the fact that most German-speaking Swiss had no desire to become German, and felt no affinity towards Germany, especially not a Germany ruled by Hitler. There were, however, hundreds of Nazi and Pan-German organizations in Switzerland and the largest of these was the NSDAP itself. Behind this overt façade of political influence lurked the Abwehr and SD, both of which established a large presence in Switzerland from the mid-1930s. The Stuttgart SD station and Abwehr Ast, together with their branches in Munich and Vienna, all operated against Switzerland with varying results.

The most important centre of German espionage inside Switzerland was the German Embassy in Berne and the German consulates in Basel, Lucerne and Geneva. These ran a network of spies, agents and informers that numbered thousands. The Swiss Federal Police (Bupo) concentrated its efforts, often with impressive results, on finding and eliminating German spies. During the war some 865 German agents, of whom 523 were Swiss, were caught and out of 37 condemned to death 17 were executed for their activities. Another task of the Bupo was to keep track of the influx of refugees from the Nazi regime. By September 1939 there were some 7000 German and 5000 Jewish émigrés in the Federal Republic. The Bupo was concerned that they might compromise the country's neutrality, becoming a fifth column of anti-Nazis that could drag Switzerland into the war by angering the Germans.

LEFT: Zürich in 1940. Its orderly, quiet and peaceful air concealed the intensive and often dangerous espionage war being fought there between the belligerents.

ABOVE: A German Bf 109 fighter. Bf 109s were sold in large numbers to the Swiss Air Force. Their subsequent use against German aerial intrusions prompted the farcical Operation Eagle against Swiss airfields in 1940.

As early as 1935 the SD had given notice to the German émigré community that anti-German activities would not be tolerated. Early that year SD agents lured the fiercely anti-Nazi journalist, Berchtold Jacob, to Basel where he was grabbed, bundled into a car and driven across the border to Germany. This showed how deep the roots of the SD agent network had grown on Swiss soil and why the Swiss Government feared provoking the Nazis. However, the Swiss refused to be intimidated and put great pressure on the Germans to return Jacob unharmed, which they eventually did. Meanwhile the Swiss Nazis became louder and more arrogant. Their leader, Wilhelm Gustloff, gained both more adherents but even more enemies with his savage attacks on the Swiss political system and democratic structure. On 4 February 1936 Gustloff, who had pushed his enemies too far, was assassinated. Hitler chose at this point not to make an issue of it, but Ernst von Weizsäcker of the German Foreign Office summoned the Swiss envoy to give the Swiss *Bundesrat* (Parliament) a stern warning to maintain "law and order", a piece of German insolence that did not go down well with the Swiss press and public.

Another far-right organization which had a potential for trouble was the Swiss *Nationale Front* (NF). Created in the early 1930s, it was a staid and pale replica of the German NSDAP, and never enjoyed the electoral support or success of Hitler's movement. In June 1941 the Bupo acted with force and determination to deal with this noisy totalitarian minority, which posed an overt if ineffective threat. The Bupo took no chances, and cracked down hard on the Swiss Nazis.

Neutrality was never an easy line to hold for Switzerland. The Swiss were torn between appeasing Germany, a view held by Federal Premier Marcel Pilet-Golaz, and standing up to the aggressor with every means at the country's disposal; the opinion of the wartime commander-in-chief of the Swiss Army, General Henri Guisan, who has been called, with some justification, the only Swiss hero of World War II.

Operation Adler: The Invasion of Switzerland

Relations between Germany and Switzerland remained calm on the surface, and the two countries even agreed to an important arms deal. From 1938–40, the Luftwaffe delivered 90 Messerschmitt Bf-109 fighters to the Swiss Air Force. On 8 June 1940 this was to backfire on Germany. Göring, who had scant respect for Swiss territorial integrity, deliberately sent 32 bombers over Swiss airspace. The Swiss Air Force tested their new German fighters against the Luftwaffe, attacking the bomber force and inflicting heavy casualties. Unlike its political masters the small Swiss Air Force, guided by General Guisan's orders to meet every German violation of the republic's territorial integrity with force, was eager to fight. This did not go down well with the Germans, and soon afterwards Göring approached Canaris to do something about the Swiss fighters. If they could not be shot down in the air, argued Göring, could Canaris not send his Brandenburger commandos to destroy them on the ground. Canaris, with some reluctance, agreed.

Operation Adler was organized, if that's the right term for this bungled operation, by the Stuttgart Ast which had detailed Abwehr Major Kluge to recruit eight Brandenburgers. They were equipped

ABOVE: *Switzerland's tough commander-in-chief, General Henri Guisan, flanked by Swiss officials in the early 1940s. Guisan expanded the Swiss Army and resisted German incursions into Swiss airspace.*

with identical German-style packs, clothes cut from the same surplus Luftwaffe stock, black berets and Czech pistols. They also had their Wehrmacht ID tags removed and were each given brand-new Swiss franc notes. The group crossed the border into Switzerland at dawn on 14 June 1940 and came to the Kreuzlinger Station. Splitting up into pairs, they boarded the train bound for Zürich. The first pair handed the conductor invalid train tickets. He asked them to pay for new ones and was handed a brand-new 100 Swiss franc note. He got very suspicious when this process was repeated twice over. At the next station the conductor phoned the Bupo and at the station after that the sabotage group was picked up. They spent the rest of the war and years after in jail. In its poor preparation and execution Adler was similar to Lobster or Lena.[2] Canaris had learnt a lesson about Swiss preparedness, and did not attempt to infiltrate the border with armed saboteurs again. Switzerland was on alert to the German threat and its people were well aware of the dangers spies posed to their country's freedom.

Colonel Masson's Secret Service and *Bureau Ha*

The Swiss Defence Minister, Rudolf Minger, chose well when in 1939 he appointed Colonel Henri Guisan, a patrician Francophone Swiss officer, as general and Switzerland's commander-in-chief. Minger chose Guisan not only for his professional record but also because he was fiercely patriotic and a staunch democrat. Guisan would stand up to the Germans and had an inherent understanding of the importance of intelligence, the republic's secret defence. Once in charge, Guisan expanded the army to 400,000 troops and reinforced the National Redoubt in the Alpine region as a last line of conventional defence against an "inevitable" German invasion.

During the summer of 1938, as the war clouds gathered over Central Europe, Swiss Army Intelligence (SAI)[3] had a paltry budget of £2500 and only five full-time officers. In charge was Colonel Roger Masson, another Francophone Swiss, who had urged the *Bundesrat* and the Federal Government time and again to take the need for espionage against Germany more seriously, but to no avail. During the Munich crisis in October 1938 the SAI was increased to six officers. It was only in September 1939 that Masson finally had something like a proper budget (£20,000) and 10 officers. This allowed him to build a small network of agents just across the German and Austrian borders. General Guisan, who took over as commander-in-chief the same month, was shocked at the small size of the intelligence service. Luckily, as a result of a private initiative by a conservative, Major Hausmann, who was hated by the pacifist social democrats, a semi-private intelligence service had been established.

BELOW: Swiss troops in the southern region of their small country scanning the border with Italy. This citizen army was fighting fit and disciplined.

Hausmann had set up *Bureau Ha*,[4] and it was Hausmann, rather than Masson, who kept Guisan up to date on German moves.

As well as the information from *Bureau Ha* and the SAI, Guisan had another source of intelligence. Agent "X" seems to have been a member of the German High Command, who kept the Swiss general up to date with direct reports.[5] In early 1940, for example, "X" sent Guisan prior warning that Germany was about to invade Scandinavia. This attack in April 1940 sent shock waves through Switzerland and made the small republic's 130,000-strong German community suspect as a possible fifth column. Far worse was the fall of France in June, that not only cut off Switzerland's access to the West but made her even more isolated and threatened by Germany. It seems that the work of Masson, Guisan and Hausmann had come just in time.

Guisan's main agent, a member of the German High Command, kept him up to date

Bureau Ha

Hausmann set up the *Bureau Ha* in September 1939 as an independent intelligence service because in the months prior to the outbreak of war, he had feared that the official military intelligence agency, the SAI, was too tiny to provide Switzerland with protection. In 1941 *Bureau Ha* provided Premier Pilet-Golaz with intelligence that the Gestapo was keeping a close watch on Swiss diplomats in Germany. Pilet-Golaz protested vehemently against this to the Germans, though an investigation later showed that Swiss diplomats were guilty of great indiscretion and incompetence.

This kind of mistake left *Bureau Ha* open to attack from Pilet-Golaz and other Swiss appeasers. But the *Bureau* always found a staunch ally in General Guisan who protected the *Bureau* because he wanted to know when and where the Germans could possibly strike against Switzerland, and wanted German intelligence blocked by an efficient

LEFT: *Rudolf Rössler: the most successful and valuable agent of the entire war. It was thanks to his sources that the USSR, despite Stalin's bungling, survived the German offensives of 1941 and 1942.*

Swiss counter-intelligence system. On both counts *Bureau Ha* was the best instrument available. The *Bureau* had a direct link with Hitler's HQ via the "Viking Line" network, which provided Guisan with the German order of battle, movements, plans and intentions during the war. This way Guisan was forewarned of any move the Germans may make.

Bureau Ha also gave its protection to the most famous spy ring of the war, Rudolf Rössler's "Lucy" ring of contacts that eventually became a part, indirectly, of the Soviet/GRU[6] "Dora" group operating in Switzerland. Though officially neutral, the Swiss, through *Bureau Ha*, became part of the most damaging spy ring of the war and a contributor to Germany's military setbacks on the Eastern Front.

The Mapmaker: Agent "Dora" and his Network

Sandor Rado, Agent "Dora", was a former agent of the Hungarian communists who was recruited by the GRU in Moscow in October 1935. He was sent to Switzerland in early 1936 with funds to set up a cover business, Geopress Ltd., in Geneva. Once there, two major Soviet spy networks were subordinated to his control as GRU Director of Operations in Switzerland. One was headed by Swiss socialist, Otto Pünter, who ran the International Socialist Agency (INSA) and had, through groups of Italian anti-fascists, an excellent intelligence network inside Italy. After 1933 Pünter added Nazi Germany to his list of intelligence targets and provided the Swiss with non-Nazi news from that country. During a fact-finding trip to Spain in 1936, Pünter was seconded by the GRU resident "Carlos" and given the cover name of "Pakbo". The Dora and Pakbo networks were united at the end of 1936 after a meeting in a Berne restaurant. Another agent of Dora's was "Sonia" who provided the network with a courier (Anna Müller), a reliable "pianist" (radio operator) agent Jim (Allan Foote), and a very skilled "cobbler" (forger), Max Habijanic. Habijanic worked as a Swiss police official in Basel and provided the Dora network with blank Swiss passports. Foote was a

ABOVE: This signpost in Lucerne clearly shows not only Switzerland as the neutral heart of Europe but also its central role as the very epicentre of wartime espionage on the European continent.

Yorkshireman who had moved from being a conservative in the early 1930s to being a communist, and had fought with the International Brigades during the Spanish Civil War (1936–38). He was the most professional of all Dora's agents and possibly more cold-blooded and intelligent than Rado himself. Rado also recruited a Swiss couple, Georg and Olga Hameln, who owned a radio shop in Geneva located only a stone's throw away from the offices of Geopress Ltd. They were invaluable since they not only repaired and built radios for the network but agreed to act as Dora's "pianists".

Another vital link in the network was Agent "Sissy", an intelligent and tough Polish Jew by the name of Rachel Dübendorfer. She ran a network of agents inside the International Labour Office (ILO) in Geneva. One of these was a short, gloomy man with a sour outlook on life, Agent "Taylor" or Christian Schneider, who worked as a translator at the ILO. Until the spring of 1941 Taylor only provided Sissy with political information, but then suddenly a stream of military intelligence of the absolutely finest top-grade quality flowed into Sissy's hands. She was curious to know who the source, codenamed "Lucy" was, but Schneider only told her that his source was safe and reliable but that he could not, under any circumstances, reveal its identity. Sissy respected this, secured the source and resisted all attempts by her nominal superior Rado and the GRU headquarters at the Moscow Centre to reveal it. She argued, intelligently and shrewdly, that this high-grade intelligence pointed to a source inside the German High Command who was desperate not to reveal himself for fear of the Gestapo. What did the identity of the source matter as long as it proved of value and was reliable?

Rudolf Rössler and his German Generals

Who, indeed, was source "Lucy"? It was Rudolf Rössler, born to a Protestant Bavarian family in 1897. He had been a journalist in Germany and head of the Bühnenvolksbund (Popular Association of Theatre) until 1933 when this organization, having caught the greedy eye of Alfred Rosenberg,[7] was taken over by the Nazis. Rössler, a liberal conservative and pacifist, became a determined opponent of the Hitler regime.

During his years in Berlin Rössler had been a member of the city's most prestigious gentlemen's club, the *Herren Klubb,* where he met and befriended a group of senior army officers. A number of these officers were later to become Rössler's source inside Germany. Another vital contact was Xavier Schnieper, who in June 1933 urged the journalist to leave Germany before it was too late, and who found a flat for Rössler and his wife, Olga, in Lucerne. Once in Switzerland Schnieper also helped Rössler set up Vita Nova Publishing Ltd. with offices in Lucerne's old city.

On 30 May 1939 Rössler was visited by two of his *Herren Klubb* contacts. General Fritz Thiele was deputy head of the German High Command's Communications Department, while his colleague, Baron Colonel Rudolf von Gersdorff, would eventually become head of Army Group Centre's Intelligence (Ic) Department on the Eastern Front.[8] The two German officers had with them an Enigma machine and the latest model of the German short-wave transmitter. Thiele would transmit highly sensitive intelligence to Rössler, who would decipher these messages using the Enigma machine. Thiele was stationed in the Bendlerblock on Bendlerstrasse, which housed the headquarters offices of the Army High Command. The Bendlerblock itself contained two massive halls with hundreds of Enigma machines sending and receiving encrypted messages 24 hours a day. Thiele's superior, General Erich Fellgiebel, was also a member of the conspiracy and allowed Thiele to recruit a small, select group of telegraph officials to send messages to call-sign "RAHS" (Rössler's cover). They were not part of the conspiracy but simply relayed messages without knowing what they were or to whom they were being sent.

In September 1939 Rössler advertised for a proofreader to work at his Vita Nova publishing house, and by pure chance "Taylor" (Schneider) answered the ad. For 18 months, perhaps longer, neither knew of the other's intelligence work. It was, again, by sheer chance that in April 1941 Rössler made it known to Schneider that he had contacts inside Germany whose intelligence, although provided to *Bureau Ha*, was not being used actively against the Nazis. Schneider replied that he could help since he was in touch with a group of GRU agents inside Switzerland. They could make better use of the intelligence than the Swiss organizations. Rössler agreed to the idea, but insisted his identity be kept a secret. From that date onwards, "Taylor" made regular trips from Lucerne to Geneva, handing over material

BELOW: The Swiss did not take any chances with their German potential foe, and built defences, such as this one, along its vulnerable borders.

from his secret source to his controller, Sissy. She in turn gave it to Rado for transmission, via Foote and Hameln, to the Moscow Centre. On the eve of the German invasion of the Soviet Union (20–21 June 1941), Lucy/Dora provided the Centre with detailed and accurate intelligence about the German military build-up on the border: 148 divisions in total, including 19 panzer and 15 motorized divisions. The overall plan was to destroy the Red Army west of the Dnieper and Dvina rivers before they had a chance to escape eastwards. Rado, the loyal communist and Stalinist that he was, relayed the intelligence but did not believe the Germans would act. He believed that Lucy was too good to be true and that it could be an Abwehr plant. Lucy's intelligence was listed in Moscow under "unreliable sources".

The German invasion put an end to these doubts, and from 23 June 1941 Lucy/Dora became Moscow's most reliable source of intelligence on Germany. Intelligence from this source was now labelled "Vyrdo" or "Urgent, decipher at once". The Moscow Centre paid Lucy 7000 Swiss francs per month and was open to receive any intelligence from it day or night. "Taylor" stopped working for ILO in Geneva and instead had daily communications with Rössler, who devoted his afternoons and most of his nights to deciphering the mass of intelligence flooding in from Bendlerblock. One set would go to the SAI (which, flaunting with the Swiss policy of neutrality passed it on to SIS in London), while another went to Rado via Taylor/Sissy. Lucy provided Moscow with up-to-date orders of battle for the German Army on the Eastern Front. It also confirmed the Japanese would not attack the USSR, which allowed the Soviets to launch the Moscow counteroffensive on 5 December 1941 with troops from the Far East. In the spring of 1942, the flood of messages was such that the whole of Otto Pünter's network was mobilized. Rado recruited 22-year-old Margrit Bolli, Agent "Sofie", who was trained by Foote to become another radio operator. "Sofie" would

LEFT: Marshal Timoshenko. Soviet Generalissimo and Commissar of Defence (1940–42), who was defeated in 1942 partly because of faulty intelligence from Lucy.

become the third and final "pianist" in what the Germans would call the Swiss "Red Three".

The Red Three

During the latter part of 1942 the German Radio Security Service, the Funkabwehr, became aware of the work of this radio ring when its long-range monitoring stations at Dresden and Prague reported extremely heavy radio traffic from three short-wave transmitters operating in Switzerland. One was in Lucerne and the other two were in Geneva. The Soviet agent "Kent" of the broken Red Orchestra ring, who was collaborating with the Gestapo, confirmed he had been to Switzerland in March and December 1940 to deliver radio schedules and codes that were to be used by the Swiss network. The Funkabwehr christened this new nest of spies the *Die Rote Drei* (The Red Three), and could confirm that this network used the same codes and radio signals as the Red Orchestra.[9] With the assistance of Kent the Funkabwehr deciphered some of the Red Three's messages and concluded, quite correctly, that their source had to be inside the German High Command itself.

BELOW: Combat scene from the Battle of Kursk during the summer of 1943. The German defeat was due in no small part to intelligence supplied to the Russians by Lucy.

The Soviets were very pleased with the intelligence that Lucy was providing them. But in the spring of 1942 there was a serious hiatus in the flow of intelligence. Marshal Timoshenko, acting partly on intelligence from Lucy, launched a disastrous counteroffensive at Kharkov, and for a while it seemed Lucy would be discredited. But as Hitler prepared an offensive south towards the River Volga and the oilfields of the Caucasus, the Bendlerblock source provided Lucy with the entire offensive plan, the 10-page Directive 41 for Operation Blue. By July 1942 it was taking just 6–10 hours between decisions being taken in Germany and Rössler knowing about them. During the subsequent campaign for Stalingrad, which began that August, Lucy fed Moscow with the plans and intentions of the Germans. The order of battle of the Hungarian and Romanian troops on the southeastern sector at Stalingrad provided the Red Army with the ability to strike at the weakest point of the front. The result was the encirclement and destruction of the entire German Sixth Army.

Lucy provided the Centre with detailed information on the German Panther tank

Citadel: Lucy's Finest Hour

Despite the victory at Stalingrad, Lucy's finest hour was yet to come. In early March 1943, the Germans planned a massive counteroffensive against the gigantic Kursk salient, and hoped with Operation "Zitadelle" (Citadel) to turn the tide of the war in the East. Thanks to a strengthened Red Army, and Lucy, these hopes were to be smashed. On 15 April 1943 Hitler signed Order No. 6 unleashing Citadel. Within 24 hours Foote was transmitting it to the Centre. On 7 May 1943 the Centre instructed Rado to get all the intelligence possible on Citadel and two days later a huge message promptly arrived. In response the Soviets began constructing three massive defence lines to protect the Kursk position.

Lucy's intelligence was not just strategic. On 12 June Rado, thanks to Lucy, provided the Centre with detailed information on the new, formidable German Panther tank. This information was to assist the Soviets in defeating the Germans during the coming tank battle.

On 1 July, Hitler chaired a conference at his forward headquarters, the Wolf's Lair in East Prussia, in preparation for Citadel which was to be launched in three days. One of those present was General Fellgiebel, who transmitted the content of that crucial meeting to Lucy. The following day Stalin read about his enemy's intentions at his desk in the Kremlin. At 04:30 hours on 5 July 1943, General Hoth's Fourth Panzer Army struck the southern sector of the salient while Marshal Model's Ninth Army attacked from the north. By 9 July the German attack had bogged down completely and on the 12th the Red Army counterattacked at Prokhorovka. The Battle of Kursk, the largest tank battle of the war, was fought over seven days . Hitler, bitterly disappointed and depressed that his surprise attack had failed, finally cancelled Citadel on 13 July having lost 70,000 troops, 3000 tanks and 1400 aircraft. The Red Army counteroffensive rolled on until November 1943, when the whole of the USSR east of the River Dnieper had been retaken.

The Elimination of the Red Three

As the war on the Eastern Front turned in the Soviets' favour, the Red Three worked on. Walter Schellenberg, as head of SD intelligence, was in charge of finding and liquidating them, but despite sending literally hundreds of agents to Switzerland even the wily SD chief was unsuccessful. The task was handed over to Heinz Pannwitz and the double agent "Kent". Pannwitz sent the agent "Yves Rameau" to penetrate the Swiss ring. Rameau was in fact Ewald Zwieg, a German Jew forced to serve the SD to save his own skin. Rameau arrived in Switzerland and tried to get in touch with Dora, but Rado suspected a Gestapo plot. He ordered his go-betweens to break off all contact with Rameau. Then the Italians had a try. In July 1943 an Italian agent, "Paolo", who worked for Dora, requested that he be

RIGHT: Walter Schellenberg. Despite his cunning and good Swiss contacts (including Roger Masson), the SD chief was never able to track down and liquidate the Lucy ring.

SCHELLENBERG

LEFT: *The Quiet American: Allen Dulles, not a man to be underestimated. He was the head of the OSS in Switzerland with a finger in every intelligence pie in the country.*

provided with a new passport from "Max the Cobbler" (Max Habijanic). Max provided the passport and a Swiss courier travelled to Como in Italy to deliver it to a tailor's shop. The courier was cautious and found the placed surrounded by Italian agents of the SIM.[10] The whole thing had been an Italian-orchestrated plot on behalf of the Germans, since Paolo and his agents had been arrested and turned in June of that year. What it revealed to the SD was the size and complexity of the Dora network.

Pannwitz and the SD did not give up. Instead Kent requested that the Centre send money to him via Switzerland, and the Centre, not knowing he was compromised, agreed. Kent had informed Pannwitz that it was the efficient and conscientious Foote who was in charge of the Dora network's finances. Foote met the courier who was to take the money to Kent, but he was surprised when the courier mentioned that he needed to contact the Centre with information and handed Foote a large book wrapped in orange paper. Foote, being an experienced and intelligent man, was not

fooled for a minute. The SD had committed several errors. Firstly, a Soviet courier would not disobey orders by talking to a contact. Secondly, the book obviously contained a radio beacon. Thirdly, Foote realized immediately that their meeting place was near the frontier and perfect for an SD abduction. Finally, the enciphered message in the book, being an SD plant, would be perfect for tracing the ring's transmitter. Foote hid the book and returned home in a long and torturous route to shake off any SD trail. Kent and Pannwitz realized they had been unsuccessful.

Having failed three times to penetrate the Dora ring, the Germans gave up their own attempts and instead put pressure on the Swiss. In a series of personal meetings Schellenberg tried to persuade Colonel Masson, the SAI chief, to detect and liquidate the Dora/Lucy ring. When the Germans occupied northern Italy on 8 September 1943, the Swiss decided to act since the Germans now had them sealed off on every side. Lieutenant Maurice Treyer, from the Swiss Army's radio surveillance section, was given command of a squadron of radio troops and set about hunting down the Red Three. He identified Hameln's radio set during the night of 11/12 September, and the following night that of Rosie. But it took him a few weeks to locate their sets. Once this had been done, the task of elimination was handed over to the Geneva Canton Bupo Chief, Charles Knecht, who placed the two buildings under strict surveillance. An agitated Rosie met Rado in a Geneva cafe at the beginning of October, telling her chief that strange men were loitering around her house and a man from the electricity board had visited her. Rado realized that the Bupo was on the case and ordered Rosie not to go home, and to return to her parents in Basel. Instead Rosie chose to stay with her lover, Hans Peters, in his flat.

RIGHT: *A Swiss policeman patrolling on a sunny day. The picture belies the efficiency and thoroughness of the Swiss secret police, the Bupo's, counter-intelligence service section.*

On 13–14 October, the Bupo struck against the Geneva "pianists". At 00:30 hours a Bupo agent picked the lock of the door to a villa owned by the Hamelns and stormed up the stairs to the attic, where Olga was transmitting frantically to the Centre. Edmond was asleep. Both were arrested and shipped off to the Bois-Mermet prison. Then Knecht raided Rosie's flat where they found enciphered messages and radio schedules that Rosie had thoughtlessly left behind. Then it was the turn of Peters' flat, where the Bupo found the Peters and Rosie in bed. When Rado called at the Hamelns' shop he realized that he was a hunted man, and took refuge with a friend in the university quarter of Geneva. From there Rado kept in touch with Sissy, Taylor and Lucy and relayed messages to Foote. But Lieutenant Treyer had located Foote's transmitter in Lucerne. Knecht was called in from Geneva to assist. On the night of 21/22 November, Knecht's policemen broke down the door to Foote's flat. Foote swiftly burnt the messages he was sending and with exemplary English nerves simply smiled broadly and asked, with a welcoming gesture: "Ah, gentlemen. Dropped in for a drink? A whisky perhaps?" Knecht, with a wry smile and a Gallic shrug replied: "Ah, Mr. Foote, it's more serious than that!"[11] Foote would survive the war, despite a harsh interrogation by the NKVD/GRU on his return to Moscow.

Acting on Rosie's confession, the Bupo picked up Sissy (Dubendorfer) on 10 April 1944, and she in turn led the Bupo to Schneider and Rössler, both of whom were arrested the following month. Rado was also eventually found. The Red Three were no more, but from a German point of view it was far too late, as they had already done a great deal of damage.

The OSS in Switzerland

In 1943, a few weeks after the Germans had occupied the neutral territory of Vichy France, an unobtrusive American crossed the border from Vichy into Switzerland in his capacity as legal advisor to the US Embassy in Berne. His real job was to be head of the OSS in Switzerland and head of US espionage directed at Nazi Germany. He was a shrewd, calm, pipe-smoking East Coast lawyer by the name of Allen Dulles, who had been in Berne as a spy during World War I and had returned to his old hunting grounds. Dulles advertised on the secret

BELOW: *The city of Berne, Switzerland. Allen Dulles, the "legal advisor" at the US Embassy located there, was in fact the head of OSS in Switzerland.*

intelligence grapevine that he and the OSS were open for business. There were many takers. He recruited Agent 476 (Gero von Schulze-Gävernitz) who was a German half-Jewish millionaire playboy. He had excellent contacts, via his sister, to members of the German nobility, economic élite and political leaders. Gävernitz was also making a fortune by trading with Germany and others, and this enabled him to make new contacts such as Hans Gisevius, who had contacts within the Abwehr itself. As it turned out, Gisevius, with Canaris' support, was looking for OSS support for the German opposition.

A Golden Opportunity

Dulles' greatest intelligence coup fell into his lap by sheer good fortune. The British were not interested in contacts with the Germans, and when an anti-Nazi German came calling at the British Legation in Berne the British military attaché, Colonel Cartwright, directed him to call on the US Embassy instead. The man arrived at the US Embassy and asked for an official, Gerald Mayer, in the mistaken belief he worked for the OSS. Mayer agreed to see him, whereupon the German pulled out three pages of documents. Mayer excused himself and went upstairs to talk to Dulles, who agreed to see the man and a mysterious friend of his from the German Foreign Office (AA). On the evening of 18 August 1944, the two Germans called at Mayer's flat a few minutes after midnight and brought a thick bundle of documents with them. Dulles, posing as Mayer's assistant "Mr Douglas", asked the Germans why they should not take them for an SD plant. The Germans replied, with some truth, that if they were plants, why bring 186 documents with them and not just one or two? Mayer and "Douglas" looked over the documents, which covered subjects as varied as a German spy ring in Mozambique to Ribbentrop's talks with the Japanese. The documents were genuine and a treasure trove of intelligence. Dulles dropped the pretence and suggested to the AA official, whose name was Fritz Kolbe, that he call on him at his residence at 23 Herrengasse. The day after the meeting Kolbe was given the cover name "George

Wood" and agent number 805. Kolbe was a devoted hater of the Nazis and wanted no payment for his espionage, only American goodwill and fair treatment after the war. In return 805 supplied Dulles with 1600 top-secret AA documents during the next 20 months.

Agent 805

Kolbe was an insignificant-looking man of 43 years who had worked for 20 years at the AA in a lowly but key position. He was assistant to Karl Ritter, who was an ardent Nazi and an AA liaison officer with the OKH and OKW. This gave Kolbe access to a host of documents and top-secret messages, mostly of an intelligence and military nature. Kolbe was not some sad, middle-aged failure unhappy with his lot, but was a social charmer who had sense enough to hide his ardent hatred of the Nazi regime. Kolbe used his considerable charm on a friend, Fräulein von Heimerdinger, to get him the courier's job to Switzerland. The AA had stringent security, and when he returned from his first trip to see Dulles a security officer asked Kolbe where he had been during the evening of 18 August. Kolbe, with a wink and a nod, claimed that he had struck lucky with a Swiss woman. Unfortunately she had been "tainted" claimed Kolbe, as he pulled out a doctor's certificate for a blood test and preventive medication. Kolbe, so grey and dull in appearance, was anything but. He was cold-blooded and imaginative, two qualities any spy had to possess. During a later visit in October, Kolbe delivered another package of AA documents to Dulles, and in December when he returned to Berne, brought news of the activities of Agent Cicero in Ankara. Dulles informed OSS headquarters in Washington, D.C., which in turn got the British to deal with this very dangerous leak. By this time Dulles had nothing but the greatest confidence in his best agent.

In March 1944, Dulles wanted to know what Berlin knew of the Japanese Navy but had no way of knowing when or where Kolbe would turn up. He sent a postcard to Zürich, asking his "friend" to find out if those clever Japanese toys were still available since his son's birthday was coming up. Kolbe, who was in

Kolbe was not some sad, middle-aged failure but an ardent hater of the Nazi regime

Berlin, eventually received the card and realized what Dulles was looking for. A few weeks later Kolbe arrived in Berne with 200 microfilmed documents on the Japanese Navy. Dulles was delighted and cabled Washington that Agent 805, in the guise of the Easter Bunny, had been generous, delivering 200 Easter eggs. Washington replied: "What a bunny!"[12] Indeed "George Wood" proved as loyal and dedicated a servant of the Americans, as Rössler was to the Swiss and Russians.

If Switzerland was the setting of Germany's worst espionage and counter-intelligence failures of the war, then Turkey was the setting of her greatest triumphs. Modern Turkey was the creation of Kemal Mustapha – Atatürk[13] – who had led nationalist forces that overthrew the Ottoman

BELOW: General Mustafa Kemal (centre), better known as Atatürk, shown in his tall fur hat. This picture was taken after the Turkish Civil War had ended in 1923.

ABOVE: *The Iranian oil pipelines that pumped the black gold of Persia (Iran) down to the Persian Gulf at Bandar Abbas for exportation to Europe and the belligerent powers.*

Sultan in 1924, defeated the Greeks, proclaimed a republic and began the work of modernizing the ancient state. Atatürk was suspicious of the Germans, Turkey's ally in World War I, and instead began making friendly gestures towards the USSR. He was no admirer of Hitler and kept Turkish xenophobia and anti-semitism under control. He died prematurely in November 1938 and was replaced by Izmet Inönü. This premier was more amenable to German aims and steered a neutral course during the war, which in effect opened his country up to German espionage.

From the 1930s Istanbul served as a base for German spies throughout the Middle East. The Abwehr station (KO) chief in Istanbul was Rohde, who hoped that the Turks would aid Germany in capturing the British oilfields of Mosul in Iraq and the Russian ones around Baku, Azerbaijan. In 1941, Paul Leverkühn became the KO chief in Istanbul and began to intrigue with Arab nationalists. The Iraqi coup of early 1941 failed but its pro-Nazi leader, General Rashid Ali Gailani, found a temporary refuge in Istanbul before travelling safely on to Berlin. Leverkühn had better luck with the proud and sensitive Turks, who were often treated with contemptuous arrogance by the British and who proved willing helpers to the Germans. One of these was a Turkish employee at the British Consulate, who proffered Leverkühn, free of charge, copies of the contents of the consulate's safe. Thus Leverkühn gained access to top-secret and confidential correspondence and documents, many of which exposed British

secrets. It showed how easily British diplomatic security could be breached.

Another character in the Turkish melting pot was Franz von Papen. As a former Chancellor of Germany and an outspoken critic of Hitler, he should have been shot in the general bloodbath that was the great purge of July 1934 (Night of the Long Knives) , when many of his former colleagues fell victim to SS bullets. But Papen had his uses and was appointed, in early 1939, as German Ambassador to Turkey despite the fact that he and Ribbentrop hated the sight of one another.[14] Papen was well liked by his British colleague, Sir Hugh Knatchbull-Huggesen, who found the German ambassador polite, friendly and well-informed. Although Papen favoured an alliance with Turkey, he was shocked and dismayed with Inönü's pronounced admiration for Hitler and the Nazi leaders. Despite links with the German opposition, Papen collaborated closely with Leverkühn and they exchanged intelligence with each other. Papen also kept Canaris, an old contact, abreast of political and military events in Turkey, while the admiral kept Papen updated on events in Berlin.

Papen neither liked nor trusted the Turks and kept his distance from the strongly pro-German Turkish officer corps. His attitude made him enemies, and on 24 February 1939, as he and Frau

ABOVE: *Franz von Papen as German Ambassador to Turkey and looking more than ever like the cunning fox and political survivor that he was. He survived the war and died in Germany in 1969.*

von Papen were making their way down the main avenue in Ankara, a bomb exploded right behind them, killing an innocent Turkish woman but leaving the couple unscathed. The Turkish Government offered its profuse apologies but Papen found these protestations unconvincing, leaving him with the uneasy feeling that the Turks were behind the outrage. Four days later, as a way of deflecting blame, Turkish police surrounded the Soviet Consulate in Istanbul and forced its occupants to surrender. A Macedonian Turk, Omer Tokat, was arrested for the attempted assassination of Papen. On 10 March, the Soviet newspaper *Izvestia* accused the SD of being behind the outrage, and said the Turks, for political reasons, wanted to blame the bombing on the Soviet Union. This

charge was strongly rebutted officially by Papen, although he privately believed the SD had persuaded the Turks to make the assassination bid and then blame it on the Soviets. This narrow escape with death made Papen more determined to work towards a peace with the Western Powers or Russia as long it ended Hitler's aggression.

Talks with "Magnolia"

In 1943, with the war turning in the Allies' favour, Canaris sent Helmut von Moltke to Istanbul. He was sent ostensibly to talk with the Turks, but his real mission was to establish contact with the OSS in Turkey and to discover what peace terms, if any, the Americans would be willing to offer a post-Hitler Germany. Moltke's was to make contact through OSS agent "Magnolia" (Professor Alexander Rüstow), who was close to Lanning Macfarland, the head of OSS Turkey. Macfarland ran the successful "Cereus" network centred on the Czech agent "Dogwood", who had an Istanbul-based firm, Vestern Elektrik Ltd., as a cover for his activities. "Dogwood" favoured contacts with the German opposition. Canaris must have believed that Moltke stood a good chance of establishing good relations with the OSS, but when Moltke arrived in Istanbul in December he was to hold talks, not with the senior member of the OSS he was expecting, but with the elderly and cautious US military attaché, General Richard Tindall. Nothing came of that meeting because Tindall treated Moltke as a spy.

This had not been the first contact between the German opposition and the Americans. Two months earlier "Magnolia" had served as the conduit between OSS agent Theodor Morde, who was acting on his own initiative, and Ambassador Papen. Morde called on Papen at the German Embassy residence in Ankara on 5 October 1943. The OSS agent made it clear that this was a private, not official, visit and emphasized that the Americans would have no dealings with the Nazis, who would have to be removed from power before any peace talks could take place. Papen in turn pointed out President Roosevelt's mistake in demanding Germany's unconditional surrender, and the Americans' underestimation of the

ABOVE: *A typical Turkish restaurant in Ankara — the perfect meeting place for agents and spies to discuss their trade and deals under the table. During World War II many such meetings took place in similar surroundings.*

communist-Soviet threat to Europe. Morde agreed on both accounts.

A second meeting took place a few days later in a villa on Krinkipo Island, just outside Istanbul. Papen felt safer in Istanbul and was more relaxed. He agreed with Morde that those "animals" – the Nazis – had to be deposed even if it meant Hitler's assassination. But he pointed out that this was easier said than done, and that such a plot could only be carried out by officers of the Wehrmacht. Nothing concrete was decided by these talks, and Morde's action was not approved by OSS senior staff either in Ankara or Cairo.

> ***Papen agreed that those "animals" – the Nazis – had to be removed from power in Germany***

A few weeks after these events took place in Istanbul, the actions of a Turkish valet working at the British Embassy in Ankara would rock the British diplomatic establishment and present the SD with its greatest intelligence coup of the war.

On 26 October 1943, Frau Janke, wife of the German first secretary, phoned Ludwig Moyzisch, the SD chief in Ankara,[15] to tell him that there was a stranger who wanted to speak with a representative of German intelligence. Moyzisch rushed over to the embassy and found the man sitting in the Janke's living room. He spoke poor French, called himself Pierre and promised to supply Moyzisch with top-secret British documents on microfilm for £10,000 per roll. Moyzisch agreed, pending the approval of Papen and Berlin. On 29 October Pierre reappeared at the embassy, handed Moyzisch a roll of film, got his money and left. Moyzisch rushed to develop the film,

LEFT: Elyasna Bazna, agent "Cicero", the Turkish butler who betrayed his British employers for German forged pound notes, seen as an old man in the late 1960s.

and after four hours of backbreaking work had 52 enlargements. The intelligence they contained was of top quality. They revealed how Stalin was complaining about the lack of Allied support and how weak the Allied forces in Italy were. Papen, impressed by this new source, named his eloquent agent "Cicero" after the Roman philosopher.

"Cicero" Goes to Work

New meetings were arranged and Moyzisch was provided with £200,000 in cash to pay the new agent. As an expensive and potentially first-class source, Ernst Kaltenbrunner, who had taken charge of the SD following Heydrich's death, wanted to know more about Cicero, and ordered Moyzisch to report to Berlin for a face-to-face meeting. The SD officer took the night train to Istanbul, from where he flew to Berlin via Bulgaria. In Berlin Kaltenbrunner told Moyzisch that Ribbentrop believed Cicero was a plant by the British and had consequently wasted the important intelligence the agent had brought. From now on Moyzisch was told, the Cicero material was to come to Kaltenbrunner alone to prevent this happening again. Moyzisch returned to Ankara on 22 November, having wasted two weeks embroiled in the Nazi regime's infighting. In Ankara, though Papen was delighted Moyzisch had made it back safely, he was also furious about the gossip-mongers in Berlin who could not keep quiet about Cicero, the main culprit being Ribbentrop himself.

In time Cicero revealed his motivation. It turned out the SD's new star source was an Albanian who had a score to settle with the British. Apparently his father had been shot accidentally by an Englishman during a shooting party, and that he had not been paid compensation or even received an apology. He also revealed that while Sir Hugh, the British Ambassador, was a very decent man his subordinates treated their Turkish servants no

New meetings were arranged and Moyzisch was provided with £200,000 to pay Cicero

better than dirt. From this information the Germans hoped to find out Cicero's identity. They never did.

As the weeks went by the deliveries of intelligence from Cicero escalated, and as the agent grew richer he also grew in confidence. December 1943 was the peak of Cicero's clandestine deliveries. He provided a full account of the Allied summit conference in Tehran, including the news that Premier Inönü and his foreign minister had attended. This was bad news for the Germans, who hoped to keep the Turks neutral for as long as possible.

A Lucky Escape

During the second week of December 1943, after another meeting, Cicero and Moyzisch were shadowed by a car and it was only with the greatest difficulty that Moyzisch managed to shake off the tail. A few days later, during a diplomatic reception, a senior Turkish police official Moyzisch knew in his capacity as the German police attaché (his SD cover) came up to him and told the German that he was, judging from his constable's report, a most reckless driver. Their tail had been the Turks and not the British SIS. Nonetheless, December 1943 witnessed the beginning of the end for Cicero. Firstly, Moyzisch was prevailed upon to hire a girl called Elizabeth, the daughter of the German military attaché, as a secretary, a decision that he was to bitterly regret. Furthermore, the OSS had received a tip-off from "George Wood" (Fritz Kolbe) about an agent inside the British Embassy. The British Foreign Office sent out a team to improve security at the embassy, and Cicero's intelligence productivity fell off just as Ribbentrop and Kaltenbrunner were finally convinced his material was genuine. Cicero, having learnt the new security routines by heart, set about his nefarious activities again in February 1944, but the results were so unimpressive that Moyzisch refused to pay him. Cicero had by this time delivered hundreds of documents and had been paid a fortune of £300,000 – though of this hoard of

cash only £40,000 turned out to be genuine. The other £260,000 was forged.[16]

Meanwhile, Elizabeth had gained the confidence of her employer and Moyzisch had entrusted her with the key to his safe. One night Moyzisch could not sleep and returned to his office, only to find Elizabeth typing away at some documents with the key in the safe's lock. He told her to go home and hand him the key. Elizabeth found a document that talked of Cicero, but Moyzisch refused to tell her about him. Elizabeth protested strongly about this lack of trust and the matter of the safe key, and as a way of saying sorry Moyzisch agreed to take her shopping. They went to a lingerie shop in the city centre. As they picked their way through different items in walked none other than Cicero. To Moyzisch's utter horror, Cicero then intervened to assist the young lady while he looked on in the background. When they left the shop, Cicero bowed in servile style with a wry smile on his lips and a wink to Moyzisch regarding his blonde "girlfriend".

ABOVE: Sir Hugh Knatchbull-Hugessen, British Ambassador to Ankara (right), deep in conversation with the Turkish President Izmet Inönü (left) in 1939. Inönü was a devious character but nonetheless very able.

Despite the incident with the open safe, Moyzisch, preoccupied as he was with Cicero, had no inkling that Elizabeth was a double agent. On 6 April 1944 he called at Elizabeth's apartment only to find it empty and the girl gone. He tried for a whole week to locate the errant secretary, but had no luck. The following week Moyzisch got a strange phone call during which an English-speaking voice tried to convince him to join the Allied cause before it was too late. Moyzisch rejected the offer angrily. A month later, in May, Turkey broke off diplomatic relations with Germany and Moyzisch was sent to an internment camp in Britain.

Moyzisch's account of Cicero's activities gave the German side of the story, but the agent's account would have to wait until Cicero himself stepped forward in 1962. The SD's Ankara spy was not an

Albanian but an ethnic Turk who had grown up in Albania, where his father was in fact a large landowner and a man of means. When Albania became independent the Turks were expelled and his family lost all their property. "Cicero" was forced to become a butler not by choice but from necessity. The spy's real name was Elyesa Bazna, he was married and had his family in Istanbul. He had been a servant to the Janke family, who dismissed him when they found him rifling through their private papers in search, no doubt, of secrets to sell. Bazna had decided as he entered his fifties to rebuild his own fortune by selling secrets he unearthed from working at the European embassies. Bazna's main motivation was not personal revenge but just greed. He worked for a short time at the American Embassy and was then hired by the British Legation's secretary, until he was transferred to the personal service of Sir Hugh whom he liked. This did not, however, stop Bazna from buying a Leica camera, photographing sensitive documents and touting them to the Soviets or the Germans: whichever side took him up on the offer was irrelevant. He was left with a small fortune, despite being predominantly paid in fake SD-produced pound notes, that allowed him, for a while, to play at being a Turkish gentleman of means. Bazna, like many other spies, ended up disappointed and forgotten after the war.

Franco's Spain

If Turkey had yielded good results for the German secret services, another neutral country, Spain, seemed to offer the hope of even greater rewards. Franco owed his victory in the civil war to Germany's intervention, and it was a blood debt that the Spanish dictator was determined to repay in full. He began first of all with deliveries of wolfram (used to harden steel for arms manufacture), mercury (the mines at Almeida produced 80 percent of the world's output) and other strategic raw materials. He also began to cooperate closely with his old friend Canaris in the secret war against the Allies.

The first major German secret service operation in the Iberian peninsula concerned Portugal, however.

That country's dictator, Don Antonio Salazar, was a mild-mannered conservative and professor of economics who had little liking for the socialist-minded Nazis and their extremist leader. He was, if anything, a loyal if unenthusiastic and often cynical ally of Britain.

The Duke of Windsor in Spain

On 19 June 1940, the self-exiled Duke of Windsor and his wife Wallis fled France in order to escape the advancing German Army, and made their way to Spain. They arrived safely and unscathed in Madrid on 23 June, to the relief of the British Embassy. The couple only stayed in the Spanish capital for nine days before heading on to Lisbon, the Portuguese capital. Salazar was determined to make the Duke feel safe and welcome in Portugal, and charged the chief of the Portuguese Secret Police (PVDE), Dom Agostinho Lourenço, with the task of protection. The duke rented a villa near Estoril called *Boca de Inferno*, which was owned by one of the his right-wing, upper-class playboy friends, Dom Ricardo Espirito Santo Silva. Lourenço, meanwhile, erected a security cordon around the villa and more or less confined the ducal couple to house arrest.

In Germany Hitler and Ribbentrop, wildly exaggerating the duke's real power, influence and political clout in British politics, believed that the Duke of Windsor still had an important role to play. The deluded Nazis believed that if the duke could be lured to Spain he would willingly become an ally of the Germans. If Britain did not come to her senses and surrender peacefully, then after the success of Operation Sea Lion the duke might become the puppet king of a German-dominated Britain. During the night of 23 July Ribbentrop called Schellenberg to appoint him, on the Führer's direct orders, head of Operation "Willi": the luring or abduction of the duke and his wife to Spain.

In his post-war memoirs, Schellenberg claimed that he opposed Willi for practical and moral reasons. One cause for Schellenberg's concern was the deep hatred that Heydrich, his boss, had for Ribbentrop, whom he called a "bloody old fool" when in a good mood, and far worse when he was

in a bad one. Since Willi was Ribbentrop's brainchild, Heydrich hoped the operation would fail and leave egg on the foreign minister's face. Schellenberg was hard pressed, not knowing which way to turn in the crazy and dangerous game of Nazi political infighting. Nevertheless, Schellenberg flew to Madrid where he received a less than warm welcome from the Spanish and a scarcely more friendly greeting from German Ambassador Baron Eberhard von Stohrer, who disliked the Nazis and the SD-Sipo especially. Schellenberg's mere presence and his unsavoury reputation for abduction and other dirty dealings, including the Venlo incident,[17] convinced Stohrer

that the "criminals" in Berlin had decided to make good on their threat to abduct the Duke of Windsor. The ambassador was, of course, correct. As soon as Schellenberg arrived in Madrid he began organizing his abduction team. He contacted Winzer, the German police attaché (in reality the SD representative in Madrid), and an Abwehr agent, "Angel" Alcazar de Velasco: a former matador and ardent Falangist fascist. Though he had been a member of Canaris' service since 1935, during talks with Schellenberg the Spaniard promised not to breathe a word about Operation Willi to the admiral. Schellenberg wanted the Abwehr chief kept out of this dirty business. In return Velasco would get a prominent role in the plot that might, if it succeeded, turn the war in Germany's favour.

On Friday 26 July, Schellenberg flew into Lisbon airport. He was determined not to use violence in order to compel the duke to leave Portugal and seek sanctuary in a German-dominated Spain. But this would not stop him from using strong means of persuasion. He had decided to set up a network of agents around the duke and create an ambience of uncertainty and fear around the royal couple which he hoped would compel them to leave for Spain. To this end he contacted an old friend, the Japanese head of intelligence in Lisbon, who quickly acquired maps, plans and drawings of their villa and the surrounding area. Then Schellenberg contacted his agent, "C", who was none other than one of Dom Lourenço's trusted deputies, Colonel José Catela, who provided 18 PVDE agents to watch over the duke. On 27 July Schellenberg's network was up and running when his SD hit squad, led by Winzer, arrived in Lisbon. At the same time Velasco arrived to see the Duke with the Spanish offer of sanctuary against British plots. The duke thanked the Spaniard for his offer but asked for 48 hours to think it over.

As German agents closed in on the duke, on Sunday 28 July, a Bristol flying boat arrived from

Britain carrying the formidable figure of Sir Walter Monckton. Monckton was a trusted Churchill man, as well as being a close friend and legal advisor to the Windsors. He was closely connected to British intelligence, and on 26 July he had actually been interrogating suspected spies in Holloway Prison when he was called to a secret meeting with Churchill in Downing Street. Monckton was told by the premier to rush to Lisbon and see to it that the duke, who was wavering in his conduct and willingness to sit out the war in the Bahamas as governor, was on the New York liner as planned. Monckton was as good as his word. His arrival meant a slump in Schellenberg's fortunes and he noted in his log book on 29 July, "Willi will nicht" (Willi does not want to go). From Berlin came direct orders from Ribbentrop for Schellenberg to abduct the duke with or without His Royal Highness' cooperation. Schellenberg, in a final attempt to get the Windsors into his grasp, sent a half-hearted warning about British plots to the duke, but his message was sent too late. Schellenberg was forced to see his quarry leave for New York, as scheduled on 1 August, accompanied by Monckton and a CID officer. Willi had failed abysmally.

Some wanted to launch a parachute assault on Gibraltar combined with a Stuka attack

Operation Felix

Even after the abject failure of Operation Willi, Spain remained a crucial secret battleground, mainly because of the key British base of Gibraltar. After the fall of France, during the summer and autumn of 1940, Canaris made several trips to the area of La Linea and Algeciras with officers, both regular Wehrmacht and Abwehr, from the German military headquarters in Bordeaux. The Spanish, especially the Chief of Police of La Linea, cooperated with the Germans and gave them every facility to spy on Gibraltar and check all the photographic and human intelligence they possessed on the "Rock" and its defences, which included tunnels in the Gibraltar mountain itself, which were large enough to house some 20,000 troops. The British were quite complacent about

the impregnability of Gibraltar, and did not consider a German attack likely. In fact the Germans had gone so far as to give the attack an official codename, Operation "Felix". Felix was to coincide with the arrival of the German Army in Spain, when and if Franco gave the Führer permission.

After a tour of inspection of the area surrounding the Rock, which revealed the inadequacy of the Spanish road and railroad system, the Abwehr began to have doubts about the wisdom of the operation. Some of the experts wanted to launch a parachute assault on Gibraltar combined with a Stuka attack, but the nearest airfield was too small and the one that was adequate in capacity was too far away. This meant that heavy artillery would have to be transported on Spain's rundown and inefficient railroad network. After many months of planning, great expenditure in effort and a great deal of Canaris' personal time, the plan was finally dropped in early 1941. The final stumbling block on which everything hinged was the word of Franco, and the generalissimo made it abundantly clear that he was not willing to gain Gibraltar if it meant Spain becoming a vassal state of Germany.

The Impregnable Rock

Having failed in their endeavours to secure Gibraltar by force, the Germans reverted to sabotage using their Spanish agents to try to do so. They were confronted by a formidable enemy, however: the British MI5. Gibraltar housed MI5's largest overseas station, set up to screen the massive influx of refugees from Spain during the civil war, some of whom might have been German agents using Gibraltar to reach Britain by the backdoor. Colonel John "Fishpaste" Codrington was in overall charge of Gibraltar's security. Given German and Spanish interest in the Rock, the British set up the Gibraltar Special Police (GSP), whose duty it was to check ships' crews entering the port, the 6000 Spanish workers who entered the dockyard every day to work, as well as every refugee entering the territory – a difficult task but essential to security. Any one of these groups could contain enemy agents, and thus they required thorough vetting. Major H.G. Medlam was in charge of the MI5 station, headquartered in the Irish Town area, and he in turn cooperated with the SIS Iberian section. The British knew that the Germans used a row of villas in Algeciras, across the bay from Gibraltar, to spy on shipping movements in the port.

Abwehr Spies in Gibraltar

The first Spanish spy working for the Abwehr and its local chief, Dr. Hans Höberlein based in Algeciras, was a half-Gibraltarian by the name of José Keay, who had contacts with the Spanish fascist Falange in La Linea. Keay had first been suspected and catalogued as a subversive in 1936 and was arrested on 4 March 1942. He was taken to London, sentenced to death for treason and hanged on 7 July, in Wandsworth Prison, under the terms of the Treachery Act of 1940.

Undeterred, the Abwehr tried again. A Gibraltarian loyal to Britain, Charles Danino, approached British security officer Kirby Green in November 1942 with the news that a Spaniard, Luis Cordon-Cuenca, had approached him about doing a job for him in Gibraltar. The Spaniard had also threatened to harm Danino's wife unless he cooperated. Green told Danino to keep in touch with Cuenca while he investigated his identity. Green soon found out that a 27-year-old Spaniard by that name worked in the Imperial Fruit Shop at 114 Main Street in Gibraltar Town, and that he had no criminal record. The owner of the shop was Hungarian but utterly loyal to Britain and beyond reproach. Thus if Cuenca was a spy and saboteur he was acting on his own initiative. A GSP officer, Bill Adamson, suddenly developed an intense urge for bananas, and called at the shop to befriend Cuenca. On 22 June 1943, Cuenca phoned Danino to arrange a rendezvous the next day at 18:00 hours.

He chose his spot well since Sir Herbert Miles' Promenade was a favourite and crowded meeting place in town. At 17:30 hours Green, Medlam and Adamson met at the Commandant's Office, which overlooked the spot chosen by Cuenca. Danino turned up early and sat down on a bench. Cuenca arrived by bike at 18:10 hours and sat down next to Danino. Adamson, in uniform but unarmed, approached the bench and asked the pair in a commanding voice what they were doing. Cuenca blurted out that they were watching the game of football taking place. Adamson, informing him he was watching hockey and not football, grabbed the stunned Spaniard by the arm. Other GSP officers arrived to take Danino away. They headed for the Irish Town HQ of MI5, where the detonators that Cuenca planned to hand over to Danino were found in his jacket pocket. They were concealed as fountain pens, gadgets commonly used by the Abwehr. Meanwhile the GSP raided the fruit shop, where they found the explosive charges hidden in the toilet.

Death of a Spy

When Cuenca was shown the explosives, he broke down and confessed that he was spying for the Abwehr. He claimed his family had been killed in the Spanish Civil War and that a Falange officer, Blas Castro, had threatened his surviving relatives with extermination if Cuenca did not serve the new regime. He said he was taken to see two German friends of Castro's in Algeciras, where he was offered £1000 to make two runs with explosives into Gibraltar. He was offered more if he agreed to carry out sabotage as well. Cuenca was tried and sentenced by the British Special Court and hanged on 11 January 1944. Danino was given a medal for his role in the arrest.

Barely a week after Cuenca's arrest a huge explosion rocked the port area. The GSP went through the security index and found one José Munoz, who had not reported back for work after the explosion and was suddenly spending a great deal of money. Munoz was later arrested in town. He had hidden a second bomb in the Imperial Cafe on Main Street, but the bomb disposal squad found and deactivated it. He was sentenced to death but was reprieved.

While Switzerland, Turkey and Spain were undoubtedly the most important spying centres in the neutral states of Europe, other nations also became battlegrounds in the secret war between

ABOVE: *Spanish Moroccan troops marching on the Moroccan side of the Gibraltar straits with the Rock, shrouded in mist and dust, forming a dramatic backdrop.*

the SIS and Abwehr. The Republic of Ireland, for example, housed a number of German agents, though there were no spectacular intelligence coups in Eire during the war. Operation Osprey, the planned series of sabotage attacks on US forces in the British province of Northern Ireland, never took place, though it is believed that a number of the agents handpicked for Osprey were subsequently parachuted into Eire. There was also some collaboration between the terrorist Irish Republican Army (IRA) and the Abwehr, mainly aimed at gathering intelligence prior to a German invasion of Britain, though this ended in 1941 and the threat from Ireland lessened. The IRA's aim was to use armed force to end British rule in Ireland, but its activities in World War II was at odds with the government of Eire, which maintained a strictly neutral policy.

Chapter 7

War without Mercy

"The Bolsheviks are our superiors in one field only – espionage!"
Adolf Hitler

FEW STATES COULD BOAST BEFORE OR DURING WORLD WAR II a better intelligence service than the USSR. Military intelligence of the highest order was provided by the Soviet equivalent of the Abwehr, the GRU, sometimes with spectacular results. The Soviets were masters of the spying game, and far better at it than any of their enemies or allies, since their intelligence service had been perfected under a totalitarian system that had sympathizers in the form of idealistic communists throughout Europe and the USA. The GRU headed two spy networks that penetrated deep inside Nazi-occupied Europe and provided the Centre (the GRU's headquarters in Moscow) with invaluable intelligence during the war. But as time wore on the Germans improved their espionage skills, and in fact copied their Soviet taskmasters' methods. Not only did they expose and utterly crush one of the Soviet spy networks, but they had their own spies working deep inside Soviet territory – a greater feat in the more rigidly controlled totalitarian Soviet state than in Nazi Germany.[1]

During the early 1930s the Germans had, as the USSR's only allies, unparalleled access to the Soviet military. In 1932, for example, General Erich von Manstein attended Red Army training exercises which left him decidedly unimpressed, since even

very senior Soviet officers lacked imagination, training or command skills. However, the commanders whom Manstein had met were purged during 1937–39, by which time the USSR was a closed book to everyone including the Germans. General Köstring, the long-serving and insightful German military attaché in Moscow, pointed out that the Red Army never displayed its latest equipment in public or during the famous parades in Red Square. Before the invasion of June 1941, the German Army's Foreign Armies East (FHO) intelligence organization completely failed to find out what the Russians had in reserve. This highlighted the problems with German intelligence in general: a lack of long-term planning, lack of coordination between departments, a failure to direct the intelligence service with developing priorities, and finally a disastrous lack of centralization.[2] Göbbels noted glumly (10 September 1941): "The depressing thing is that we have not the faintest idea what Stalin has left in the way of reserves."[3] He was quite right. One of the elements the Russians had in reserve was the T-34, the best all-round tank of the war, whose appearance on the battlefield in the autumn of 1941 came as a most unpleasant surprise to the Germans on the Eastern Front.

In October 1939, Stalin's decision to incorporate the independent Baltic states of Lithuania, Latvia and Estonia into the Soviet Union, through a series of "mutual assistance treaties" appeared to confirm Nazi fears that his intentions towards Germany were

LEFT: *Harro Schulze-Boysen, a Luftwaffe officer who was assigned to the Reich Aviation Ministry, a position that gave him access to sensitive information. He was a member of the communist Red Orchestra spy ring.*

ABOVE: *The Soviets, masters of deception and subterfuge, kept the very existence of the T-34 tank (shown here) a closely guarded secret. Its appearance on the Eastern Front in 1941 gave the Germans a nasty surprise.*

aggressive. This was because his decision transformed the buffer of neutral states who would defend themselves against German aggression into most unwilling satellites.[4] Canaris, who had a close relationship with the Estonian military intelligence service (they shared information about the USSR), saw to it that the entire staff of that service was evacuated to Germany when the Soviets moved in. Based in Berlin, they retained their agents and contacts in the Baltic States and the western USSR. So they were able to provide the Abwehr – their protector and benefactor – with invaluable intelligence about the common enemy. This German influence, though disliked by many Balts, was preferable to that of the Soviets and communists. The Balts combined a virulent hatred for the Russians with a strong distaste for communist ideology. The anti-Russian and anti-communist Germans were therefore perceived as allies against a common foe.

There had been 60,000 native Baltic Germans in Latvia before the Soviet occupation, and there were 260 Nazi-run organizations. But from October to December 1939, 52,000 were evacuated to Germany. As a consequence the Abwehr lost a potential source

of agents, but there remained enough willing Baltic volunteers. The Germans tried to gain consular status for their representative offices in the region, but the Soviets, aware of their "ally's" real intention of using them for espionage, refused to oblige. Despite these difficulties, the Abwehr had contacts with the anti-Soviet underground in all three states, with one Abwehr agent in place within the Latvian Foreign Ministry itself.

As it was, the NKVD[5] had its work cut out combating the Baltic underground and the Abwehr's network of agents. The intelligence war against the USSR never stopped from the German side as it never did from the Soviet side. But in the Baltic states the Germans had all the advantages. During 1940 and up to June 1941, the NKVD unearthed 75 Lithuanian nationalist groups, and during the same period 66 resident Abwehr agents were also caught. Such "criminal anti-Soviet elements" were either shot at the NKVD headquarters in Moscow or deported to a long, lingering death in Siberia. In total there were 1596 German agents inside the USSR, of which 1338 were in the Ukraine, the Baltic states and ex-Polish Byelorussia (White Russia). The rest operated inside the 1939 borders of the USSR, which was much harder to do given the longer period of communist terror there.

In Berlin, the Lithuanian military attaché (to the now defunct Lithuanian Government),[6] Colonel Kazys Shkirpa, founded the Lithuanian Activist Front (LAF) on 17 November 1939. His intention was to set up a nationalist underground inside Lithuania to fight the Soviet occupation. To avoid NKVD infiltration or detection the LAF had only small cells (each numbering 3–5 men) with specific tasks to perform, such as cutting telephone lines, attacking isolated Soviet police (*Militia*) stations or assassinating specific Soviet representatives. By 1941 the LAF had an estimated membership of 36,000, with command headquarters in Vilnius (Vilna) and Kaunas (Kovno). In Latvia the countryside was not

safe for the Soviets, except in armed convoys or groups, and even inside Riga, the capital, it was not unknown for Russians to "disappear" after drinking bouts in the city's taverns.

As a strongly anti-communist conservative, Canaris had never trusted the Russo-German Non-Aggression Pact of August 1939 and he did his best to ignore it. He encouraged the Estonian exiles in Berlin to set up, with the connivance of the Finnish authorities, training camps outside Helsinki for Estonian volunteers from Finland's Winter War with Russia. The Finns and the Germans equipped and trained these Estonian partisans for future operations in Soviet-occupied Estonia.

Distrusting both the Balts and the Germans, throughout 1940 and early 1941 the Soviet military authorities took steps to strengthen their hold on the

BELOW: German troops during Operation Barbarossa in 1941. The Wehrmacht's progress through the Baltic states was aided by a number of uprisings in the area.

three Baltic states. The Red Army withdrew the XXII, XXIV and XXIX Territorial Corps (the former Baltic armies) from the region, while the NKVD's response was suitable brutal and comprehensive: anyone suspected of being an opponent of Stalinist rule was rounded up. Beginning on 13 June 1941 some 250,000 Balts were deported to Siberia. This operation was under way when the Germans invaded, launching Operation Barbarossa on 22 June. The invasion had an immediate effect on the Baltic states. As the panzers rolled over the Soviet border the LAF rose up in Lithuania, taking over the town of Kaunas as soon as Barbarossa was launched. Some 200 LAF partisans died in seizing control of the radio station, telegraph exchange and the prisons, where political detainees were immediately set free. Any Soviet official or NKVD man who fell into LAF hands was shot, and local communist collaborators were dealt with in a similarly swift and brutal manner. That same morning a young Soviet officer was shot as he emerged from a restaurant in Kingisepp, Estonia, while in the Latvian capital, Riga, only occupied by NKVD officers and cadets, the city was bombed by German planes and armed nationalists ("Aisargi") took to the streets. A colonel in the Latvian underground engaged in an armed battle with the NKVD, while a Latvian woman warned a Soviet journalist, Vladimir Rudny, to get out while there was still time.

Germans in Riga

The following morning the Luftwaffe showered Baltic towns with propaganda leaflets proclaiming the end of Soviet rule. By the early hours of 24 June Riga was no longer a Soviet-controlled city. As German paratroopers dropped nearby and panzers approached from the south, Latvian nationalists began to fight the Soviets in open combat. The Soviets were sniped at, their officers were shot in the streets and areas of the city became unsafe for Soviet soldiers to patrol in. On 29 June, after the NKVD failed to blow the bridges across the Dvina River, German panzers broke into the city as Soviet troops fell back in confusion. The following day the

The Abwehr could read the confidential messages the Red Army was sending

German XXVI Army Corps held a victory march down Bausky Chaussé, Riga's main avenue. The largest city and sea port in Baltic region had fallen to the Germans in less than a week, and with little cost in lives due to the German-supported "Aisargi".

Events in Lithuania showed, however, that the Nazis were no better than the previous occupiers and that whatever advantages had been gained by cooperating with the Baltic nations would be squandered by the Germans. When General Georg von Küchler's army arrived in Kaunas on the morning of 25 June the city was already in LAF hands (some 100,000 Lithuanians had joined the uprising against the retreating Russians). Instead of capitalizing on this wave of goodwill for Germany and treating the Baltic population with respect as an ally, the Germans instigated a policy of repression, motivated by their racist National Socialist ideology.

Soviet Paralysis

During their rapid advance the Germans captured Soviet field ciphers, which meant the Abwehr and the field intelligence units (Ic) could read the confidential radio and telephone messages the Red Army was sending. These could be used to sow confusion. For example, the German radio field units could interfere with Red Army radio traffic by using Soviet frequencies. Not only did radio communications in the Baltic region between the Eleventh Soviet Army and the Northwest Front headquarters break down, but the Soviets began to fear the use of the radio. This was a major German intelligence triumph, which only complicated and delayed Soviet operations. The Abwehr even managed to convince the Soviets that the Germans were preparing a major parachute landing near Leningrad (St. Petersburg).

Meanwhile the Estonians, who were still under Soviet occupation, could count down the days until the Red Army was sent packing by the advancing Germans. On 6 July the Germans captured Pärnu and the road to Tallin (Reval), the capital, was open. Since the Soviets had not made any plans to defend the port city from a land assault, no defences had been erected. The Germans could have captured the

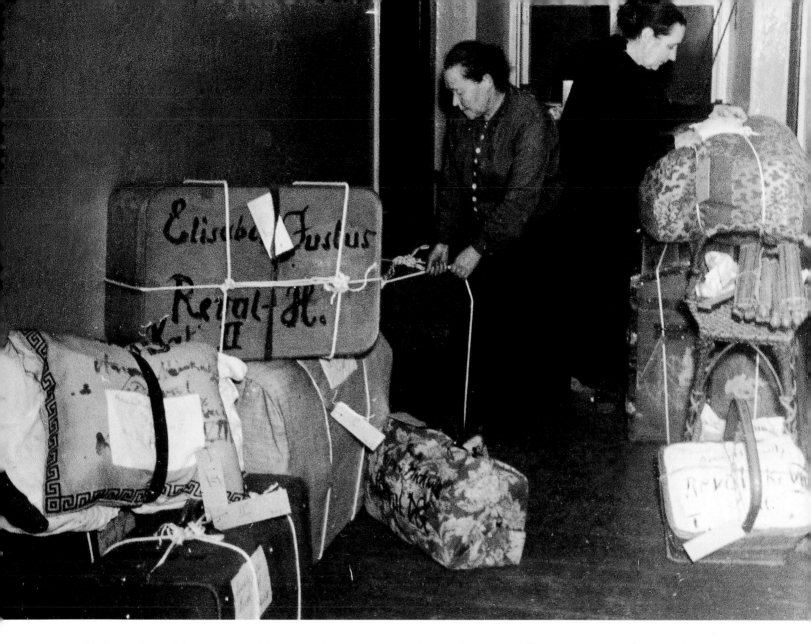

ABOVE: Members of the German Baltic community, some who were evacuated to Germany under the terms of the Nazi-Soviet Pact. Many proved valuable Abwehr agents operating against the USSR in 1941.

city without much of fight, like Riga, but the advance slackened because the armoured column heading for Leningrad was given priority. Instead, specially German trained Estonian partisans, the Erna[7] battalions, landed on the coast (some 40 fighters led by 2 Abwehr officers), while others were parachuted into the countryside. They landed on 9 July and linked up with Estonian nationalist partisans, making the countryside very dangerous for the Soviets. Soviet Admiral Pantalayev was almost shot by an Erna sniper when he inspected the defence lines being built only 19–22km (12–14 miles) outside Tallin. The Estonian Soviet "Government" forced 25,000 "volunteers" to build the lines, as the NKVD unleashed a wave of terror to keep the population down. But the front was crumbling. By 8 August Tallin was cut off from Soviet-held territory. The Soviet journalist, Nikolai Mikhailovsky, who had been a valued customer at the Golden Swan Inn in Tallin, was greeted by the usually attentive headwaiter with indifference and the less than warm greeting: "All is finished, 'respected' comrade." A few weeks later the entire Soviet Baltic Fleet evacuated the port with enormous losses, and Soviet rule came to a bloody end. The departure of the Russians was due in no small measure to the Abwehr's secret war against them and clandestine support for the Erna and Estonian nationalists.[8]

One of the "what ifs" of World War II lies in the attitude of the German Army towards population of the Ukraine. During the 1930s Stalin's grandiosely bungled policy of forced collectivization, which reduced most of European Russia to starvation, hit the Ukrainians the hardest. Stalin's brutalities against this proud and defiant nation might have cost him the war had it not have been for Hitler, who made the same error of mistreating and humiliating the fiery Ukrainians.

The people of the western Ukraine (Galicia) found themselves divided between bloody Stalinist oppression and milder Polish suppression, and viewed Germany as a protector and benefactor. During the 1920s the Abwehr had found many willing agents in Poland among the disaffected Ukrainian population. During 1917–18 the Germans had put Ataman[9] Skoropadsky in charge of a pro-German Ukrainian administration, which collapsed when the Germans withdrew. Skoropadsky removed himself to the safety of Berlin where he was supported and sponsored by the Abwehr until 1937, when the intelligence service tired of paying him for no results. The Red Army had invaded and occupied the Ukraine in 1919 – the eastern and central part of the country fell into their hands – but it was not until 1926 that the USSR took full control of the country. This was only won through the most violent and brutal oppression of all manifestations of Ukrainian national feeling. Yet despite all this, Skoropadsky and other nationalist leaders continued to have support and influence in the occupied country (though Skoropadsky failed to carry out any sabotage or more active agent activity in the face of the NKVD).

ABOVE: A German soldier from Army Group North is lifted aloft by a deliriously happy population in Riga on 2 July 1941, following the Latvian capital's liberation from the hated Soviet occupation.

The OUN

The Abwehr hoped for more from the younger, radical and dynamic Commander Konovalek and his OUN (Organization of Ukrainian Nationalists). Even in exile the Ukrainians were not safe from the reach of the NKVD, though, and Konovalek was murdered by one of its assassination squads. His place as head of the OUN was taken by Andrei Melnyk, but the more radical wing rallied to the leadership of Stephan Bandera. The OUN was thus split into two separate and hostile factions: OUN-M (Melnyk) for the "moderates", and the OUN-B (Bandera) for the "radicals'.

What few people knew was that both Ukrainian leaders were in the pay of the Abwehr. When Bandera founded the Ukrainian Insurgency Army (UPA) the Abwehr set up training camps, in 1938, for young Ukrainian militants. Located outside Berlin at an isolated holiday camp on the Chiemsee, these ardent nationalists were trained in partisan warfare. They were then sent on a course of Abwehr sabotage at Quenzgut, outside Berlin, where they received training for missions in Poland and Soviet Ukraine. Since they had a common foe in the USSR and there was a large Ukrainian population in Manchuria, the Japanese supported the Abwehr II's Ukrainian activities with funds and intelligence expertise. This Japanese connection proved most useful.

RIGHT: *Petro Vershigora, Ukrainian partisan leader, and a deadly foe of the Germans and the Ukrainian nationalists alike. He commanded thousands of partisans in the Ukraine.*

German relations with the various Ukrainian organizations were never easy or trouble free. Ukrainian loyalty to the Germans was sorely tested in March 1939 when Hitler, more concerned with gaining Hungarian favour, handed the Ukrainian-inhabited Czech province of Ruthenia over to the Magyars. The Ruthenians rose up against this decision, raised the blue and yellow Ukrainian flag and were promptly crushed by their Hungarian occupiers. Even greater strain was placed on German-Ukrainian relations when Hitler made his pact with Stalin and ordered, at the end of September 1939, Abwehr II's training of Ukrainians to cease. However, the Abwehr simply handed over their Ukrainian wards to their Japanese partners, who continued to fund the training schools. Their value was to be amply demonstrated during Operation Barbarossa, when they slipped across the frontier before the offensive commenced. Behind the lines they sabotaged Soviet communications by cutting telegraph and telephone lines and blowing up bridges. They were also instrumental in lessening the impact of Soviet partisans in the German-occupied territories by infiltrating and liquidating these units.

The Nightingale Commandos

During the autumn of 1940, with Operation Sea Lion in abeyance in the West, the OKH/OKW began to plan the invasion of the USSR. During the winter of 1940–41 a new Ukrainian training camp was set up at Neuhammer, near Leignitz in Polish Silesia. The partisan/agent recruits came from Bandera's OUN and UPA troops and were led by an outstanding Ukrainian military leader: Commandant Skonprynka. Other recruits came from the Ukrainian (Galician) troops who had capitulated or deserted to the Germans during the invasion of Poland. Skonprynka showed no mercy in the training of his unit, and he made it clear that they were being prepared for the liberation of their occupied homeland.[10] The unit's German military commander was Lieutenant Albrecht Herzner and

its Political Officer was Professor Oberländer. Abwehr II named this Ukrainian unit after a famous Cossack choir: the Nightingales. It may have had a fancy name but its weaponry was not much to brag about.

In June 1941 the Nightingales began operations attached to the Brandenburgers. During 29–30 June they went into action several hours before the Brandenburgers were supposed to strike because they had received intelligence of an impending mass slaughter of their compatriots in the NKVD prison of Lvov (Lviv in Ukrainian). Like the Lithuanians, the Ukrainians were naïve enough to believe in German assurances of an independent state once liberated from the Soviets. With the Lvov radio station under their control, the Ukrainians proclaimed an independent state. The Germans responded by denying any such state existed and announcing that the western Ukraine had been incorporated into

Hans Frank's General Government of Poland. Morale slumped in all the Ukrainian units, especially in the Nightingales, and the Germans decided to close it down.

An infuriated Oberländer, who was a warm friend of the Ukrainian national cause and an expert on the country, gained access to Hitler personally and remonstrated with the Führer at this mishandling of the most valuable ally Germany had in its war against Stalin. Hitler was not impressed. With a mixture of ignorance and sheer crass stupidity he told Oberländer: "You don't know what you're talking about. Russia is our Africa, and the Russians are our niggers." The professor was stupefied by this reply and when he returned to report the outcome of the meeting to the Brandenburger commander, Oberländer blurted out: "That is, sir, Hitler's conception, and that, sir, is a conception which will lose us the war."[11]

Oberländer was correct in his analysis. In his ignorance and arrogance Hitler had made the mistake of identifying the long-suffering Ukrainians with Stalin's communist rule. Nothing could have been further from the truth. If there were any people

ABOVE: Enthusiastic and warmly welcoming Ukrainians greet their German liberators from Stalin's murderous yoke in August 1941. Their generosity of spirit was squandered by Hitler's racist ideological policies.

who had every reason to relish the thought of Stalin and his crew hanging from the walls of the Kremlin, it was the Ukrainians. Hitler compounded his mistake by not identifying the completely separate nationalities of the Ukrainians from the Russians and not realizing that he could, by supporting the Ukrainians against Russian oppression, win the Ukrainians' devoted loyalty and support. But to make a bad situation worse, Hitler, by treating all the Slavs as nothing more than illiterate and primitive savages, turned the hitherto friendly population against their new German occupiers.

What initially saved the Germans in the East was the fact that Stalin's disastrous economic policies, wholesale massacres and deportations had bitten so hard into the Ukrainian psyche that they were prepared, even after the events of 1941, to serve the Germans in large numbers. After all, in choosing between two evils, the Ukrainians, like the Baltic peoples, would rather have the devil they did not know. Amazingly enough, some 200,000–250,000 Ukrainians were still serving in the ranks of the German Army and SS a year later. As for the Balts, despite three years of humiliation and mistreatment at the hands of the Nazis, they rallied to those SS units set up to defend their countries in 1944 from the advance of the Red Army.[12]

The Fremde Heere Ost (FHO)

The OKH was not satisfied with the FHO's work during the Barbarossa campaign, which reflected the ineptitude of the head of the FHO: Colonel Eberhard Kinzel. Kinzel had served in the ND under Nicholai's command but he was inefficient, slow and easygoing. On 1 April 1942 Kinzel was dismissed and replaced by his deputy, Reinhard Gehlen, who undertook a complete remodelling of the FHO. Gehlen replaced Kinzel's men with younger and more determined personnel who shared his devotion to duty and energetic intelligence work. He divided the FHO into three sections for each army group operating on the Eastern Front, and a fourth for partisans was added. Colonel Baron Alexis von Rönne, a Baltic German noblemen who spoke fluent Russian, headed Group III, which paid more general attention to Soviet policies and the USSR.

Gehlen's order to Rönne was to gather every scrap of intelligence he could about the Soviet enemy. Rönne was also in charge of liaison with the Abwehr, SD, OKH and the OKW. A special interrogation group was set up in the fortress of Boyen, near Lötzen in East Prussia, under Captain Bernhard von Blossfeld, who had managed the Hotel Rome in Riga before the war. He was assisted by the ex-Soviet Major Vasili Sakharov, who did the main part of the interrogation work. Separate POW camps for Cossacks, Ukrainians (at Luckenwalde) and non-Slavs were set up. Gehlen also set up a giant archive of information on the USSR and the Balkans, which was constantly updated and held an enormous amount of detail concerning every aspect of the enemy's economy, society, leaders and military capacity. Elsewhere within the FHO, a forging department was established that became so proficient that the SD and Abwehr used it to produce documents for its own agents operating inside

ABOVE: *Professor Oberländer, the man who dared to remonstrance with Hitler's Eastern policies and orders to treat the Ukrainians and the other Slavs in the region as no better than primitives.*

Soviet-occupied territory. The FHO, of course, had many agents operating behind enemy lines, though Gehlen was not enamoured of all of them.

One such agent was "Ivar" in Leningrad. Gehlen had inherited "Ivar" from Kinzel and, unlike his predecessor, was not impressed and noted that Ivar was sending him "old rags". But Ivar had been at his post inside the city since February 1941, and in February 1943 he sent intelligence that the Thirty-Third Army, led by General Yefremov, was about to attack on the central sector of the front around

Rhzev. The OKW acted on Gehlen's warning from Ivar and made preparations to meet the Soviet thrust by placing a strong force at Yachnov, which attacked the Thirty-Third Army and encircled it. General Yefremov, rather than face Stalin's wrath, shot himself. This was a major success for the FHO and Gehlen personally, vindicating his promotion to head the most important intelligence organization of the Third Reich. This ensured that Gehlen gained control over the Abwehr's Luckenwalde camp and eventually the other POW camps, which gave him a larger pool for the recruitment of agents.

Colonel Tavrin

One of those recruited in the camps was Piotr Ivanovitch Tavrin, who had been captured in the Rzhev sector in May 1942. He agreed to become an FHO agent despite his high Soviet decorations and seemingly impeccable communist record. He crossed back to the Soviet side in September 1942 and after a thorough NKVD interrogation (for which Gehlen had briefed him), he was passed back into the ranks of the Red Army. Gehlen's high hopes for Tavrin were not to be disappointed, and over the next two years Tavrin was promoted and again decorated.

Tavrin held several important posts in the Soviet Ministry of Defence in Moscow, the Stavka,[13] and was promoted to the rank of colonel. He then joined the staff of the brilliant Marshal Ivan Chernyakovsky on the Bryansk Front, south of Moscow.[14] Tavrin sent by radio regular, detailed and extremely valuable reports that were of enormous value to the German forces' ability to block or counter the Red Army's offensives. In August 1944 a worried Tavrin radioed the FHO that he was fearful the NKVD suspected him, and Gehlen, showing exemplary loyalty to his Russian agent, readily agreed to send a plane to pick him up. Tavrin and his wife set out on 5 September for the rendezvous with the Messerschmitt plane that Gehlen had dispatched. However, travelling on a motorbike, the couple were stopped by a patrol who found in their luggage a German radio and cipher codes written on cigarette papers in the lining of Tavrin's coat. Tavrin

Tavrin sent by radio regular, detailed and extremely valuable reports on the Red Army

realized the game was up and openly admitted to being a German spy. He was taken away for torture and interrogation. Tavrin and his wife, the FHO found out from their close monitoring of the Soviet press, were shot shortly after their capture. Gehlen pitied the loss of such a valuable agent as Tavrin, and noted that his intelligence had been most valuable and filled three fat dossiers in the FHO's growing archive.

Operation Thrush (Drossel)

Vasili Antonovich Skryabin was born in 1920 and as a young man lost both his parents during Stalin's purges of the 1930s, despite being related to Foreign Minister Vyacheslav Skryabin, better known under his communist *nom de guerre* as "Molotov".[15] Skryabin served in the 38th Guards Regiment until on 17 August 1941, he, like hundreds of thousands of other Red Army soldiers, surrendered to the German Army. Skryabin impressed his captors with his intelligence, eloquence, reliability and his excellent German. He was recruited by the FHO as "Igor" and teamed up with the experienced FHO agent Albert Muller or "Gregor". "Gregor" was born in St. Petersburg in 1909 to a German father and Russian mother. He had emigrated to Germany in 1928 when his father died, and before the war had worked as an agent for Colonel Rauch at the Abwehr's Königsberg Ast. In 1942, however, Gehlen enticed him to work for the FHO. "Gregor", who was fluent in German and Russian, worked to begin with as an interpreter. But Gehlen was preparing him and "Igor" for Operation Thrush – to infiltrate them deep inside Moscow. Gehlen hoped Igor would eventually get a high post in the Red Army or possibly the Soviet Government given his education, class and intelligence, while Gregor as the more experienced agent was to be employed for ordinary tasks.

Gehlen's FHO subordinates gave the two agents the most meticulous and thorough training. They were issued with several perfectly forged documents and briefed to the minutest detail of life in wartime Soviet Russia. Igor was dressed up in the uniform of a General Staff major and Igor that of a first lieutenant with suitable war decorations. Gehlen personally inspected the pair before they set out on their mission. In these disguises the duo were taken to airfield 304 outside Vitebsk in northern Byelorussia, and flown across the frontline and dropped into the sector of a General Koslov. Early on the morning of 10 August they buried their parachutes and overalls and made their way to the headquarters of the 11th Guards Division at Ostrova. Once there, General Staff Major "Posyutchin" and his ADC, Lieutenant Krassin, presented their forged Soviet credentials – forged FHO orders that claimed that Posyutchin was on Stavka chief Marshal Vasilevsky's staff. Koslov not only accepted the forgeries as real but gave the agents full hospitality: a tour of inspection, a massive banquet in the evening and access to his HQ plans. Two days later Koslov, ever the good host, provided the pair with a staff car and driver. Koslov was also generous

BELOW: Soviet POWs proved, despite their mistreatment at the hands of the Germans, willing to both divulge intelligence and serve as agents for the Abwehr.

enough to provide "Poyutchin" with secret staff plans sent by army and front headquarters. These were sent in Soviet code by Gregor to the FHO, where they were quickly decoded and provided most interesting reading for the army group command and OKW.

During their tour of inspection along the lines of the Soviet Central Front the pair changed identity twice, before switching into civilian garb and finally making their way to Moscow. Since Gehlen wanted to know all about Soviet arms production, Gregor, faking war injuries and presenting forged documents showing he was war veteran, got a job as an electrician in an arms factory run by Gosplan.[16] The younger Skryabin got his own job, a girlfriend called Marfa and a flat in Moscow. Once established inside the Soviet capital, the pair, posing again as Red Army officers, had no problem in renting a *dacha* (cottage) outside Moscow where they developed the microfilms they had taken. These were transported across the frontline by Vlasov,[17] an officer who was the courier "Peter"'. These regular despatches were so bulky it took weeks to deliver, but provided Gehlen with a wealth of information unknown to any intelligence service working against the USSR.

By October 1944 it was becoming very difficult to get the intelligence out, and so Gehlen recalled Igor and Gregor back to Germany. He arranged a pick-up in a meadow near the village of Dzerzhinsk, some 70km (44 miles) west of Moscow, for Igor, Marfa and Gregor. But when the pilot landed only Gregor had turned up on time – the pilot had no wish to linger. He set off as quickly as possible just as Igor and Marfa arrived, only to see the plane take to the sky with Gregor frantically waving to them. He tried to get the pilot to return but the airman quite sensibly decided against such a precarious move. Gregor pleaded with the FHO to make another attempt and Gehlen arranged for a new pick-up in January 1945, in what was now Soviet-occupied East Prussia. But no one turned up and nothing further was heard of Skryabin or Marfa.

BELOW: Reinhard Gehlen doing what he was best at: working hard at fighting the secret war against the USSR. He shared Oberländer's views on Hitler's policies.

If the adventures of the Operation Thrush agents in Moscow seem remarkable, then they pale in comparison with Gehlen's greatest intelligence coup. During a trawl through the Ukrainians in Luckenwalde camp, the Germans found a *Politruk* (Political Officer) who had served on Marshal Zhukov's West Front command and had been captured during the battle of Vyazma in October 1941. There seemed nothing remarkable about Vladimir Minishkiy, but he was in fact a high CPSU (Soviet Communist Party)[18] official and before the war had served as one of seven secretaries to the party's Central Committee. In May 1942, having endured eight gruelling months in the unpleasant surroundings of Luckenwalde, Minishkiy was ready to collaborate with the Germans. He was deeply pessimistic about a Soviet victory and was a lukewarm communist. Gehlen, who conducted the interview with Minishkiy personally, won the Soviet officer's confidence and trust by treating him well,

ABOVE: The sorry aftermath of Timoshenko's failed offensive in July 1942 when, for once, the intelligence tables had been turned on the Soviets. The Red Army lost 250,000 men and 1249 tanks in the abortive attack.

speaking to him with respect and showing concern for his and his family's welfare.[19] Gehlen promised that Minishkiy could have any position he wished in Germany, and that his family would be smuggled out of the USSR.

At this point Gehlen, remarkably enough, already had a radio operator inside Moscow, and he was ordered to relay Minishkiy's messages back to the FHO. Minishkiy, now given the designation "V-438" and the codename "Flamingo", was thoroughly briefed, and to help his cover as a returning POW, was sent back with some genuine intelligence to feed the NKVD. Minishkiy crossed the lines, was thoroughly interrogated as a former POW and his story of a daring escape was believed, as was his intelligence. Minishkiy made contact with the radio operator and returned to his senior role in the CPSU, and was subsequently promoted to be a member of Stalin's inner war cabinet, the GKO.[20] "Flamingo" could report a most interesting and momentous meeting at the GKO on 14 July 1942 which was

attended by Shaposhnikov, Voroshilov and Molotov, as well as members of the American, British and Chinese military missions. The meeting revealed that there would be a deliberate retreat towards the Volga River leaving only scorched earth behind, but that it was imperative that the Red Army held Stalingrad, the Caucasus and the port of Novorossisk on the Black Sea. The Red Army would therefore launch diversionary offensives at Orel and Kalinin (south and northwest of Moscow) to draw off German forces.

Through land and aerial reconnaissance V-438's report could be verified since they showed, quite clearly, that Soviet forces were retreating slowly towards the Volga. Gehlen warned the OKW about the planned offensive, which was launched in July 1942 by Marshal Timoshenko. The Germans, through V-438's reports, could make the right dispositions and Marshal Timoshenko lost 250,000 troops, 1249 tanks and over 2000 artillery pieces in the offensive. During the summer of 1942 "Flamingo" kept sending valuable reports on the order of battle of the Red Army, Soviet plans, and discussions at the GKO. He continued this activity during the autumn, but was gripped by a sense of increasing gloom and depression. In October 1942

German lines. He and his family, thanks to Gehlen, survived the war.

FHO Special Operations

At the end of 1941, the Abwehr had created a special unit made up of former Red Army troops under a White Russian émigré, Colonel Sakharov. It was based in Byelorussia outside Orsha in a place called Osintorf. The unit's official name was Experimental Organization (Versuchsband) Osintorf (Mitte) but was called Graukopf (Greyhead) after Sakharov's grey hair. By the end of 1941, the Graukopf unit numbered 350–400 men and by July 1942 it had grown to 3000. It was therefore renamed, to give it more dignity and standing, the RNNA[21] – the Russian National Peoples' Army. Colonel Sakharov's RNNA was used to good effect against the Soviet partisans in German-occupied areas of the Ukraine and Byelorussia. By December 1942 the RNNA numbered 10,000, but as usual with the Nazis these enthusiastic anti-communist Russians were not given their proper due or the support they deserved against the common Stalinist foe.

In the spring of 1942, to compensate for the weakness of the FHO under Kinzel's leadership, Canaris intervened to put some backbone into the organization by ordering the chief of Abwehr III, Major-General Eccard von Bentivegni, to set up commando units. Bentivegni established three groups, codenamed "Walli", for infiltration, reconnaissance and intelligence gathering behind Soviet lines. Walli I, under Major-General Hermann Baun, was located at Sulejowek east of Warsaw for the main thrust. Major Seeliger was in charge of Walli II (sabotage), while Lieutenant-Colonel Heinz Schmalschäger's Walli III trained commandos to operate in Soviet uniforms behind enemy lines – as the Brandenburgers had done in 1941.

The Walli teams infiltrated the central sector of the front during the summer of 1942 to spy out Soviet defences west of Moscow – intelligence that could prove invaluable should Hitler decide to launch an offensive there. As this seemed less likely given the increasing strength of Moscow's defences, the Walli teams were switched to other targets farther south. Meanwhile Canaris' SD rival, Schellenberg, set up rival commando teams known as Zeppelin

ABOVE: *Walter Schellenberg, the loyal and smartly uniformed SS officer. He set up the Zeppelin commando teams in 1942. However, the SD did not, like the Abwehr, become a major player on the Eastern Front.*

Gehlen who believed, like Canaris, that loyalty and generosity shown to agents would be repaid in the same measure, arranged for German commandos to pick up Minishkiy and his family. Unlike Tavrin and Skryabin, they managed to escape back to

detachments, in February 1942. They were led by SS-Sturmbannführer Hengelhaupt, who in turn reported directly to the OKW's Colonel Schildknecht and the SD (i.e. Schellenberg). Otto Skorzeny served for a while as a temporary commander of the Zeppelins, but these SS units did not prove as adept as the Wallis in infiltrating behind Soviet lines.

One such experiment rebounded badly on the SS when it created the SS-Verband Druzhina[22] (SS Unit Druzhina) under Kuban Cossack V.V. "Rodionov" Gill's command. The Druzhina had good relations with the Russian population and conducted several outstanding operations against the Soviet partisans. But due to Nazi arrogance and the suspicion displayed by the SS command, the unit was again not utilized or appreciated enough. Fed up with their Nazi masters' racism, the Druzhina defected to the Soviet side on 18 August 1943. The Wehrmacht had to initiate Operation Spring Feast in April 1944 to destroy this rogue SS unit. On that sad and bloody note ended yet another Nazi failure to win the hearts and minds of the Soviet people.

Heroism and Treason

When the FHO picked up intelligence from "Flamingo" that Stalin had given orders that the oilfields at Grozny and Maikop in the Caucasus would be blown up if the Germans threatened them, the FHO decided to act. Gehlen got together 25 men (15 were Soviet ex-POWs), and they were dropped near Grozny with orders to secure the oilfields from Soviet sabotage until the advance units of the First Panzer Army could arrive. Using machine guns with silencers, all the Soviet saboteurs left behind to blow up the oil wells were killed. But triumph almost turned to tragedy when the German troops arrived. They mistook the commandos for Soviet stragglers and almost had them shot.

Another group of commandos, one company of Caucasians and 36 South Tyrolean mountain troops, were not so lucky. They were dropped on 25 August 1942 into the Caucasus mountain region near the villages of Tschiscki and Datsku-Borsoi, where Soviet troops were lying in wait. Many of the unlucky

Whatever the young officer revealed was soon radioed to GRU headquarters

troops were shot before they even hit the ground. Only five exhausted men made it back to the German lines. They had been betrayed by an unwitting member of the Abwehr, who revealed their drop and several other Abwehr commando operations on the Eastern Front to his married lover. Her name was Mildred Harnack, an American woman married to a senior German bureaucrat. Both she and her husband worked for the GRU, and whatever the young officer revealed was soon radioed to the GRU Centre in Moscow.

The Red Orchestra

If Gehlen had Flamingo working for him in the Kremlin, then his enemies in the GRU had their agents – the "Red Orchestra" – working in the very corridors of power in Berlin itself. The only difference was that Flamingo was a single spy, while the "Red Orchestra" was an entire network. On 26 June 1941, only five days after the beginning of Barbarossa, a radio monitoring station at Kranz in East Prussia picked up radio signals from a transmitter in Western Europe communicating with Moscow. It was using the same frequency, PTX, as the French Resistance. Radio surveillance was the responsibility of the Funkabwehr (Radio Security), headed by Lieutenant-Colonel Hans Kopp, and his headquarters staff at Matthäikirchplatz in central Berlin. It was situated between the Gestapo and Abwehr headquarters in the city. In early July a second transmitter, also using a Soviet-style code, had begun transmitting, and in September Kopp sent three radio-monitoring squads into the streets of central Berlin to track it down. Kopp realized that there was a Soviet spy in the very centre of Berlin itself. The three vans disguised as postal vehicles operated together and identified three locations in central Berlin from where this radio transmitter was being used. Kopp had now located the other PTX operator to Belgium, and he went to Tirpitz Ufer to speak with Colonel Rohleder, head of Abwehr IIIF (counter-intelligence) – the largest and most efficient counter-intelligence

department in Germany. Rohleder sent Abwehr Captain Harry Piepe to Brussels where he set up, as cover, a trading firm.[23] Meanwhile Kopp had sent a Funkabwehr squad to Brussels, where a PTX operator had been located in the Etterbeek district. A plainclothes Funkabwehr man carrying a "suitcase" was sent to patrol the streets, and he located the transmitter in Rue de Atrébates.

The Rue de Atrébates Raid

Piepe mobilized regular troops and the GFP[24] for a raid on 101 Rue de Atrébates on 14 December 1941. During the operation a man tried to flee but was caught. He claimed to be a Uruguayan, Carlos Alamos, though he spoke French with a heavy Slav accent, while the two women with him were Belgian Jews. Piepe assured the women that he was not from the Gestapo but from the Abwehr. One of the women, Rita Arnould, relieved by his reassurance, told Piepe to check the walls, which he did. He found a secret darkroom where a forger had his workshop. Piepe withdrew but placed two GFP officers in the house, who later caught one more Soviet agent (David Kamy) but let another escape. The latter was as a well-groomed character who produced an identity card made out to Jean Gilbert and an OT[25] special pass. What the two GFP men did not realize was that "Jean Gilbert" was in fact "Grand Chef" – the head of Soviet military intelligence in Western Europe. Another mistake the Germans made was not to wait until they found all three transmitters at work in Brussels.

In Berlin the Gestapo was called in to "assist" Piepe, and Karl Giering was selected. Giering linked the South American, "Carlos Alamos", caught during the raid with a GRU officer called Mikhail Makarov. Giering set up his headquarters in Brussels, but torturing "Alamos" revealed nothing except that he was indeed Makarov. The remaining prisoners were sent to the SS prison fortress at Breendonk outside Brussels, where the commandant, Major Schmitt, greeted them with the friendly statement: "This is hell and I am the

LEFT: A German Radio Surveillance Unit (Funkabwehr) operating on a Paris rooftop in the hunt for radios operated by the French resistance.

ABOVE: Abwehr Captain Harry Piepe in full Wehrmacht uniform. This was not his usual garb, since his cover was that of a successful and well-to-do German businessman with offices in Brussels.

Devil!" He was not exaggerating. Kamy and Makarov were "interrogated intensively" in true Gestapo fashion, but they revealed nothing.

Piepe, through an Abwehr IIIF officer – Lieutenant Bödiker's V-Man Police inspector – located the "Cobbler" (forger in Abwehr parlance),[26] who was none other than Adam Raichmann – "Adash" – who had been trained by the GRU Berlin "Apparat" before 1933.[27] In February 1942 the PTX transmitters burst into life again in Berlin and Brussels. The Berlin transmitter operated only intermittently, but the one in Brussels sent messages for hours on end, which assisted the Funkabwehr to locate it. At 03:00 hours 15 Luftwaffe troops and 10 GFP men went into action led by Piepe. The radio operator escaped through a skylight as the Germans burst in, and he ran from house to house until he

ABOVE: *The OGPU headquarters in Moscow. Its operatives within the Nazi machine were highly effective at providing the Red Army with timely and accurate intelligence about German Army movements on the Eastern Front.*

crashed through another skylight. Again the GFP/Luftwaffe patrol burst into the house and finally found the radio man cowering underneath an overturned bath tub. He was beaten severely as he resisted arrest.

The radio man was more important than just someone tapping at a radio key. The captured Soviet agent was none other than Johann Wenzel, a senior German communist who had been an associate to Ernst Thälmann – the pre-1933 leader of the KPD[28] – and who had run his own spy ring in Belgium, the "Group Hermann". Piepe returned to Berlin with Wenzel's messages and showed them to his superiors, Rohleder, von Bentivegni and Canaris. They were shocked. The messages gave a wealth of detail of the forthcoming Operation Blue: the attack on the Caucasus and Stalingrad. Giering ordered Wenzel to the

Breendonk prison where, after eight weeks of interrogation and torture, the communist agent was willing to cooperate with the Germans.

Wenzel's collaboration yielded a rich harvest of communist agents and German traitors. Dr. Hans Kummerow, an electrical engineer who had been supplying the GRU with intelligence on German inventions since 1932, was arrested with his wife after an arranged meeting with a "courier" at Potsdamer Platz U-Bahn station. Wilhelm Fellendorfer and Erna Eifler (GRU agents parachuted into East Prussia during 16–17 May 1942) were also picked up, as was the *Comintern*[29] head of the Hamburg section, Bernhard Bastlein. The "cobbler" workshop in Berlin was smashed when the entire Hübner family was arrested. Wenzel had proven his worth as a double agent and was installed in a flat, under Gestapo supervision, in Brussels. One cold morning in January 1943, as the Gestapo guard was lighting the fire in the stove, Wenzel knocked him out and fled the building. A major source into the workings of the Red Orchestra[30] had been lost.

The Gestapo in Paris raided a house in the city where a Jewish couple, Hersch and Myra Sokol, ran a transmitter for the Red Orchestra. They were transported to Breendonk where Hersch died from his mistreatment, while Myra was shipped off to a concentration camp in Germany where she later died. They only revealed one important piece of intelligence: that the Conductor of the Orchestra used the alias "Gilbert". The torture of Sokols had revealed no new avenues into the Orchestra, but then, in July 1942, having put the cobbler Raichmann in contact with V-Man Inspector Mathieu, there was a breakthrough. Raichmann arranged a meeting between Mathieu and a Soviet agent in need of a passport. The meeting took place on 30 July in the Royal Botanical Gardens in Brussels, and just as Mathieu[31] was about to hand over the document both were arrested. The tall, blonde fellow with Mathieu protested that he was a Finn called Eric Jernström studying at the Brussels Polytechnic. However, when "Jernström" was confronted by Wenzel he confirmed he was "Bordo" – in reality the Ukrainian Konstantin Yefremov, a Red Army captain infiltrated into Belgium in 1939 to head the GRU network there. Yefremov promptly agreed to collaborate with the Abwehr, and then betrayed several agents of the Red Orchestra.

A Fatal Meeting

Another meeting was set up in the Botanical Gardens, and this time the Abwehr/SD netted the "cobbler" and his Czech mistress, Malvina Gruber. They revealed that the GRU ran its operations through the firm of Simexco, whose office was next door to his own "firm". Piepe got Abwehr IIIN (the Abwehr's telephone-tapping service) to place a 24-hour tap on Simexco's phones. But this surveillance did not yield the promised harvest of information on the Orchestra that Piepe and Giering had hoped for.

A crucial, and for the spies in Berlin, fatal breakthrough had already come in October 1941 when the Centre – for reasons only known to itself – sent the following message in plain language to its Brussels radio operator. Agent "Kent" (Petit

In one month, 60 members of the Berlin section of the Red Orchestra were arrested

Chef) was to travel to Berlin where he could find "Charo" at 19 Altenburger Alle (Neu Westend), 3rd floor right; "Wolf" at 26A Fredericiastrasse, Charlottenburg, 2nd floor left; and Bauer at 18 Kaiserallee, Friedenau, 4th floor left. "Kent" was to use the password "Director". When the Funkabwehr handed this message to the SD it was sceptical, since it seemed to be too good to be true, though it investigated the leads nevertheless. The identity of the agents were quickly established. They were Lieutenant Harro Schulze-Boysen, a Luftwaffe desk officer in the Ministry of Aviation ("Choro"), Dr. Arvid Harnack, senior civil servant at the Ministry of Economics ("Wolf"), and "Bauer", who was the prominent writer Dr. Adam Kuckhoff. The tentacles of the Orchestra reached deep inside the bowels of the Third Reich. A meeting took place between Schellenberg, Bentivegni, Canaris and Kopp. While the SD appointed Johann Stübing and Horst Kopkow to expose the Berlin nest, Piepe and Giering would continue their work in the West.

Death of the Orchestra

The main agents were watched closely until the lesser characters in this remarkable spy network had been exposed. Schulze-Boysen was arrested at the Reich Ministry of Aviation on Sunday 30 August 1942, his wife Libertas Schulze-Boysen was arrested when she tried to board a train bound for the Moselles at the Berlin Anhalter railway station, while Dr. Harnack and his wife Mildred were caught on 7 September in a hotel in East Prussia. "Bauer", or Adam Kuckhoff, was picked up on 16 September. In one month 60 members of the Berlin section of the Red Orchestra were arrested by the Gestapo. Friedrich Panzinger, an experienced and ruthless Gestapo interrogator, headed a 25-man special investigation team to work on the spies.

What were the motives of the members of the Red Orchestra? Both Kuckhoff and Harnack were old GRU agents and committed communists. In other words experienced spies and hardened

ABOVE: *The brilliant Soviet spymaster himself: Le Grand Chef (Leopold Trepper or M. "Gilbert") – head of the GRU in Western Europe and head of the Red Orchestra, one of the most successful World War II spy rings.*

conspirators for whom no mercy whatsoever would be shown. Harro Schulze-Boysen and his wife Libertas were very different. Harro was badly beaten – losing half an ear in the process – during the Nazi accession to power back in 1933 and his motive was emotional: revenge. His wife Libertas was only a very foolish and uncomprehending fellow traveller. They were indiscreet and far too conspicuous in their opposition to the regime. In May 1942, for example, Harro forced members of the Orchestra to partake in his risky sabotage of Göbbels' propaganda show against the USSR in Berlin.

For once the Gestapo, no doubt under the "moderating" influence of the SD, whose aim was to get as much intelligence as possible about the Red Orchestra, employed subtle methods rather than hammers, cold baths, thongs and other "tools of their trade". During hours of interrogation

between Stübing and Schulze-Boysen the latter revealed nothing about his network. All the members of the Red Orchestra kept quiet about their activities. But there was one fatal weakness in this front. Alfred Göpfert, employed to interrogate Libertas, Harro's wife, realized that she was weak, foolish and easily led. Göpfert persuaded his secretary to engage Libertas in an "after hours" conversation, just "between the two of them". These talks betrayed additional members of the Berlin section of the Red Orchestra. The first talk led to the arrest of Hans Coppi that same evening.

Under Torture

Panzinger was not as pleased with the rest of the Red Orchestra, and after a week of with no progress he took the gloves off. The prisoners were handcuffed day and night, then dragged down to the basement of Prinz Albrecht Strasse to the Gestapo's infamous torture chamber – the aptly named Stalin room. Several of the prisoners tried and failed to commit suicide. One tried to throw himself and Panzinger through a window, but this too failed. The Germans, through Wenzel, contacted the Centre in Moscow and requested a courier be sent to Berlin to assist the Orchestra. The Centre, unaware of the trick, sent GRU agent and German communist Heinrich Könen, who was dropped at Osterode in East Prussia on 23 October 1942. His contact at Saalestrasse 36, Ilset Stöbe "Alta", had been arrested already on 12 September. Five days after landing Könen reached Saalestrasse where he met Alta and arranged for another meeting a few days later. This "Alta" was in fact Gertrude Breiter, Libertas' off-the-cuff conversation partner. Breiter was convinced Könen would not make the second meeting having smelt a rat, but he did. Breiter was well briefed by Panzinger and Göpfert on Ilse Stöbe, and when Könen said he brought greetings from her husband, Rudi, she was able to correct him. "Rudi" or Rudolf Herrnstadt, a German communist in Moscow exile, was only her lover. This correction was enough to convince the GRU agent that Breiter was the genuine article, and he arranged a third meeting. They met at a cafe where both were arrested. Könen was carrying a receipt for 5000

Reichsmarks paid to First Counsellor Rudolf von Scheliha. This receipt was to be used to blackmail Scheliha, GRU agent "Arier",[32] into increasing his flow of intelligence that had been slackening. Scheliha was on vacation in Switzerland but was set to return to Konstanz, whence Panzinger flew to. As the train from Switzerland pulled into the station "Arier" was arrested by Panzinger.

Trial and Executions

The arrest of Arier completed the search for members of the Berlin Red Orchestra and it was quite a bag. By the end of 1942 some 117 agents had been netted from the original 60 betrayed by the revelations of Arvid Harnack, Harro Schulze-Boysen and his wife Libertas. Since the Libertas family were neighbours and friends of the Görings and the Reichsmarshal had accepted Harro into his service, Hitler ordered Göring to set up a special military court martial. Göring appointed "Hitler's Bloodhound", Dr. Manfred Röder, as prosecutor. Hitler had ordered, for reasons of security and prestige, that the entire proceedings be kept secret. Most of the defendants were sentenced to be executed. On 22 December Harro and Libertas Schulze-Boysen, Arvid Harnack, Ilse Stöbe, Hans Coppi and Scheliha were all executed, the men by hanging and the women by guillotine. Executions were carried out until 5 August 1943, when the last members of the Red Orchestra were killed.

The Berlin Red Orchestra had, by October 1942, been smashed but "Kent" (Petit Chef) and "Jean Gilbert" (Grand Chef) remained at large. The hunt for them was headed by Piepe and Giering, who set up a headquarters in the French *Suréte* offices at 11 Rue de Saussaies in Paris. Raichmann and his lover, Marina Gruber, were now working for Piepe.

BELOW: Berlin after the ravages of Allied bombing. The city was the active nerve centre of the Red Orchestra until it was smashed in 1942.

They were unable to find the Grand Chef but they had a break when they discovered that Kent had fled into Vichy France. This was an unsafe sanctuary since the Germans, following Operation Torch (the Allied invasion of French North Africa), invaded and occupied Vichy in November 1942. Gestapo SS-Sturmbannführer Bömelburg headed south towards Marseilles accompanied by the cobbler and Malvina, who quickly establish Kent's whereabouts. On 12 November 1942 five French policemen raided a flat and apprehended Kent and his girlfriend, the tall, blonde and beautiful Czech girl, Margareta Barcza. They were taken to Berlin via Paris, and after only four days in the cells of Prinz Albrecht Strasse "Kent" was willing to collaborate. His real name was Viktor Sukolov-Gurevich, a GRU captain who had entered Belgium in July 1939 via Montevideo as the Uruguayan citizen Vincent Sierra, and had set up Simexco as a cover for his operations. He had, using generous GRU allowances and the profits of Simexco, lived a life in luxury and wined and dined Belgians and Germans alike. But not even Sukolov-Gurevich had any idea where Jean Gilbert or Le Grand Chef was.

Ineptitude

Piepe and Giering set 24 November as the date for raiding Simexco in Brussels and Simex in Paris. They left Kriminalobersekretär Eric Jung in charge in Paris while they were absent in Brussels. Instead of awaiting his superiors' return, Jung, on his own initiative, decided to act and on 19 November raided the offices of Simex. All the employees were arrested and carted off to the Fresnes Prison in Paris. Jung called on the Simex manager's wife, Mme. Corbin, the day after and left two Gestapo officers to keep an eye on her. On 23 November a furious Giering was back in Paris and gave Jung a violent dressing down for his insubordination. He called on Mme. Corbin and informed her that her husband was a spy, but that if the Gestapo could get its hands on "Jean Gilbert"

LEFT: Heydrich the Potentate in full SS regalia as head, not only of the SD, but also in his new post as Reich Protector of Bohemia and Moravia.

with her help then his crime would be viewed in a very different light. The distraught woman did not have any clue where the elusive Grand Chef could be, though. Suddenly she had an inspiration. "Gilbert" had complained about a toothache and she had recommended her dentist, Dr. Maleplat, located at 13 Rue de Rivoli.

An Appointment with the Dentist

Giering called on the dentist who, after a thorough search of his appointments ledger, found a Jean Gilbert and confirmed that this gentleman, whom he had not met, did indeed have an appointment for 14:00 hours on 27 November. While Giering waited impatiently for the day and hour to arrive, Piepe was in Brussels arresting and cleaning out Simexco, while the Simex branch in Marseilles was similarly "cleansed". Picpc flew back to Paris, and in the morning of 27 November entered Dr. Maleplat's surgery. He and Giering took up position in an adjoining room to the surgery and exactly on time "Gilbert" entered. He sat down, chatted and said: "Things are looking up, aren't they? Did you hear the news on the radio?" The Sixth Army had just been surrounded at Stalingrad. Dr. Maleplat could only nod as he was in a cold sweat, but nevertheless tried to hide his nervousness. He wondered why the Germans didn't act soon. Suddenly Piepe and Giering burst in brandishing their pistols. "Gilbert" was utterly calm and simply told Piepe: "Bravo. You've done a good job.". Piepe, like Giering, a nervous wreck from waiting, simply replied: "It's the result of two years of searching."

The most dangerous Soviet spy network inside Nazi-occupied Europe had been eliminated. During a year and a half it had fed the Centre in Moscow with a great deal of important intelligence. The Red Orchestra proved the effectiveness of "humint", or human intelligence, when organized professionally and run by an effective service. Although the existence of the Red Orchestra is proof of how Nazi Germany was riddled with spies and is testimony to the triumph of Soviet espionage, the destruction of the spy ring proved to be the greatest triumph of the Abwehr and SD's counter-intelligence services.

Chapter 8

Special Operations

"Who Dares Wins"

The motto of the British Special Air Service (SAS)

FOR SOME STRANGE REASON THE REGULAR ARMED FORCES of the European powers during World War II had a deep and abiding aversion to anything associated with irregular warfare. It appeared that the professional soldiers' contempt and hatred for armed civilians, be they partisans or guerrillas, tainted any similar tactics that might be used by regular troops. None suffered more from this phobia than the German Wehrmacht, and the mere mention of irregular warfare to a General Staff officer would have him dropping his monocle in his soup or reaching for his service pistol.

It is refreshing to know, however, that not all German officers of the regular armed forces were this moribund. There were some who could think in a more unorthodox manner. One was Captain von Hipel, who had served under the brilliant General von Lettow-Vorbeck in German East Africa (Tanganyika)[1] during World War I. By using the tactics and strategy of irregular warfare, Lettow-Vorbeck had managed to pin down huge numbers of Allied (British, South African, Belgian and Portuguese) troops, until he capitulated in late November 1918 (his command was the only German force in the war not to have been defeated in open

combat). During the 1930s Hipel persuaded Canaris that the Abwehr should set up an irregular warfare company, based on the experience of Lettow-Vorbeck's campaign.

What Hipel had in mind was a special unit that would advance across the enemy's frontier, well ahead of the main body of the German Army, and use methods that were, as Hipel put it, "not those of a Prussian gentleman". The fear of widespread infiltration behind the lines would divert enemy troops away from the front. The unit would only accept volunteers, preferably men who had experience of travel in foreign countries and who spoke foreign languages. Thus when the unit was forming the majority of recruits were Germans from the former overseas colonies, as well as Germans from Latin America and Volksdeutsche – Sudeten, Baltic and Volga Germans.[2] By the summer of 1939, the "No. 1 Construction Training Company" had been set up under Hipel's command and under Canaris' personal supervision. The company commander was Lieutenant Grabert.

A second company was formed on 15 October 1939, made up of mainly Romanian Germans from the Banat and Transylvania (Siebenbürgen), Baltic Germans and Germans who had settled in Palestine. This second company went under the name of "Bau-Lehr Battalion z.b.V.nr. 800" and was based at an estate at Brandenburg-Havel outside Berlin. It was because of the location of their camp that these units

LEFT: Otto Skorzeny (left) and Mussolini (centre) surrounded by victorious German commandos after the Gran Sasso operation in September 1943.

ultimately became known as the Brandenburgers. Eventually there were four companies. Company I was made up of recruits from the Baltic and Russia. Company II comprised those who could speak English, Portuguese and some African languages, i.e. Germans from the old colonies. Company III was made up of Sudeten Germans who could speak Czech, Slovak and Ruthenian. Finally, Company IV contained Poles, Byelorussians, Russians and Ukrainians.

The language skills of such troops would be in great demand as the Third Reich expanded across Europe after September 1939. At the Brandenburg estate, which was rented by the Abwehr, these troops for "special purposes" were faced with a gruelling training routine that included marksmanship, bomb making, commando-style warfare, survival and camouflage skills. One of the techniques which made the Brandenburgers especially feared was silent killing: their ability to sneak up and kill using steel wire (the fine art of garroting) or a razor-shape knife.

By September 1939, Canaris was confident that he had an excellent combat unit that he could use to support the German Army's offensives in Europe. Even if he lacked enthusiasm for Hitler's war, he was determined that if his unit could help achieve a speedy victory it would do so. However, Canaris was determined that the Brandenburgers should comply with international law and not fight wearing enemy uniforms. When they went into the combat phase of operations they were to shed their disguise and fight as German troops in German Army uniforms. If they were captured, then at least they would not be shot as spies but treated as prisoners of war (or so the theory went). Furthermore, as part of Canaris' code of conduct the admiral insisted, and Hipel agreed, that guile rather than force was to be the Brandenburgers' trademark.

As noted earlier,[3] Canaris fundamentally disagreed with Hitler's illegal tactic of fabricating a border incident to justify the war against Poland. For this reason it was the SD, under Heydrich's personal command, which undertook Operation Canned Goods; attacking the Gleiwitz radio station and the German Customs House at Hochlinden. The Brandenburgers' role was to cross the Polish frontier in secret and lead the way for the German assault troops, sappers and panzer units by securing bridges, road crossings, killing sentries and causing general mayhem behind the lines. Likewise, their role in the occupation of Denmark (Operation Weser South) was to secure the bridges across the Little and Great Belts connecting Jutland on the mainland with Zealand, where the capital Copenhagen was located.

Until 1940 the enemies of Germany were barely aware of the Brandenburgers' existence. However, they were to shoot to fame during the invasion of the Netherlands in May 1940. In Case Yellow, the codename of the operation that would see the whole of Western Europe fall into German hands in a matter of weeks, the Netherlands was at the very northern tip of the great German drive to the English Channel.

The Brandenburgers were given three separate objectives to aid the advance of the army. Firstly, the Meuse bridge at Massyk was to be taken by Company III. Secondly, the bridges across the Juliana Canal at Berg, Uromon, Obicht and Stein were to be seized by Company IV. Finally, the railway bridge at Gennep,

the most important objective, which would open the road to central Holland through the River Peel Line, was to be captured and held by Company II.

The German offensive against the Netherlands[4] depended on airborne units, landing near The Hague, Rotterdam and Amsterdam, being given rapid support and protection by German Army land forces. For that to succeed the Gennep railway bridge[5] had to be seized and held to prevent the Dutch blowing it up. That required the Brandenburgers, in Dutch uniforms or other disguises, slipping across the frontier undetected before the invasion and hiding themselves. Then, before zero hour, they would have to attack and seize the bridge. Behind the Brandenburgers would come two trains filled with German infantry. Some of these troops would secure the bridge and relieve the

BELOW German paratroopers landing deep behind Dutch lines inside "Fortress Holland" on 10 May 1940. The Netherlands capitulated four days later.

Brandenburgers, while the rest would, with the assistance of an armoured train, push on to punch a hole in the Dutch defence line along the Peel River.

The three Brandenburger companies involved were moved to a training camp at Asperden, near the Dutch frontier, where they were given general training and some specific skills needed to carry out the Gennep operation. However, to preserve complete security the men were not told anything about their actual mission. Only their officers knew what the intended target was. All fluent in Dutch, the commandos would slip across the frontier in civilian clothes and as unobtrusively as possible observe the bridge, its approaches, the surrounding landscape and where the Dutch frontier troops were stationed.

The Gennep Bridge Mission

During the evening of 9 May, the men of Company II were told that their objective was to be the Gennep bridge. At 23:30 hours they set off across the frontier led by a Dutch-speaking corporal who had reconnoitred the terrain already. He led the group, some of whom were wearing Dutch Military Police (MP) uniforms, across the frontier and then into the flat land between the Nieus River and the railway embankment. They reached the road between Heien and Gennep without being detected, although this road was frequently patrolled by Dutch troops. They then made their way down to the marshy meadows along the bank of the Meuse (Maas) River. Once there they took cover in the bushes to await the dawn and the beginning of the German offensive. The Dutch Army had been placed on alert at 22:00 hours, but there were no patrols in the Gennep area and all was quiet at the bridge.

Just before dawn two German trains made their way slowly across the frontier. Sentries at the paper factory, which was located next to the railway line, began shouting a warning for the first train to stop. When it did not they fired warning shots in the air. The German locomotive driver simply ignored them – his train was armoured and impervious to Dutch fire – and continued his slow, yet inexorable advance towards the bridge. A Dutch border MP phoned the

Four days later the Dutch capitulated, but the queen and her government escaped

guardhouse at the bridge's eastern end to warn it that the Germans intended to capture the bridge, and that it was time to blow it up before it was too late. His frantic, incoherent chatter was not understood. Meanwhile six men, two of them in Dutch MP uniforms and the others in raincoats, approached the bridge on the eastern bank. The three Dutch guards were suspicious, but before they had time to react the Brandenburgers had overpowered them.

The Germans now controlled the eastern side of the bridge and one of the Brandenburgers, speaking fluent Dutch, picked up the phone to tell his "colleagues" at the midway section of the bridge that two MPs were bringing in four suspects. The Dutch swallowed the bait, the "Dutch" MPs moved back across the bridge and the "suspects" were taken back to the west bank. This left only one old sergeant to guard the detonator, but before he had time to react the German armoured train arrived, seized the middle section of the bridge and made him a prisoner. The "suspects" pulled out their concealed weapons, made prisoners of their own guards and opened fire on the small Dutch force holding the western side of the bridge. This group was forced to capitulate as it came under cross-fire from the German assailants. The German trains, filled with jubilant troops from the 481st Regiment, sped into the heart of Holland past the crestfallen Dutch guards.

The Advance Through Belgium

Four days later the Netherlands capitulated, though the queen and her government escaped to London. The Belgians continued to resist and flooded the Nieupoort area, which halted the German advance to the sea for a week. To prevent the Belgians from repeating this tactic by flooding the River Yser south of Ostend, thus blocking the German approach to the British bridgehead at Dunkirk, the OKH called for the services of Canaris' Brandenburg specialists. Lieutenant Grabert assembled 12 men in the Ghent area. They were given a Belgian Army bus, greatcoats and caps and ordered south to take the sluice and pump houses at the foot of the

ABOVE: Soviet tanks bogged down on a river bank in the western part of European Russia during Operation Barbarossa in the summer of 1941. The Brandenburgers were used to secure river crossings during Barbarossa.

Neiupoort–Ostend road bridge. In the confusion of retreating Belgian troops and fleeing civilians, it took them hours to cover the 24km (15 miles) from Nieuport to Ostend. The Brandenburgers only reached the bridge at 19:00 hours, and were immediately shot at by the British (a detachment from the 14th Lancers) as they poured out of the bus.

At nightfall Grabert, accompanied by Corporal Janowsky, made their way towards the bridge on their bellies. Inch by inch they crawled their way to the bridge and then, very slowly and carefully, cut the detonation wires to the explosive packages placed on the side of the structure. This was nerve-racking and dangerous work, especially as the British were firing Very lights into the air which lit up the entire landscape and frequently forced the pair to halt their work. With the demolition charges disabled, the two commandos made their way down to the other end of the structure. Once there Janowsky, carrying an MP38 submachine gun, opened fire at the guard house while Grabert threw a number of grenades at

it. This was a signal for the other 10 Brandenburgers to rush across the bridge and support them. The Grabert Detachment charged and seized the pump houses, where luckily the British had failed to place any charges. The Brandenburgers braced themselves for a British counterattack that never materialized. The German Army could now march on Dunkirk thanks to the Abwehr's "specialists". Janowsky was given an Iron Cross for his efforts.

It was in Russia that the Brandenburgers were used with greatest effect. In preparation for operations against the Soviets Canaris, through his station chief in Helsinki, Commander Alexander Cellarius, received surplus stocks of Soviet military materiel that the Finns had seized during the Winter War of 1939–40. This materiel included uniforms, greatcoats, caps, weapons, even trucks and motorcycles. As in the West, disguised Brandenburgers had preceded the German Army, slipping across the border where they made contact with Ukrainian and Byelorussian partisans fighting against the Soviet occupiers. Most of the men, however, sat tight and awaited zero hour – the early hours of 22 June 1941. A roar of artillery and Stuka dive-bombers strafing parked Soviet aircraft signalled the start of Hitler's war in the East. Border

ABOVE: Hitler's favourite trouble-shooter – Otto Skorzeny. He wears his new Knight's Cross at his neck and is attired in a smart SS uniform.

posts were overwhelmed in minutes, and then mysterious unmarked trucks filled with men dressed in the drab, brown-grey uniforms of the Red Army drove east. These men secured the passage of the spearhead of Army Group North towards Estonia and Leningrad (St. Petersburg) by capturing the bridges across the Dvina River intact.

Farther south, Guderian's Second Panzer Group had advanced into a morass – it had entered the outer rim of the vast Pripyat Marshes which stretched east from the new (1940) border to the Dnieper River. A roadless, featureless area of reeds, ponds, lakes, forests and soggy marshy meadows, every road bridge and river crossing was invaluable. Guderian

himself called for the assistance of the Brandenburgers to capture and hold one such bridge.

A Splendid Coup

They were called to Guderian's HQ on 26 June, but only arrived in the operational zone the following day, having been delayed by clogged roads and the fear that if they asked for priority clearance this would alert Soviet spies as to what they were up to. The lieutenant in charge of the Brandenburgers wanted to attack the bridge towards dusk when the landscape would be lit by the setting sun, which would also blind the Soviet sentries. His plan was simple: two trucks filled with retreating "Soviet" stragglers would make their way across the bridge. The first truck would make it across while the second, to delay the detonation of the charges and give the lieutenant time to find them, would suffer a mechanical breakdown in the middle of the bridge. The lieutenant was perfect for the role of Soviet officer since he spoke flawless Russian with a Leningrad accent and had found, among captured Soviet loot, an NKVD officer's uniform. This green uniform with the blue peaked cap was both feared and loathed by the ordinary Red Army soldiers, and would give him additional time.

To begin the show, Stukas made a mock attack at the western approach to the bridge, which allowed the Brandenburgers' "fleeing" trucks to get to the bridge where they encountered retreating Red Army troops. It took the NKVD officer (the lieutenant that is) all his authority to prevent a Red Army officer putting his wounded on the truck. Having crossed the bridge he engaged the engineer officer in a pointless argument. While the second truck made its way across, the lieutenant spied out the charges, which his men dealt with. When that was done he pulled off his uniform. A firefight broke out and the lieutenant was killed in the melee. For half an hour the Brandenburgers had to fight off a series of Soviet attacks, since the panzer force that was supposed to have supported them was held up by heavy enemy fire. At last light the Stukas returned unexpectedly and pounded the Russian positions to pieces. The original plan was for the Brandenburgers to hold the bridge for only 15 minutes – they held out for two hours. But it was

BELOW: Skorzeny's superior officer, Luftwaffe General Kurt Student (in peaked cap), shown here inspecting paratroopers.
BOTTOM: Field Marshal Kesselring (with cane), flanked by an Italian general, inspects Italian troops. Kesselring fought a spirited defensive campaign in Italy in 1943–45.

the panzer troops who got all the glory for capturing the bridge intact, while the specialists limped off to lick their wounds.

The Brandenburgers were used to great effect during the offensive phase of the Russian war, but as German fortunes began to turn during late 1942 and early 1943 there seemed to be little they could do to stem the tide. Many of the enemies of the "specialists" in the ranks of the Wehrmacht now saw their chance to have the Brandenburgers disbanded. Not so Hitler who, from February 1943, saw the use of German commandos as crucial in giving him spectacular victories to bolster German morale. Otto Skorzeny was the man who would lead those commandos in their most daring operations. Skorzeny, a huge, scar-faced Austrian, had been made commander-in-chief of German commandos on 20 April 1943. He then sat down to study Abwehr files on the British commandos, Special Air Service (SAS), Long Range Desert Group (LRDG) and US Marines. He was planning raids into Persia and the

ABOVE: Mussolini's prison in the Abruzzi Mountains: the
"Alpine" resort hotel of Gran Sasso. While he was there he
learned that the Italians had surrendered and that he was to
be handed over to the Allies.

Ural mountains of Russia when news arrived, on 25
July, that the Italian Fascist Grand Council had
removed Mussolini from power and replaced him
with Marshal Badoglio.

The telephone rang at Skorzeny's headquarters
outside Berlin, which had the inappropriate name of
Friedenthal (Peace valley). Skorzeny was summoned
to Berlin, from where he was flown from Tempelhof
to the Wolf's Lair in East Prussia. Skorzeny had
never heard of this place or ever met Hitler. Hitler
walked in and selected Skorzeny from among a
group of other officers. "I have a mission of the
highest importance for you," Hitler blurted out, and
then launched into a tirade against the treacherous
Italians who had "dared" to defy his wrath by
toppling his friend Mussolini. "He has got to be
rescued before those traitors can surrender him to
the enemy. You, Skorzeny, are going to save my
friend. You will succeed," continued Hitler holding
the 35-year-old officer in his gaze, "and your success
will have a tremendous effect upon the course of the
war. This is a mission for which you will be
answerable to me personally." Hitler shook the

officer's hands with a double handshake and a
bewildered Skorzeny left, now under Paratroop
General Karl Student's personal command.

Early in the afternoon of 27 July, Skorzeny and
Student landed at Rome airport and immediately
sped off to Frascati – the headquarters of Field
Marshal Kesselring, German Commander-in-Chief
in Italy. Kesselring naïvely still believed in Italian
assurances of goodwill and assurances that the *Duce*
(Mussolini) was still in Rome. But the suspicious
Badoglio, without the Germans knowing, had the
deposed dictator whisked off in great secrecy to the
island of Ponza. Both sides kept up an elaborate
game of deception and false friendship, to postpone
the inevitable showdown until the split could be used
to best advantage. After weeks of laborious detective
work, Skorzeny had Mussolini's whereabouts pinned
down to a small island in the Tyrrhenian Sea off the
Italian west coast. Then, as he laid his plans for a
rescue, the Italian Government moved the ex-
dictator to a small island off the northeastern corner
of Sardinia. The island was called Maddalena.

Through Abwehr agents and contacts in Italy it
was not too difficult for Skorzeny to confirm
Mussolini's presence on the island. Aerial
reconnaissance confirmed signs that the island's
defences had been improved and enhanced, which
confirmed the presence of an important prison

there. On one such mission Skorzeny and his companions were shot down by the Royal Air Force. The aircraft plunged into the sea, but Skorzeny and his men managed to get out and were, ironically, rescued by an Italian anti-aircraft ship there to guard Mussolini against a German rescue attempt. Undeterred, Skorzeny and his companions returned to Maddalena, this time disguised as German sailors. Lieutenant Warger was sent to find the exact whereabouts of Mussolini. After trying to find out information in the local bars, Warger had success with a vegetable trader who showed him the Villa Weber. The German spy and his Italian guide lay in wait and there, surrounded by guards, was a familiar shaved head and Roman profile of the *Duce*. Warger paid the trader a handsome sum for his help and returned to Skorzeny to tell him the good news. Skorzeny made new plans: this time for a full-scale

commando assault. This was scheduled to take place on 28 August, but the constant and intrusive interest by the Germans made the *Duce*'s guards very nervous and apprehensive. On 27 August, a civilian seaplane with Red Cross markings took off from Maddalena and flew east towards the Italian mainland. Warger made his rounds again and found out that Mussolini had been moved. He alerted Skorzeny to this fact and the operation was cancelled at the last moment.

It was back to the drawing board for Skorzeny. He had a lucky break when an SS officer, Herbert Kappler, turned up at his office in Rome to tell him that something odd was taking place in the

BELOW: Student giving Skorzeny his final orders to rescue Mussolini from Gran Sasso during a formal inspection parade of the latter's unit at Prarira Aerodrome.

Abruzzi Mountains east of the city. The Italians had stepped up security measures around the ski resort of Gran Sasso for no apparent or logical reason. Only one explanation could be deduced – the Italians had moved Mussolini to this isolated and remote spot. Skorzeny thanked his SS comrade profusely and decided to follow up the lead as quickly as possible. He had by this time surrounded himself with capable subordinates, such as Warger, and a good network of Italian informers (in the employ of the SD and Abwehr) who could keep him informed about interesting leads. Skorzeny discovered that there was a hotel high on the Campo Imperatore plateau at Gran Sasso, and that it could only be reached by a single cable car from Assergi. The hotel was impossible to reach by road or track, and therefore very easy to defend against an assault – consequently it was perfect for incarcerating Mussolini.

One false move and Skorzeny would alert the Italians, who were now both alert and nervous that the Germans knew the whereabouts of the *Duce*. To confirm that Gran Sasso was the place without raising suspicions, General Student got hold of a German medical officer (MO), Leo Krutoff, and ordered him to find out if the Italians would be willing to let the

ABOVE: A unique shot of Skorzeny's commandos having just landed on the plateau outside the hotel at Gran Sasso, and deploying for an assault upon the impressive stone edifice to rescue Mussolini.

Wehrmacht use Gran Sasso as a convalescent centre for its troops. Krutoff turned up at Assergi to take the cable car to the hotel, but was brusquely turned away by irate Italian Carabinieri[6] guards. Krutoff was told that the Gran Sasso was off limits and under military control. Krutoff returned to Rome distraught at this news, and a sympathetic Student and Skorzeny could only regret the behaviour of their Italian allies towards the good doctor. Skorzeny, thanks to the credulous MO, now had enough intelligence to confirm that Mussolini was at Gran Sasso.

Skorzeny presented an audacious plan that left his superiors utterly shocked: he would take 100 German paratroopers in towed gliders through the mountain passes to Gran Sasso and land on the plateau. The gliders, being silent, would not be detected by the Italian guards until it was too late. Senior officers expressed extreme doubt as to the practicality of the plan, but Hitler – a great admirer of guts, determination and complete daring – approved it forthwith.

At 13:00 hours on 12 September 1943, 12 German aircraft towing gliders set off from an airfield outside Rome and flew towards the Abruzzi Mountains. Skorzeny's right-hand man, Radl, had a brainwave and brought along the fascist and Germanophile Carabinieri commander, General Soleti, to accompany them. The daring and adventurous Soleti readily agreed. It was only when they were in the air that Skorzeny, whose bulk was not easily accommodated in the cramped glider, had an opportunity to glance out and discovered, to his utter horror, that two gliders had vanished into the clouds. That would not have mattered too much had it not have been for the fact that they contained the advance party and their guide. Skorzeny now had to guide the glider towards Gran Sasso from memory.

The hotel came into view. Skorzeny ordered the pilot of the glider to crash-land as close to the hotel as possible. With a tremendous jolt the glider landed and the paratroopers, with Skorzeny leading them, rushed towards the hotel. Skorzeny, having glanced at what he thought was Mussolini in an upper window, bounded up the stairs while Soleti ordered

THIS PAGE: SS Colonel Mari (right) congratulates the Skorzeny paratroop commander, Ralph von Berlepsch, after the conclusion of the risky operation at Gran Sasso (above). The victorious Skozerny commandos and paratroopers bask in the glory of the brilliantly executed and daring Gran Sasso operation (below).

the Italian troops to lay down their arms. As Mussolini was led from the hotel, a small Stork (Storch) observation aircraft landed on the plateau. Both Skorzeny and Mussolini prepared to fly out in it, but the pilot, Captain Gerlach, was reluctant to risk taking off carrying so much weight. Skorzeny admonished him not to be a coward and fly. At full throttle, while paratroopers held the wings, Gerlach gave the signal and the plane took off over the edge of the cliff and sank fast into the ravine below – all three men believed their last moment might have come. But Gerlach, a skilled pilot, managed to stabilize the aircraft and fly on to Rome, where Mussolini was met by his wife. From there the Italian dictator travelled to Germany, where on 14 September Hitler gave his old ally a fulsome welcome at the Wolf's Lair at Rastenburg.

Overnight Skorzeny was transformed into a household name, and his exploit served as a tonic for the tired and increasingly hard-pressed German people. More importantly, Mussolini could set up a fascist state in northern Italy and the southern front

RIGHT: For once the German propaganda magazine Signal *(here in French guise) did not need to exaggerate its claims. The Gran Sasso rescue was a propaganda dream come true for Göbbels, and a welcome morale boost for the Germans.*

would hold. Italy would be the scene of a prolonged and bloody war led, with enormous skill and determination, by Marshal Kesselring.

Skorzeny's new-found fame made him the candidate for any similar operation across Europe that Hitler or Himmler thought up. One which Skorzeny greeted with a total lack of enthusiasm was Himmler's flight of fantasy that a U-boat, rigged out with ramps, was to carry a V-1 rocket and fire it at New York in retaliation for the US bombing campaign against Germany. Skorzeny pointed out the technical as well as practical problems that such a plan would entail. Skorzeny, with the enthusiastic support of Hanna Reitsch – one of Germany's test pilots – cooked up another scheme whereby a pilot would man a V-1 rocket and crash it into the British Houses of Parliament. Air Marshal Milch put a stop to this madness in time to stop any risk of Reitsch, the most famous female pilot in Germany, being killed.

Skorzeny had to wait a while until his special talents were called for again. This time his theatre of

BELOW: Skorzeny (with binoculars) and Mussolini (in black overcoat) surrounded by German troops and Italian admirers after their safe arrival in Rome.

Signal

Un communiqué historique:

«Haut les mains!» ordonna à la garde de l'hôtel Otto Skorzeny, qui conduisit l'entreprise de libération du Duce. Désorientés et effrayés les carabinieri obéirent aussitôt.

La libération de Mussolini

the Yugoslav communist leader and deal his partisan movement a fatal blow.

Operation Knight's Move

The OKH came up with Operation Knight's Move (Rösselsprung), which called for a massive land offensive against the partisan forces in western Bosnia, while airborne troops in gliders and SS paratroopers would attack Tito's headquarters at the town of Dvar. It was to this part of the assault that Skorzeny would be involved, acting as an advisor.

From information gathered by Abwehr and Brandenburg agents, the Germans knew that the Soviet and Allied military missions were present at Tito's headquarters, so the plan was to capture or kill these officers as well. German intelligence sources noted that Tito was protected by 350 handpicked élite troops from his Escort Battalion. The headquarters also benefited from Dvar's location. The town is set in a bend of the River Unac, and is defended by water on three sides. It could only be reached by fighting through a narrow defile between wooded hills on either side of the narrow river valley.

The assault would be launched on 25 May 1944, with H-hour set at 07:00 hours. When Skorzeny arrived at Belgrade and heard that Serb agents in the pay of the Abwehr knew of the impeding offensive, he wanted to cancel the operation. The Belgrade Abwehr told him that this knowledge might not matter and that Rösselsprung should go ahead. Despite his misgivings Skorzeny agreed. In fact the partisans' intelligence bureau, although it knew the Germans were planning an offensive, had no idea that it included a large aerial assault. Neither did the men of the unit chosen to do the job – the 500th SS Parachute Battalion. Only its commander, SS-Obersturmführer Rybka, and his senior officers knew. His men, some 350 of them,[8] were only told during the night of 24/25 May.

Take-off for the first assault wave was just before dawn. Within 55 minutes the Ju 52 transport aircraft were nearing the Dvar valley, which was covered in smoke from a massive Stuka raid on the

operations would be the Balkans, where a bloody sideshow in Yugoslavia was becoming an ever greater liability for Hitler's crumbling empire. Having failed during 1943 to come to an agreement with the partisan leader, Marshal Tito,[7] Abwehr agents inside partisan-held areas reported that there was a major slump in morale among Tito's fighters. In early 1944 it was decided to exploit this and deal with Tito in another fashion. If the Germans could not come to an agreement with him, then they would seek to abduct or kill

ABOVE: Female Yugoslav communist Partisans. They were used, to the shock and disgust of their enemies, as frontline troops. They proved both brave and disciplined.
RIGHT: Josip Broz, a Croat-born communist who only took up arms after the invasion of the USSR in 1941. The German attempt to capture him in 1944 was a failure.

town. The Ju 52s kept a tight formation to avoid dispersal and out jumped the SS paratroopers. Meanwhile, the DS 230 gliders, expertly handled by their Luftwaffe pilots, crashed their wooden craft near the mouth of the "Citadel", Tito's main cave headquarters. The German and Bosniak (Bosnian-Muslim) airborne troops were successful at first, storming and capturing the partisan communications centre, which was savagely defended by women partisans. However, what Abwehr/Brandenburg intelligence had failed to discover was that the Citadel's defences had undergone some last-minute improvements. Soon partisan resistance began to stiffen. The SS paratroops, having landed near Dvar, took an hour to secure it, and by the time they arrived at the Citadel most of the glider troops were either dead or wounded.

The situation for the Germans was deteriorating rapidly. The paras could not make a flanking attack because well over 100 partisans, including élite officer cadets, had arrived to counterattack, while the 1st Battalion of the 1st Partisan Brigade was attacking Dvar from the east. The paras were caught in a deadly pincer, and when the second wave of paras dropped at 12:30 hours they were met with murderous mortar and machine gun fire.[9] As if this was not bad enough, Rybka was badly wounded. He ordered his men to fall back on Dvar. The ruined cellulose factory could not be held because it was too large and open to defend for the hard-pressed SS troops, but a small walled cemetery proved a stronger position. Meanwhile, Tito had escaped through a side exit from his living quarters in the Citadel, which led out to a dried-up riverbed. From there he made his way, accompanied

by his entire General Staff, HQ staff and the Allied liaison officers, to the village of Potoci, where a waiting train took him out of western Bosnia. He set up an almost invincible new headquarters on the Adriatic island of Vis.

The SS paratroopers, knowing that the Partisans would not take prisoners, fought with utter desperation against a series of massive attacks. The fight continued into the night and reached as far as the cemetery. The following dawn, Tito, having made good his escape, ordered his troops to withdraw, but not before they were pounded to pieces by a Stuka attack. This prepared the way for the arrival of the 13th Regiment of the SS *Prinz Eugen* Division, which fought its way into Dvar to relieve the surviving paratroopers. "Knight's Move" had been a failure, but it had disrupted partisan operations for a considerable time. Skorzeny, who had acted only as an advisor, and who had not taken part, blamed the ground forces for not reaching Dvar faster. He was determined not to preside over a similar mess again.

As Hitler took stock of the situation on the Eastern Front, which by mid-1944 was moving uncomfortably close to the Reich, there were more opportunities to use Skorzeny and his "men of steel".

On the southern edge of the front, the risk to Germany's ally Romania was becoming acute. If Romania fell to the Soviets then the whole southeastern sector across the Balkans would unravel and Germany's largest source of oil would be lost.

When, in August 1944, Romania switched sides after King Carol's coup against the pro-German dictator Antonescu, a German withdrawal became inevitable. Now it was a case of "save what could be saved". This meant holding the passes through the Carpathian Mountains against the advancing Red Army. Skorzeny was the right man for this and he appointed a fellow Austrian, Walter Girg, to do the job. Girg was a firebrand and a commando veteran. He was aged only 22, but already had a reputation for utter fearlessness and determination. Skorzeny sent Girg to hold the passes with two platoons formed at Timisoara (Temesvar) in Transylvania. Girg's troops were Russian speakers and commando specialists. Girg divided his men into four groups of 10 commandos each, and these troops armed every local Transylvanian German they could to help hold the passes. Girg also found and mobilized 2000 idle Luftwaffe troops. By using partisan-style warfare behind the Soviet lines, the offensive against the passes was dissipated. The line held and the whole southeastern sector was saved from catastrophe.

Operation Panzerfaust

The Carpathian Front may have stabilized, but behind it there was another problem brewing for Germany. By the autumn of 1944, there were reasons to doubt the loyalty of their hitherto loyal and effective Hungarian allies. Hungary was ruled by a Regent, Admiral Horthy, who, while he hated the communists, was having doubts about his Nazi ally. For years Germany had exploited Hungary's agriculture and oilfields for very little return. Horthy was also determined to defend all Hungarians, Jew or not, against any attempt to have them deported to the Nazi death camps in Poland. Horthy was in fact determined, albeit subtly, to emulate the Romanians' example and switch sides before it was too late.

To the east of the Hungarian border, the Carpathian Front was held by over a million German and Hungarian troops, but if Horthy betrayed the alliance the front would collapse and the Soviets could pour into Greater Germany through Austria. After events in Romania, Hitler suspected that Horthy might change sides and took steps to have him removed from power. On 10 September 1944 he called for Skorzeny and gave him a note with carte blanche for anything he might need to do the job. Skorzeny, disguised as the tourist "Dr. Wolf", travelled to the Hungarian capital Budapest. The plan was to depose Horthy but leave the Hungarian Government intact. Should the Regent-Admiral, who was venerated by most Hungarians, be wounded or killed the Germans would face a country in uproar. The innocuous-looking German tourist "Dr. Wolf" reconnoitred the government buildings inside the castle on Castle Hill and saw its impressive array of defences. It was obvious that a direct assault on this massive structure, with its big garrison of loyal troops, was not a viable proposition.

From Abwehr and SD representatives in Budapest Skorzeny found out that Horthy had already begun negotiations with the Russians through two of Marshal Tito's officers, who were holding secret talks in Budapest with the Regent's son, Nicholas Horthy. Abducting Nicholas would compromise the Regent's plans and provide a means to force the admiral's abdication.

Skorzeny's first abduction planned failed when the Regent suddenly arrived at the apartment building where Nicholas was holding the negotiations. The abduction was aborted. The second time Nicholas would not be so lucky. Skorzeny had his commandos and some members of the GFP[10] surrounded the building again, and he had four SD agents in a room above the flat where the negotiations were taking place. This was on 14 October 1944. Outside several cars were parked, and the GFP and commandos lounged on benches awaiting Skorzeny's signal. Then they bounded into the building without warning and Nicholas' guards open fire. All hell broke loose, with bullets flying in all directions. Skorzeny blew the whistle three times. This was a signal for Fölkersam[11] and his group to storm into action. Fölkersam's commandos dealt with Horthy's guards while the SD agents arrested and overpowered Nicholas. He was bundled into a Persian carpet and flown to Germany.

It was now time to deal with the Regent, who made an anti-German tirade on the radio that same day, proclaiming that Germany had lost the war and that Hungary, as a consequence, had signed an armistice

BELOW: Admiral Horthy (in black overcoat), the Hungarian Regent and Dictator since 1921, shown here with Deputy Führer Rudolf Hess (with hand on belt) in pre-war Germany.

with the USSR. Skorzeny now knew that Castle Hill was held by 2000 élite troops, and that one single German division in the Budapest area was outnumbered three to one. But he had no intention of storming or bombing the castle and leaving a trail of destruction and blood along the way. The German division in Budapest would continue at its post, while Skorzeny laid his trap.

Skorzeny's coup, codenamed Operation Panzerfaust, was as cunning as it was daring and unorthodox. Two battalions made forays around the castle's walls to distract the Hungarians, while the real "assault" was launched through the front door. Half an hour before dawn Skorzeny told his men: "Do not open fire. Safety catches on. Whatever happens you must not open fire unless an officer tells you." Operation Panzerfaust could now begin. In full battle array the troops were lined up with Skorzeny and his NCOs in the leading tank (of four) at the head of the column. Skorzeny was banking on the Hungarians not firing on troops who marched into the castle peacefully. It was a daring and foolhardy bluff that could, should a single nerve among his troops crack, backfire. At 05:55 hours on the morning of 15 October the column, like some field-grey caterpillar, made its way up the single road to the castle's main gate. The Hungarian guards let the German troops pass because they were presumably fooled by the latter's relaxed and non-threatening behaviour. Skorzeny was through the

> *Skorzeny was banking on the Hungarians not firing as his troops marched into the castle*

ABOVE: Budapest Castle Hill – Horthy's supposedly impregnable citadel in the heart of the Hungarian capital, which fell to Skorzeny without a shot being fired. Horthy's son was kidnapped to ensure Hungary stayed with the Axis.

first gate and in occupation of the main square without a shot being fired.

Unharmed, the column made its way past the barracks and the Hungarian Ministry of War – each building housed 1000 of the castle's garrison troops. They made for the Regent's Palace and Skorzeny, closely followed by Fölkersam and other officers, pounded up the main staircase into the palace. An agitated colonel had his pistol knocked out of his hand by Fölkersam. A Hungarian soldier training his machine gun on the intruding Germans was quickly disarmed. A commando simply threw the weapon into the palace courtyard as Skorzeny made for the commandant's office unscathed. Fölkersam informed Skorzeny that the palace was secure and that the whole Castle Hill area was quiet. The Hungarian commandant, hearing this, chose to capitulate. The Hungarians laid down their arms and Skorzeny called the officers to the Regent's throne room. Skorzeny told the Hungarians that they were his Hapsburg cousins, had no reason to quarrel among themselves and that this was a time to close ranks when the Red Hordes were knocking on the gates of their country. Germans and Hungarians should therefore close ranks. The Hungarians, reassured, agreed heartily.[12]

Admiral Horthy was captured and deported to the same Bavarian castle that housed his son. On 21 October Count Ferenc Szalasy, the Hungarian fascist leader, took over the government of Hungary. Though Horthy had almost succeeded in surrendering his country to the Allies, his capture meant that the Soviets would have to take Hungary and Budapest by force of arms. Most Hungarian Army units fought on the German side to the bitter end. This was undoubtedly Skorzeny's most brilliant coup.[13]

It is a great pity that Skorzeny's name, although associated with such inspired coups as the Gran Sasso rescue operation and Operation Panzerfaust, will also be linked to Operation Greif (Grasp), which went into action against the Americans during the Battle of the Bulge in December 1944. Germans who had lived in England or spoke English, and could speak it with an American accent, were placed under Skorzeny's command. Their task was to operate in American uniforms behind the enemy's lines to sow confusion and wreak havoc. Skorzeny was forbidden to cross the lines with his men, which angered him immensely since he believed that a good leader shared the dangers and privations of his men. "Greif" did succeed in its purpose, causing paranoia among the American troops. Even General Omar Bradley had to tell trigger-happy guards and roadblock commanders the names of the latest Hollywood stars, capitals of the lesser-known states and other trivia in order to verify his identity. Operation Greif, however, was to prove a suicide mission. Skorzeny's men who were caught were shot by US military police as spies.

After the Battle of the Bulge, Skorzeny's talents were squandered. He was tasked with conventional operations in a desperate attempt to stem the Soviet invasion of eastern Germany and occupation of the heart of Prussia east of the River Elbe. It proved pointless and cost the lives of his remaining troops, including young Fölkersam. Both he, his officers and men deserved a better fate.[14]

BELOW: *After the successful conclusion of the Budapest mission, Otto Skorzeny's (shown here, second from left, enjoying a concert) fame was firmly established.*

Chapter 9

The Worldwide Web

IT WAS NOT JUST IN OCCUPIED EUROPE that German espionage agents were active. They were also operating in the Middle East and Latin America. Here, German agents were the hunted quarry at the mercy of the native and enemy intelligence services. Closer to home, German agents were in a much stronger position because military might could be brought to bear, especially in the Balkans.

The Germans were interested in the Balkans for two reasons. To begin with the region was of enormous strategic value. It was a valuable base for a southern route into Russia when Operation Barbarossa was launched in June 1941. It was equally valuable to Germany as a route, via Turkey, to the Middle East. Furthermore, Hungary and Romania were rich sources of grain and oil, both being especially valuable after Germany lost Russian supplies.

The key to both these important strategic assets was Romania, which had been one of the victors from World War I and historically an ally of the West. Germany, however, was Romania's largest trade partner. Even before the war an Abwehr officer had raised the vulnerability of the Romanian oilfield of Ploesti (just north of Bucharest, the capital) with Admiral Canaris. The officer also pointed out that with a few well-placed barges, the River Danube, the

LEFT: Afghanistan – the violent crossroads of Central Asia and the ancient gateway to the plains and riches of India. This is a market in the Afghan city of Gazni.

main artery of oil exports to Germany, could be blocked. Canaris raised this topic with Field Marshal Keitel in August 1939. Thereafter Abwehr agents were despatched to protect Ploesti and act as "crews" on Danube oil barges.

To help secure oil supplies Canaris also reached an accord with Colonel Murozov, the head of the *Siguranza* or Romanian secret police. This collaboration prevented SIS Section D (forerunner to SOE) from running an operation to block the River Danube by sinking barges into the river.[1] It was a complete success for Abwehr that Canaris could be proud of, and it paved the way, together with other political developments, for Germany's dominance of Romania.

The Germans saw their grip tighten on the country when, on 6 September 1940, the fascist "Iron Guard" forced King Carol II to abdicate and flee the country with his mistress, Magda Lupescu.[2] Shortly afterwards, General Ion Antonescu became the dictator of Romania and fired Colonel Murozov, who was thrown into jail, despite Canaris' attempted intervention. Murozov was replaced as the head of the *Siguranza* by Colonel Eugen Christescu, to whom Canaris took an instant and enduring dislike.

Antonescu committed Romania to the Axis in November 1940 and from 1941 it provided, after Germany, the largest contingent to the war on the Eastern Front. Immediately the invasion of Russia began, the Soviet Legation in Bucharest – a huge espionage and subversion centre – was shut down, and its agents rounded up by the *Siguranza* and

Abwehr IIIF. As long as the war in Russia went well Romania fought on. But after the defeat at Stalingrad in early 1943, and increased Allied bombing raids on Bucharest, the Romanians, even the pro-German Iron Guard, began to lose heart. German defeats created favourable conditions for a burgeoning peace movement which found a leader in King Michael, King Carol's son and successor.

In March 1944, a high-ranking Romanian delegation flew secretly to Malta to negotiate a separate peace with the Allies, in the hope of preventing the occupation of Romania by the Soviets. Later on, another Romanian envoy, Prince Stirbey, flew to Cairo for talks with Major Boxhall of the SIS. Both these approaches failed because Stalin's veto and the Allied demand for unconditional surrender meant the negotiations could go nowhere. Nevertheless, the Romanians continued their preparations to quit the war. When SOE officer Colonel de Chastelain and his radio man landed in Romania, for example, Antonescu gave them protection because he knew of the intrigues around the king. In May 1944 King Michael laid plans for a coup. All this was

BELOW: Romanian oilfields in the Transylvanian Alps in the 1930s, some 80km (50 miles) north of Bucharest, outside the main petrol-producing centre of Ploesti.

happening right under the noses of the SD, but the coup plans went ahead.

On 17 August 1944 General Aurel Aldea signed an armistice with the Red Army, and six days later the king called Antonescu to the palace in Bucharest and told the dictator to resign. When Antonescu refused the king put him under arrest by the Palace Guards. Christescu and General Tobescu, Head of the Gendarmerie, managed to warn the German Ambassador, Manfred von Killinger, what was happening. Killinger was at a loss what to do and ordered an ineffective air strike against Bucharest, which only provoked the Romanians into breaking all links with Germany.

What of Bulgaria? Located to the south of Romania and bordered by Greece, European Turkey and southern Yugoslavia, Bulgaria was of great strategic importance to any power with pretensions to dominate the Balkans. However, Germany's attempt to gain control over Bulgaria was an uphill struggle, and for the Abwehr to gain a foothold the task was fraught with difficulties. King Boris III, whom Canaris knew, had echoed the sentiments of the King of Spain in 1916,[3] when he summed up the dilemma of Bulgaria: his people were Russophile, his army pro-German, and his queen Italian. "I am the only one who is pro-Bulgarian," he said. In addition the US

Ambassador, the ebulliently anti-Nazi George Earle, sought to keep Bulgaria neutral.

So the Bulgarian capital, Sofia, was no dream posting for Abwehr staff. In January 1940 Canaris simply called one of his agents to Tirpitz Ufer and told him the less than pleasing news that he had been appointed to head the Sofia KO. The officer pointed out the strong Russian influence in the country and the large, active Soviet Legation in the Bulgarian capital as a reason for Canaris to pick someone else, but the admiral wanted to hear no objection to his choice. The new KO chief flew first to Romania, where he picked the brains of local KO operatives in Bucharest and friends in Romanian military intelligence. He also asked the *Siguranza* about its southern neighbour and historical foe.[4] After briefing himself on the situation he then took the train to Giurgiu, crossed on the Danube ferry, and entered Bulgaria at Ruse without anyone taking any notice. He arrived in Sofia with the cover of "Adviser on Military Economic Affairs" to the German military attaché.

As Bulgaria began to slip into the Axis camp the KO in Sofia expanded greatly and the Abwehr began to use the country as a conduit for sending

ABOVE: Hitler (third from right) played host, in Munich during the summer of 1941, to his Romanian ally General Ion Antonescu (fourth from right) who proved a loyal ally until August 1944, when he was overthrown by King Michael.

agents to Turkey, Iran and the rest of the Middle East. On 13 January 1941, Hitler "invited" Bulgaria to join the Axis, allowing German troops to enter its territory and to participate in German military operations against Greece. German military missions were also sent into the country, and two weeks before the German occupation of Bulgaria Abwehr II sent Brandenburg troops there. They were there to collaborate with the Sofia KO in preventing British agents and the pro-communist underground from damaging the country's infrastructure. These men arrived at Sofia by air, donned Bulgarian Army uniforms and set about guarding bridges, railway stations, depots, power stations and other prominent sites.

On 1 March 1940 King Boris, after months of dithering and delay, agreed to join the Axis and German troops belonging to Field Marshal List's Twelfth Army began to cross the Danube. They received a hearty welcome from the Bulgarian

ABOVE: *King Boris III of Bulgaria (left) shown during a troop inspection of new army recruits in late December 1939. The monarch refused to hand over his country's Jews or participate in Hitler's Russian war.*

populace. With the country under occupation, the Sofia KO was transformed into an Ast with 250 agents working for it. After the invasion of Yugoslavia in April 1941, it spread its operational area into Bulgarian-occupied Macedonia and the Greek province of Thrace. Although these easy victories proved popular, that was not the case when Germany invaded the USSR. Because of its broad, pro-Russian traditions, Bulgaria did not declare war on the USSR like Hungary and Romania. The Soviet Legation in Sofia and the Soviet General Consulate in Varna remained open and its staff protected by the Bulgarian Police, with orders from King Boris to prevent any attempt by the Abwehr or SD to penetrate them.

Because of this policy, the GRU and NKVD could continue their intelligence and subversion activities inside Bulgaria and other parts of the Balkans. In late 1942, three Soviet agents were landed on the Bulgaria's Black Sea coast with orders to cause as much disturbance in German-Bulgarian relations as possible. They began by murdering some sailors in King Boris Park in Sofia. The Abwehr, assisted by the SD-Sipo, and the Bulgarian Police hunted down the assassins, who turned out to be German KPD officials who had fled to the USSR after 1933 and had been trained by the NKVD as agent/assassins. In 1943 the communist underground, with support from Moscow, began a partisan campaign which extended out from Sofia into the country-side, and encompassed Macedonia and Thrace. In response the Abwehr set up, with recruits from the police, the Anti-Partisan Platoons (APT) to fight these communist partisans. They had some success but Bulgaria remained the weak link in the Axis line across the Balkan peninsula. In 1943 the situation deteriorated further when King Boris died under very mysterious circumstances and his rule was replaced by that of a regency acting for his baby son, Simeon. By the time the Russians marched into Bulgaria in September 1944, Bulgaria was already deeply infiltrated by communist and Soviet influence.[5]

If the Abwehr can be said to have failed in Bulgaria, then it had even less success in Greece.

Like Bulgaria, Greece had experienced a great deal of political instability. Its pre-war politics had been complicated by constant changes from republic to monarchy.[6] Germany failed to take advantage of this and exploit internal divisions, if only to the limited degree of turning Greece into a reluctant satellite, as was the case of Bulgaria. Having failed to dominate Greece through politics, the Germans chose to use force. In early 1940, despite orders from OKH/OKW to leave the Mediterranean to the Italians, the enterprising head of the Hamburg Ast decided to take action in Greece, since he believed that Germany would, sooner or later, have to be involved in this strategic region. After all, Greece and the island of Crete dominated the approaches to the Black Sea and the Eastern Mediterranean. Germany would need to secure these positions if the war continued and expanded beyond the narrow confines of Western Europe.

The Greeks soon found out to their cost what it meant to be occupied by the Nazis

The Hamburg Ast's first move was to send two agents, disguised as businessmen, to Athens. Each had a light field radio (an Afu set) in his briefcase. They quickly installed themselves in an Athens hotel, established a network of agents in the field, and began to transmit daily reports to Hamburg.

Abwehr Operations

With the station in Athens firmly established, the Hamburg Abwehr chief could expand his operations throughout the country. In mid-March 1941, after German forces began their attack on Greece, the Hamburg Ast sent commandos, in disguise, to the Greco-Bulgarian border to subvert Greek attempts to stop the German Army's advance south. So well protected and cared for were the Abwehr transmitters that the Wehrmacht, whose sets were not as well cared for and broke down, had to ask its intelligence service for assistance in communicating with OKH/OKW. The Abwehr, gloating at their military colleagues' discomfit, were ready to oblige. One veteran noted that it was Norway all over again: the Wehrmacht would have been left without a line of communication back to the Fatherland had it not been for the Abwehr. Abwehr agents and commandos scored other successes during the Greek campaign. For example, one young Abwehr commando officer behaved with such confidence that the Greek admiral in charge of the navy surrendered this service intact to the Germans.

The Abwehr agent network played its role in undermining the Greek defence effort, and was instrumental in securing Greek shipping intact for the German invasion of Crete.

By May 1941, the conquest of Greece was complete and most of the country was left to the Italians to occupy and administer. Yet the Germans kept control over key areas of the country including Arcadia, Athens, Thessaloniki, plus some of the offshore islands and Crete; just in case the Italians proved unreliable. The Greeks soon found out to their cost what it meant to be occupied by the Germans, as the SD-Sipo set up offices in Athens and Thessaloniki. Kriminalrat Geissler, a fanatical Nazi and devoted SD officer, had compiled a list of prominent Greeks to be arrested and deported. He began rounding up these unfortunates, but came in for severe criticism from the Abwehr which prevailed on Geissler's superior, von Altenburg, to have the SD officer recalled to Berlin. Until 1943 the Abwehr dominated the intelligence field in Greece, which helped to keep the violence and brutality of the occupation forces under some sort of control. As early as May 1941, the Abwehr pointed out that the German forces' indiscriminate seizure of food and its transportation back to Germany only antagonized the Greeks, and increased support for the partisans. It contrasted this behaviour with that of the generous Italian troops, who distributed pasta and olive oil to the hard-pressed population, and to that of the British, who had paid for everything they consumed or used.

The GFP and the Anti-Partisan War

The threat of partisans to the security of the occupation forces in Greece soon became evident. The Wehrmacht set up the Feld Polizei to deal with these threats, and also established a more shadowy and sinister organization: the Geheime Feld

Polizei (GFP) or the Secret Military Police. The GFP was supposed to be a sister organization to the Abwehr since they were both Wehrmacht organizations. This was the theory, but the harsh, complicated reality was that GFP ran its own network of agents in the Balkans and was entirely independent of other agencies. The head of the GFP in the Balkans, Roman Loos, had a broadly based and efficient network of informants and paid agents spread across Greece. This was all well and good for the GFP, but for the broader German intelligence effort it meant diminishing available resources, because the GFP networks had to compete with the Abwehr and SD for agents' services. This created a seller's market for agents and informers such as Liana, the cabaret dancer, and Panayotis P., smuggler and casino manager, both of whom "worked" for GFP Unit 621 in Thessaloniki. The problem was that these

BELOW: *Nazi military might on display in the Balkans – German assault guns outside the Dikitiri Palace in Thessaloniki (Salonika) in northern Greece.*

informers were more interested in milking the Germans for money than they were in providing their employers with reliable and hard intelligence. To give one example. In the spring of 1944, Corfu was flooded with GFP troops and personnel after the Abwehr ast in the Albanian capital, Tirana, had tipped off the GFP regarding preparations for a major uprising on the island. The GFP station in Janina in northern Greece sent an investigation team to Corfu, only to find that the local Wehrmacht Ic section had been closed down because of a lack of "business", and that the island was entirely calm. The GFP found out that the rumour of major partisan activity had been spread by Albanian doctors resident on Corfu, who combined their medical practices with some extra-curricular smuggling and intelligence gathering for the Abwehr.

There were plenty of real partisans to hunt, however. In the winter of 1941 the Wehrmacht went on the rampage, burning down two villages in the Struma district of northern Greece, where troops killed all the male adults on suspicion that

the villages were collaborating with the partisans. Note that these atrocities were committed by regular Wehrmacht troops and not SS or GFP units. A third village, Efharpia, its inhabitants petrified by these examples, surrendered two men the Germans suspected of being partisans.

Even in the remotest corner of rural Greece[7] there were informers and agents in the pay of the Abwehr and/or GFP. But neither organization could keep a close eye on them to verify their loyalty, which was often dubious at the very best of times. The Abwehr therefore resorted to sending agents, disguised as British POWs or Greek partisans, to inspect the districts and the reliability of their agents and informers. A unit of the 117th Jäger Division revisited the village of Bozirka, only to find the home of the local informer, Georgios Benekos, burnt to the ground and the agent apparently taken by the partisans. The Jäger Ic officer was convinced that it was an elaborate hoax staged by the partisans to convince them that Benekos was not a double agent, and they did not set out to find him.

When Italy capitulated in June 1943, the Germans had to take over the entire burden of occupying Greece. In late 1943 the Germans,

ABOVE: *SS commander Jürgen Stroop (centre, with eagle on left arm and field cap) during the Warsaw ghetto uprising. His short spell in Greece was a disaster, as Stroop insulted the Greek collaborationists. He was quickly recalled.*

having occupied the island of Rhodes, believed Italian deserters had joined with the local Greek resistance. The GFP were sent to investigate and root out the threat. They launched their hunt after a German soldier was shot by a sniper in the centre of the island. It was believed that a band led by an Italian deserter "Pietro", known as the "Capo" or "Commandante', was responsible for the sniping incident, and that the man he used to recruit Italian deserters was a certain "Georgio". Using its informers, the GFP soon arrested nine Italian deserters (all young, raw recruits) and four Greeks who had helped them. The GFP commander ordered them all to be shot to set an example, and Sturmdivision Rhodos (occupying Rhodes) warned the population that any similar "incidents" would be punished severely.

From September 1943 the full force of German terror was unleashed in Greece. For the first time the SS and its different organs went amok, killing and torturing Greeks without restraint. General Löhr

ABOVE: The Butcher of the Balkans: Dr. Ante Pavelic, the bloodthirsty head of the feared Croat Nationalist extremists of the Ustashe, responsible for over half a million Serb, Jewish and Gypsy deaths in wartime Croatia.

(the Military Commandant) and Herman Neubacher, both whom were opposed to the SS, sought to keep a lid on the violence. In August 1943 Jürgen Stroop, fresh from crushing the Jewish uprising in Warsaw, arrived in Greece and began by insulting and browbeating the Greek collaborationist government and its premier, Ioannis Rallis. Neubacher and Löhr were furious with Stroop, since they hoped to build up a royalist and conservative force of Greeks that would ally with the Germans against the growing threat of communist partisans. Neubacher phoned Ernst Kaltenbrunner at the AA in Berlin and got Stroop recalled in October and replaced by Walter Schimana, who became the new resident BdS in Athens. Schimana concentrated on building up the various police and security formations and left the intelligence work in the hands of a 38-year-old

former lawyer Dr. Walter Blume, who had (by the standards of the SS) a reputation for being soft and bureaucratic.[8] In Athens, Blume created quite a different reputation, going about his counter-intelligence work with ruthless efficiency.

A concentration camp was set up at Haidari outside Athens, and by 1944 the Gestapo was working flat out to root out and deport Jews. On 25 March 1944, the Jewish quarter in Janina was surrounded by GFP troops while the Wehrmacht supplied 80 lorries to transport the victims. The SD, whose operation this was, relied on the GFP for troops and personnel. The entire Jewish population of 1700 individuals ended up in Auschwitz. Although this was proof of Wehrmacht and GFP collusion in the Holocaust, the German commandant of Corfu, Colonel Emil Jäger, opposed the deportations on principle but also pointed out the practical problem. The Greek population on the island would be enraged and frightened by the deportation of the Jews, and would fear the same fate for themselves. Jäger's objections were brushed aside by the Wehrmacht command, and Corfu's Jews met the same horrible fate as those of Janina.

Yugoslavia: Every Man a Hero and a Traitor

If German terror in Greece was bad, the situation was even worse in Yugoslavia, where by 1943–44 the national and ethnic groups in the country were at each others' throats. As elsewhere in the Balkans, the German intelligence presence there had been modest in the beginning. Instead, the lead role had been taken by Germany's allies Hungary and Italy, which had sponsored the IMRO[9] organization in Macedonia and the Croat *Ustashe* movement, led by the psychotic Dr. Ante Pavelic.

Yugoslavia was therefore no friend of either state and there was a possibility that the Germans could step into the role of its protector. By 1941 the Abwehr's resources were already stretched thin, so the lead that competing services, the SIM, SIS and the *Deuxiéme Bureau,* had in the capital Belgrade could not be reduced immediately. The Germans were also divided about which of the two main Yugoslav nations, Croatia or Serbia, they should sponsor. Ribbentrop was opposed to the SD or

Abwehr meddling in Balkan affairs, and he wanted all Yugoslav business to go through the AA in Berlin. The AA Press Chief, Dr. Paul Schmidt, was close to the Serb Yugoslav journalist, Danilo Gregoric, and Schmidt was instrumental in getting Ribbentrop to back the Serbs. Hermann Göring also became involved in German moves on the Yugoslav state. He had made a state visit to Yugoslavia in 1935, and was deeply impressed with the Serbs and their military prowess. His agent of influence, Franz Neuhausen, became the German General Consul in Belgrade before the war. The SD was convinced that Neuhausen was a Soviet spy, and he was later arrested and convicted for involvement in a currency operation.

Serbs or Croats

Unlike Ribbentrop and Göring, who favoured the Serbs, the Abwehr wanted to sponsor the Croats, as a way of ousting the Italians from influence in Yugoslav affairs. However, Ribbentrop and Göring overruled the idea. On 23 November 1940 Ribbentrop offered the Yugoslavs an alliance, and proffered them the Greek port of Salonika (Thessaloniki) as an incentive. After much vacillation the Yugoslavs signed on 25 March. Two days later the Yugoslav Chief of Staff, General Dushan Simovic, led a military coup against the Regent, Prince Paul, and the government that had agreed to this scandalous sell-out. In response, Hitler ordered a postponement of Operation Barbarossa from mid-May to mid-June in order to include Yugoslavia in Operation "Marita" (the invasion of Greece). On 6 April the Germans invaded and crushed the Yugoslav Army in nine days.

The *Ustashe* seized power in Zagreb, the Croat capital, while in Serbia General Nedic became military dictator, under German protection. However, pro-royalist Serbs, known as Chetniks, led by General Drasha Michailovitch, immediately began a guerrilla war against the *Ustashe* and the Germans. His communist counterpart, Josef Broz "Tito", only began organizing his partisans after the German invasion of the USSR. So a Yugoslav civil war began between the royalist Serb Chetniks, the Pan-Yugoslav communist partisans under Tito, and the Nazi *Ustashe* Croats. It was a war that was vicious, bloodthirsty and utterly merciless. The *Ustashe* were the worst butchers, responsible for the deaths of over 600,000 Serbs, Jews and Gypsies, while the Chetniks spared few Croats if they fell into their hands, and the partisans executed anyone who stood in their way or did not give them due support.

Abwehr Contacts with the Chetniks

To make the situation even worse, the Germans involved themselves in the civil war and committed one mistake and atrocity after another. Instead of backing the Chetniks, they supported the Croat *Ustashe* and ended up alienating the entire Serb population, which served to strengthen Tito's communists. By 1943 it was obvious that Germany could no longer afford to commit over 350,000 troops to this nasty sideshow in the Balkans. The Abwehr sent the 4th Brandenburg Regiment to Kosovo-Mitrovitza district to find or capture the Chetnik leader Michailovitch. The Abwehr instead established contact with him, and in early May 1943 the commander of the 4th Brandenburg Regiment went to Michailovitch's headquarters at Kolashin. The talks were conducted in a most friendly and constructive fashion, since the Chetniks were already cooperating with the Italians and the dictator General Nedic against the partisans. Michailovitch wanted the Germans to restore Serbia as an independent state, with King Peter II at its head and himself as Minister of War. Unfortunately the OKW rejected the proposal, Michailovitch's emissaries were arrested and deported by the Gestapo to Germany, while the 4th Regiment's commander was relieved of his command. The SS Division *Prinz Eugen* unleashed a vicious campaign that cleared Montenegro and Serbia of Chetniks, but only weakened a potential ally in favour of the communists. This disastrous decision and subsequent German policies lost Berlin the war in Yugoslavia and effectively handed it over to Tito's communists.

> *Into this hornet's nest stepped the Germans, who committed one mistake after another*

In Zagreb, the SD Station Head, Wilhelm Höttl, and the German commandant in Croatia, General von Horstenau, came up with a radical new plan which ran contrary to previous Nazi policies in Yugoslavia: if a deal could not be struck with the Chetniks then why not with the partisans? Horstenau had met with Tito's representative, "Dr. Petrovic", to organize an exchange of partisan prisoners for captured members of the army's construction organization, the OT.[10] Petrovic spent 10 days at Horstenau's headquarters as the general's guest, and revealed that he was in fact Tito's deputy and right-hand man in Croatia: General Ljabo Velebit. Velebit told Horstenau that he was willing to sign an armistice with the Germans. Horstenau spoke with Höttl, who brought the matter to the attention of Ernst Kaltenbrunner, who in turn spoke with Himmler. The Reichsführer-SS promised, but failed, to take the matter up with Hitler. Horstenau then relayed Velebit and Tito's offer to Hitler via Ribbentrop. Hitler's terse answer was: "I don't parley with rebels – I shoot them!"[11] The failure of the SD

BELOW: Tito (in centre of group, at left) seen at an inspection parade of his frontline partisans troops in 1943, a time when his forces controlled over a third of Yugoslavia.

talks with Tito created the background to the failed attempt to capture or kill the partisan leader in June 1944.[12]

The SD, in collaboration with the Wehrmacht Ic staff in Yugoslavia, had broken the codes used by the partisans in their radio communications, which enabled them during 1943 to deliver one blow after another. After a series of setbacks Tito suspected that there had to be traitor in his ranks, and he purged his staff. Despite this the setbacks continued. Someone pointed out that the codes being used might be too primitive, but instead of changing codes, radio frequencies were changed instead. These measures were to prove insufficient because the SD/Ic radio surveillance service kept track.

Tito, like Michailovitch, was disgruntled with the Western Allies and had broken off relations with them, but the SD did not believe this news until General Velebit's negotiations and other intelligence confirmed it. This new information had been picked up by the Hungarian Intelligence Service, Section II of the Hungarian General Staff, which had captured a Soviet courier from Moscow on his way to Tito's headquarters. Stalin had no illusions that his alliance with the capitalist West was only a wartime expedient, and that he needed

to plan for the post-war world. To this end his courier had orders for Tito to cooperate with the Germans should the Western Allies land on the Dalmatian coast.

The Middle East

The Middle East held some vital strategic prizes for Germany. If Rommel could invade Egypt then Britain's lifeline to India, via the Suez Canal, would be cut and the British position in the whole region would be undermined. Iraq was the key to the whole region and its position was similar to that of Romania: a politically divided, militarily weak and oil-rich state which could also function as a bridgehead for offensives against the East. Here the great prize was not Russia but the equally oil-rich state of Iran (Persia).

Egypt's corrupt and pampered élite was less than pleased with British rule, and none were more keen to get rid of the British than the country's king, Farouk (Faruq).[13] In early 1940 King Farouk sent an emissary to Istanbul to speak with Ambassador Papen, who was sceptical about involving Germany in Egypt's affairs. Not only would German support for the Egyptians anger that country's old colonial masters, the Turks, but as a national leader Farouk was incompetent and fickle. One day he would support the British, the

ABOVE: Colonel Drazha Michailovitch's Chetnik forces marching through the streets of a friendly or Chetnik-occupied town in Yugoslavia. The Chetniks were sworn enemies of Tito's communists.

next the Germans and the third Mussolini. But it was true, as the emissary pointed out, that the British hold on Egypt was weak. Its Western Desert Force was small and poorly equipped. A German-led invasion of Egypt would probably be crowned with success, and then the whole of the Middle East would be in Hitler's grasp.

Whenever Egypt and Abwehr are mentioned in the same breath, the name of the Hungarian adventurer Count Ladislas von Almaszy will crop up again and again. Almaszy was not only a knowledgeable Egyptologist and archaeologist but he had acquired, through numerous, lengthy and arduous journeys in the region, an expert knowledge of the Western Desert.[14] This knowledge, combined with his language skills, made him invaluable as an agent of the Abwehr.

In November 1940 the intrepid Hungarian nobleman accompanied the senior Abwehr agent, Karl Heinz Krämer, to Cairo where the two spies were to meet with the Egyptian military opposition. They made contact with two young officers who were the Abwehr's link to that opposition. The officers,

Anwar al-Sadat and Gamal Abdel Nasser, would both later become presidents of Egypt.[15] The Germans and the Egyptian rebels had one thing in common: they both wanted the British thrown out of Egypt and neither were particular about the methods they employed to achieve that aim. Through Nasser and al-Sadat, Krämer and Almaszy were introduced to a far more important contact: General Masri Pasha. Masri provided Krämer with copies of Britain's defences in the Western Desert, which would come in handy should the Germans join the Italians in their war on Britain in North Africa. In 1940 that seemed a likely proposition, as the Italians were being defeated by the British.

Unfortunately for the conspirators, the British captured a forward headquarters of the Italian Army where they found their stolen defence plans, and it did not take long for the British to figure out that it was Masri who was behind this

BELOW: Having narrowly failed to capture the Yugoslav partisan leader during Operation Knight's Move, these German SS paratroopers hold up Tito's captured uniform.

leak to the enemy. Masri was fired from the Egyptian Army. He was arrested but escaped. Krämer managed to get in touch with the fugitive and arranged to pick him up in a plane from outside Cairo and fly him west to Derna, in the Italian territory of Cyrenaica (which, with Tripolitania, had been ceded to Italy in 1912). The SIS Station Chief in Cairo, Captain A.W. Samson, knew of Masri's plots and learned from his network of agents where the renegade general was off to. Masri had planned his escape poorly, and he was arrested at the airstrip before he could board the plane. Masri and the pilot spent the rest of the war in a POW compound.

This did not deter Farouk from further intrigues to win the support of his German "friends". In February 1941 – the same month that General Erwin Rommel and the advance units of the Afrika Korps arrived in Tripoli to save the Italians from defeat – Farouk sent a new message promising a general Egyptian uprising when and if the German Army reached the Egyptian border. Should the Germans reach Egyptian soil, their most likely ally

would be the "Ikhwan al-Muslimin" (The Muslim Brotherhood), a violent, fanatical, fundamentalist Muslim organization founded in 1930 by Hassan al-Banna. The Muslim Brotherhood wanted to remove all "corrupting" Western influence by returning Egypt to the purity of Koranic (Sharia) law. The Brotherhood was unpopular with most Egyptians, and whatever his other failings Farouk wanted no truck with them. In early 1941 the Brotherhood attacked Jews, Christians, conservative Egyptians and the premier, Hussein Sirri Pasha, as affronts to their strict version of Islamic conduct.

Rommel's American "Spy"

The SIS kept an eye on the Brotherhood while Ambassador Sir Miles Lampson kept Farouk under the British thumb. When Foreign Secretary Anthony Eden visited Egypt he backed Lampson's hard line with the king, and protested at the large number of Italians working in the Royal Palace. Farouk's response to this behaviour was to send his cousin, the ex-Khedive of Egypt, Abbas Hilmi II, to Berlin as emissary. Abbas, who arrived in April 1941 via Turkey, was a good choice since he was not only Germanophile but a strong hater of the British. He also spoke fluent German. On behalf of Farouk, Abbas offered to place the king's considerable fortune at the disposal of the Abwehr for its operations in the Middle East. Even more astonishingly, Abbas offered to have the Turkish President Inönü assassinated.

These offers, and others from nationalist Arabs, left the Germans decidedly unimpressed. Ribbentrop shared Italian Foreign Minister Count Ciano's contempt for the Arabs as completely untrustworthy, while Otto Abetz, German Ambassador to Vichy France, pointed to the ambitions that many Arabs had regarding the Islamization of the whole of Sub-Saharan Africa and the expulsion of all Europeans, irrespective of their nationality. The Arabs were nobody's friend and the Germans viewed them, at best, as an unreliable and dubious card to play against the British.

The Arabs were nobody's friends, and the Germans viewed them as unreliable

By the end of April 1941, after a swift and devastating offensive, General Rommel had sent the British Army reeling back to the Egyptian frontier.[16] He was assisted in this by a major coup by his Ic. The Germans had broken the Americans' "Black code" used to decipher military intelligence. In October 1940, Colonel Bonner Frank Fellers arrived in Cairo as the new US military attaché at the American Legation. He was given every facility to visit the British frontline and access to the most sensitive information. He made clear, detailed and most concise reports of what he saw, what the British had said, their plans and the troops' dispositions. This intelligence was intercepted, deciphered and read by the Germans, who gave the source the codename "Rebecca". It was through the Rebecca intercepts that Rommel avoided the raid on Benghazi at the end of 1941 by British commandos out to kill him. It appeared that Rommel always seemed to know where the British lines were at their weakest, or when it was most inopportune for him to strike. When the British began to complain that there seemed to be a leak somewhere, the American High Command became concerned enough to send an investigating team from Washington. They did not find a leak, but enough concern was raised for the recall of Fellers.

Spies and Subversion in Egypt

Rommel always suspected that the "Rebecca" source would eventually dry up, and that spies would have to be sent to Egypt to replace it. It was the irrepressible yet overconfident and self-proclaimed spymaster, Nikolaus Ritter from the Hamburg Ast, who popped up to tackle the job. In early 1941 he got the idea of smuggling into Egypt a pair of spies right under the noses of the SIS. He proposed that the agents be sent, overland, across the Western Desert to sneak into Cairo via the backdoor. When he broached the idea to Canaris the admiral was flabbergasted and burst out: "Are you out of your mind, man?"[17] He told Ritter to forget the whole idea. But a month later, probably following a request from Rommel for assistance, Canaris had a change of heart. The next day Ritter flew to Budapest to see Almaszy for background information.

Ritter decided that he would take charge personally and he decided, for ease of passage, that instead of travelling overland his agents were to be flown into Egypt. The mission turned into a disaster. Flying over the Western Desert, the Luftwaffe pilot declared that he dared not land in such rough terrain, and despite threats of punishment for cowardice he turned the plane back. Unfortunately, the nearest airfield, at Derna, was under heavy British aerial bombardment, and the pilot was forced to fly on towards Benghazi, but by this time the plane was low on fuel. The aircraft was then spotted by the RAF and flew into cloud cover with tracer bullets whizzing around it. By the time the pilot reduced altitude and regained visibility he discovered that he had overshot the coast. Below them was only vast expanses of dark sea water. The plane crashed into the sea due to lack of fuel, and it was several days later that a Kriegsmarine vessel, sent out on a search and rescue mission, found and rescued the party.[18]

The Playboy and the "American"

Two months after this debacle, Canaris himself turned up at Rommel's desert headquarters to bring some order to the Abwehr's efforts in North Africa. Rommel had told the local Brandenburg unit commander that he needed two agents in Cairo without delay, and if they could not get there by plane they would have to be smuggled there by the land route. Canaris' solution was to bring in Almaszy. The Hungarian, never one to turn down an adventure, would take the new pair of spies, "Sandy" and "Buddy", through the Great Sand Sea, south of the Qattara Depression. This was the Rommel style and the general gave the Hungarian a hard smile and told him: "It's a bold plan. I hope you don't die in the damned desert. Oh well, they say that lunatics are usually lucky. Why shouldn't you be?"[19]

The agents Almaszy was to lead through the desert wilderness were an unprepossessing pair. "Buddy", or Johannes Eppler-Gafer, was a most unlikely looking German. With his short body,

tanned face and black hair he looked more Levantine than any Arab. Yet Eppler was born to German parents in Egypt. His mother had later remarried to an Egyptian judge, Gafer Pasha, who had tried to bring up his stepson in the strict Muslim faith, but had failed. Eppler instead developed a taste for the high life and a fondness for a "slow horse and a fast woman". He was recruited in Beirut in 1937 by two Abwehr officers, Haller and Rohde, the latter being German military attaché in Cairo at the time.

A Near Disaster in the Desert

Eppler was sent to Berlin in August 1937 where he was trained in the arts and crafts of soldiering, which he, the born rebel and raconteur, did not enjoy. His training in secret work was far more to his liking. Having gone through a short spell of Abwehr training, Eppler went to Istanbul to get to know the Turks better and then returned, in December 1937, to Beirut for talks with the fascist nationalist Arab leader, Antun Saadah, who in turn was in touch with the Grand Mufti of Jerusalem. The Mufti, Hadji Mohammed Amin el Husseini, was one of the most crafty and murderous schemers to come out of the Middle East during the turbulent 1930s. He was one of Germany's main contacts in the region and he hoped, with German help, to remove the British and unify the Arabs into a latter day Caliphate and pursue a *Jihad* (Holy War) against the British authorities. Eppler, however, was not authorized by Berlin to discuss politics and therefore cut the wily conspirator out. With these years of experience behind him, Eppler was not just an amateur agent out on a desert jaunt. Now, in 1942, with the Afrika Korps poised to invade and conquer Egypt, the moment that Eppler had trained for all his life seemed to have arrived.

His fellow agent and the team's radio man was Peter Monkaster, or "Sandy" (Sandberg), who travelled with a genuine US passport, while Eppler had his Egyptian passport made out in the name of Gafer. Canaris was on hand to give his agents some last-minute instructions, and was deeply worried about what these two young men would get up to in Cairo with the Abwehr's £20,000 fund. He handed

ABOVE: *Overview of the Abadan oil refinery in Iran – the main production centre of that country's petrol producing-region of Khuzestan. Such resources made the region a tempting target for German espionage operations.*

them a copy of the best-seller *Rebecca* by Daphne du Maurier. It was to be the base for their coded messages back to Rommel and the Abwehr. It was Canaris, in person, who bade them farewell in April 1942 as they left German lines in two trucks filled with Brandenburg troops.

Almaszy sped south towards the last Italian outpost in the desert, the oasis of Jalo, before reaching Kufra and then turning sharply to the east through the Japsa Pass, then Glif Kebir and the British-held oasis of El Kharga, from where Gafer and Sandberg had to take the train to Cairo. It was tough going through the desert. To get over

the high sand dunes, Almaszy had instructed the Brandenburgers to drive at full speed to the top and then down the other side at an angle. But they would get stuck and then have to take out all the supplies and dig the trucks out of the sand. When the medical officer went crazy and had to be punched unconscious and the chief mechanic collapsed from heat stroke or a heart attack, Almaszy, most reluctantly, agreed to drive back to Jalo. They set out again on 11 May. When the German troops moaned about the conditions Almaszy, incensed at their weakness and continual complaining, shouted back at them to shut up: "Have you ever thought that at this very moment, other people don't just have to exist in this heat ... they have to fight in it?"[20]

What saved the convoy from disaster this time was the timely discovery of an SAS/LRDG[21] depot

consisting of fully laden trucks hidden near a sand dune. The men helped themselves to water, food and other supplies. They set out again, and Almaszy used an old Arab Bedouin trick to keep his men's spirit up by telling them that the next objective was not far, or just beyond the horizon. But when they finally ran out of water the Hungarian pulled off his greatest motivational coup. When they reached the dark outlines of the Kebir Mountains, Almaszy told the incredulous Germans that he had hidden several

canisters of water there during his 1937 expedition. The Germans thought the crazy Hungarian had finally lost his mind, and Eppler wondered aloud if the water, even if it were found, would be drinkable. Almaszy reached a spot where he began to dig until he hit metal. He pulled out the water canisters. Eppler drank avidly and found the water surprisingly drinkable. Refreshed, the convoy set out again and after 11 days, spotted at night the twinkling lights of El Kharga. From here the agents could pick up the

LEFT: *February 1941: the newly arrived General Erwin Rommel (centre) is shown around the capital of the Italian colony, Tripoli, by a group of high-ranking Italian and German officers.*

were not just a pair of playboys but accomplished spies as well. Eppler made friends with indiscreet British officers in the bar and restaurant at The Shepherd's Hotel, a favourite haunt of both British, Arab, American and Axis spies. By being generous Eppler built up a large circle of agents, as well as picking up with some of his old friends, who were surprised to find him back in Cairo. Eppler recruited his most important agent in the Kit-Kat Club: a seductive and voluptuous belly dancer Hekmat Fahmy, who was an Egyptian nationalist and more than willing to supply information in return for a generous supply of money from Eppler. Hekmat, whom Eppler described as an unbelievable lover, proved very efficient at her "work". She told her British interrogators after her arrest: "An Englishman who has just made love to a girl don't [sic] just feel confidence for her, he can't stop talking." One senior officer was off on a top-secret mission, which he of course divulged to his mistress, and Hekmat slipped him a drink with a sleeping potion in it. She handed Eppler the officer's briefcase containing documents showing the British defences around Cairo – vital if Rommel broke through. In September 1942 a major also unwittingly divulged General Montgomery's battle plans at El Alamein, but "Sandy" could not transmit the information to Rommel in time.

Time had in fact run out for the dynamic duo on the house boat. Their indiscreet contact, Anwar al-Sadat, talked too much and was dropped from the network. But it was too late – al-Sadat was arrested by the British. The SIS had managed to infiltrate Eppler's network. In one move to get close to the German spies, the SIS chief in Cairo, Captain "Sammy" Samson, had disguised himself as a black marketeer and had actually played golf with Eppler on several occasions. On 14 October 1942 the doors on the houseboat were kicked in, and in stepped the SIS to apprehend Eppler and Sandberg. Eppler chose to talk while Sandberg

road north to the Nile and Cairo. Almaszy bid the agents farewell and turned back into the desert. Operation Condor now began.

Operation Condor

As Canaris had feared, the two young men used the Abwehr's £20,000 to install themselves in Cairo to enjoy life. They rented a luxurious houseboat on the Nile to set up their Afu radio receiver. But Eppler and his radio man, "Sandy", attempted suicide. The adventures of "Condor" were over.

"Condor" was not the only operation the Abwehr had going in the Middle East, but at least Eppler and Sandberg reached their goal. Not so two other agents, both female, who set out for the same region. Ursula Bayomi had divorced her Egyptian husband who was still in Cairo and was recruited into German service by Dr. Praetorius, head of the Hamburg Ast Economic Section. She was recruited to spy out British oil installations in the Middle East. In Hamburg, Ursula befriended an Egyptian "prince" who promised to accompany her some of the way. Ursula's lover was in fact an SIS agent who betrayed her to the British.

Waltraut Örtel

The adventures of Waltraut Örtel proved equally exotic and abortive. Örtel was another recruit of the Hamburg Ast, and operated as an Abwehr agent in Yugoslavia prior to the invasion of that country in 1941. Once she was back from her Balkan mission Örtel was given a new assignment: the Middle East. She travelled to Budapest – one of the Abwehr's way-stations to the Levant– where she "befriended" a wayward, 70-year-old British engineer, Maxwell C.B. Clapham. Already married to a Hungarian lady, Clapham adopted her and promptly slept with his new found "daughter". After Hungary became an ally of Germany, Clapham, as an enemy civilian, was soon packed off to an internment camp in Germany, leaving Örtel free to assume the identity of "Miss Clapham". Using this cover she made her way to Turkey where she claimed to be a British refugee fleeing the Germans. The British Ambassador, Knutchball Huggesen, a decent, but naïve man, contributed to her travelling funds and sped her on her way. Örtel made her way to Haifa in British-controlled Palestine and spied out the installations there, but her reports – she had no radio – never reached Hamburg. In 1942 she was finally arrested and interned by the SIS.

Though the stories of Bayomi and Örtel are replete with exoticism and adventure, they are made to seem rather mundane when compared to the intrigues of Charles Bedaux. Bedaux was a

ABOVE: Mohammed Amin el Husseini, the self-proclaimed "Grand Mufti" of Jerusalem, here basking in the sun of German friendship, was a notorious schemer who tried to use the Germans and Italians for his own ends.

Frenchman and a strong admirer and friend of the new Germany. He was especially close to Ribbentrop and his sister-in-law, Frau Janke, in Ankara. Bedaux put a proposal to Colonel Lahousen (chief of Abwehr II, the service's sabotage section) to blow up the Abadan oilfields in Persia. Lahousen was sceptical since Bedaux's previous schemes had cost a lot of money and yielded little return. Nevertheless, Bedaux went ahead and as a cover rented a series of rooms at 53 Avenue Hoche in Paris. The mansion also contained the offices of a mysterious "purchasing agency" that was an Abwehr front run by AO

Andreas Folmer, who was deeply suspicious of Bedaux's plan. But he found out that the Frenchman was up to something in Iran, and that Bedaux had a financial hold on the director of the oilfield employing 15,000 workers. Lahousen placed the plans to attack or sabotage the fields on the desk of Karl Strojil, Abwehr II's sabotage expert. Strojil concluded the operation was more than feasible and should be carried out as soon as possible, because of the enormous damage inflicted on the fuel supplies of the Allies. He also recommended that the Abwehr organize the operation itself and that Bedaux be dropped. Nothing was done, and Germany let slip another golden opportunity.

Iraq: Another Missed Opportunity

If there was one German who could call himself an expert on the Arabs then it was Dr. Grobba, who was the German Ambassador in Baghdad before the war, and was known as an advocate of a German alliance with the Arab states against the Zionist Jews in Palestine. Grobba was sounding out the Iraqis about a possible alliance against the British and was accompanied by Colonel Groscurth. Groscurth signed his own name in the hotel ledger. With proof in the spy's own handwriting that the Abwehr were in the city, the Baghdad SIS station asked the two gentlemen to kindly leave Iraq.

In November 1937, a personal emissary from King Ibn-Saud of Saudi Arabia arrived in Baghdad for talks with Grobba. The king wanted to established links, acquire German arms and enlist support against the Palestinian Jews. That same month Henry Kohn, a Persian whose stepfather was German, arrived at SD headquarters in Berlin for a similar purpose. Both the SD and Grobba urged their respective superiors to take up this lead, but the only progress made was that a German Consulate was set up in the Saudi Arabian city of Jeddah. These murky undertakings return us to the shadiest and most odious character in this twisted tale of treason and plots: the Mufti of Jerusalem. The Mufti had usurped his position, murdered rivals to keep it, and in 1938 even the British had had enough of this violent Muslim cleric and his supporters' outrages against Jews and Christians in Palestine. He fled to the French in Beirut and repaid their generosity by proposing, in August 1940, an Arab alliance with Nazi Germany.

The Mufti sent Osman Kemal Haddad to Berlin where Haddad met the ever-understanding Grobba, and a far more hard-headed and sceptical Ernst Weizsäcker of the AA, who had previously met and talked with Count Ciano about the Mufti. Ciano complained about the unreliability of the Mufti, who had been paid millions of Italian lire in return for the "sabotage" of Allied oil installations, but had inflicted hardly any damage. Ciano's advice was to drop the Mufti; advice which was followed by Weizsäcker who had a furious argument with the Mufti's emissary, Haddad. The negotiations with the Mufti ended with Ribbentrop firing Grobba and burying the plans of supporting the Arabs.

This was probably a wise decision, since nothing good could come from these dealings. Through the Mufti Grobba had had contacts with Rashid Ali el-Gailani, the new pro-Nazi ruler of Iraq. He and his fellow Iraqi Army conspirators from the Golden Square nationalist organization ousted the Anglophile premier on 1 April 1941, and alienated the British beyond the line of provocation with their talk of Arab liberation and admiration for Hitler. The British were in no mood to appease or play around with these conspirators, and in May 1941 they invaded from Palestine and through the Persian Gulf, easily conquering the oil-rich state. In August the same year, Iran was also occupied by combined Anglo-Soviet forces and thus ended, for another year, German dreams of dominating the Middle East.

Operation "Tiger"

To protect their Indian empire, the British had set up the first proper and permanent security service – the Indian Political Intelligence Bureau – that combined efficiency with ruthless guile. The bureau guarded India from both external and internal enemies. During World War I the Raj had been defended against Turco-German probes into Iran and Afghanistan. Now the British faced a far more determined foe – the Nazi German intelligence services.

It was only in April 1939 that the AA consulted the Abwehr about coordinating on a worldwide strategy should Britain prove hostile. One idea put to Canaris was to plan for a Russo-German invasion of India which would, even if it was only a threat, tie down considerable British forces well away from Europe. Johannes Eppler-Gafer played a role in the development of this plan. During his stay in Istanbul in December 1937, he made a friend of a fierce Kashgai tribal warrior from Persia by the name of Amir Azurnuch. Azurnuch suggested that Eppler make a journey east to meet with his fellow tribal leader and conspirator, the Afghan leader Ghulam Barakatullah, who had good contacts with the Afghan (Pathan) tribes of the Northwest Frontier – India's most vulnerable border region.

Two years later, in May 1939, Eppler, disguised as a Turk, travelled east from Erzerum in eastern Anatolia. After a month he approached Masuleh, Barakatullah's home village, where Azurnuch met him and introduced him to the Afghan warlord. Barakatullah had taken part in a rebellion against the pro-British government in Kabul in 1932, that had been sponsored by Soviet military intelligence, the GRU. As this was the time of the flowering Soviet-German pact, that was fine with Eppler. To undertake this new uprising,

BELOW: The port and petroleum refinery in Abadan, the target of German plans to capture or sabotage this vital installation for its supply of oil to the Allies.

Barakatullah had made contacts with the Afridi tribe who populated the area near to the famed Khyber Pass – the gateway to the plains of India. The Afghani leader introduced Eppler to an Afridi messenger by the name of Medji, who was in touch with the Faqir of Ipi, Hadji Mirza Ali,[22] ruler of North Waziristan. The talks went on until nightfall and beyond. Eppler, with one Afghan at the pedals of his small generator, sent a message back to Berlin that he was now deep inside Afghanistan. Eppler then travelled on into central and northeastern Afghanistan, where he had a meeting with the Faqir of Ipi in Kafiristan and then made his way back to Iran. Eppler had established a working network should the Russians and German combine to disturb the British hold on India, or should Germany, on her own, need an overseas diversion.

Nothing came of these nebulous plans, but the Abwehr did not give up on its designs. A Baltic German from Lithuania, Professor Manfred Oberdörfer, converted Canaris to the idea of sending a new agent to the Northwest Frontier. That agent, fluent in Iranian and Pathan dialects, was of course himself and he would use his expertise as a medical expert in leprosy to give his expedition the necessary cover. Oberdörfer was sent on his way to India with the assistance of Fred Brandt. The Leprosy Mission to Afghanistan arrived in 1940 and at Herat was joined by an Afghan guide, who was in the pay of the Indian Intelligence Bureau. The Italian Ambassador in

Kabul introduced the German doctors/agents to a British colonel who had deserted his post in India, and was now willing to serve the Germans. The colonel offered to have the pair guided into the perilous Northwest Frontier zone. Here they were ambushed by tribesmen. Oberdörfer died in the car while being driven back to Kabul.

German Spies in Latin America

Operations in Afghanistan were dangerous and unglamorous. Those in Latin America were more attractive, though often no less deadly.

In a cafe overlooking Havana harbour, the elegant gringo in the white suit, immaculate tie and Panama hat had his regular table overlooking the ships moored at the quays and anchored in the bay offshore. From the table farthest out, the man, either a Yankee or an European gringo, had a perfect view over the busiest and most important port in the whole of the Caribbean. The man wrote down nothing of what he saw, but made a mental note of events down below. Over his coffee and newspaper, this particular V-man could simply combine leisurely pursuits with the job the Abwehr or SD paid him to do: keep his eyes and ears peeled for information on any enemy shipping movements.

Neutral Cuba, ruled by Fulgencio Batista since the military coup against General Machado in 1933, was a superb place for the Abwehr to conduct spying in the New World. It was next door to the USA – less than 160km (100 miles) from Florida, in fact. Havana was chock-a-block with American, British and Allied (Norwegian and Dutch) shipping loaded with oil from Mexico and Texas bound for Britain. Intelligence sent by the cafe agent would end up aiding the U-boats to sink these ships in the Atlantic.

The agent was Enrique Luni. His real name was Heinz August Luning, born 1910 in Hamburg, a frequent visitor to the West Indies and fluent in Spanish. Luning had joined the Abwehr in 1940 and had been thoroughly trained in the art of spying in Latin America. He had used Barcelona as a conduit and sailed on the Spanish freighter M/V *Ciudad de Madrid* to Havana, where he arrived on 20 September 1941.

"Luni" set up a dress shop as a cover, and every day went to his favourite cafe at Porto Chico with its terrific view over Havana harbour. After an hour or two he slowly walked home from where he composed his daily report, which was sent to an "innocent looking" address in Barcelona. If the report was urgent he would radio it directly to Spain. So life went on for the discreet and unobtrusive German spy, the Abwehr's man in Havana, for 11 long and hot Caribbean months. It would have continued had he not, despite his meticulousness, committed one fatal mistake.

Much of the mail from Latin America, including Cuba, went through the British-controlled island of Bermuda, where the LIU[23] had its largest overseas station housed in the Hamilton Princess Hotel. The LIU station was headed by SIS officer Peter Wilson, with a large staff of young and hard-working women. This station was a major source of information for MI5 in its task of hunting down German agents in the New World. The censors became suspicious of Luni's mail to Spain when letters were found written with the same handwriting, but signed with different names. This "precaution" by Luni proved his undoing, because the LIU sent over copies of the letters to the FBI in Havana. The FBI acted on the evidence and arrested Luni on 15 August 1942. Despite howls of disapproval by Cuban Yankee haters and Nazi sympathizers, Luning was shot by firing squad on 8 November 1942 – the same day the Americans landed in North Africa. Another Abwehr agent in Cuba, Richard Dorres, was active on the island between 1941 and late 1942. Dorres was never detected, but after Luning's arrest and execution he made good his escape, no doubt realizing that it was only a matter of time before he too was discovered.

Mexico: Espionage Bridgehead against the USA

Mexico has a long and troubled history in its relations with the USA, and it was not lost on those Mexicans who hated America that Germany might be a good ally to have. During the 1930s, however, the left-leaning President Cardenas had supported the Republican side in the Spanish Civil War against the forces of General Franco and had flirted with communism. But in 1940 a new group of leaders took charge in Mexico, and the Abwehr had an opportunity to establish itself in the country and use it as a base to launch espionage operations into the USA. Soon three networks, with some 40 agents, had been set up and were supplying the Hamburg, Cologne and Berlin Asts with a wealth of intelligence on the USA. Canaris was most keen to keep a close eye on Britain's powerful and dangerous de facto ally, and prepare for the worst should President Roosevelt declare war on Germany.

Max and Morris

The two main German spymasters in Mexico were called "Max und Morris", but they were not a comical pair of German clowns but an effective double act for the Abwehr. "Max" was an arrogant young Nazi major by the name of Georg Nikolaus, who had been a banker in Colombia until 1938. His colleague "Morris" was Colonel Baron Karl von Schleebrügge, who had been a Luftwaffe commander during the Polish campaign but had lived in Mexico making a living as a representative of a German arms manufacturer before the war. Nikolaus arrived in Mexico with $10,000 and set about building up a network of agents and front companies to hide their real activities. Their agents in the USA, such as "Fred", "James" and "Harry", sent their reports direct to the Abwehr "post office" in Mexico City – the local office of the A.E.G. company. These reports were then sent to Germany from Mexico.

Fortunately for the German spy network in Mexico, in May 1940 J. Edgar Hoover had stated that "the best way to control Nazi espionage in the United States was to wipe out the spy nests in Latin America". Roosevelt agreed with the FBI boss and a new department of the FBI was created on 3 June 1940: the Special Intelligence Service, which was abbreviated for maximum confusion with their British colleagues as the SIS.

The new service started by cleaning out the Mexican nest. Schleebrügge was expelled by the Mexicans in April 1941, while the FBI/SIS in collaboration with the Mexican Federal Police put "Max" under 24-hour surveillance. By 1942 the increasing collaboration of the Americans and Mexicans, eagerly abetted by the British, put an end to Abwehr's activities south of the Rio Grande.

Brazil was also the other main centre of German espionage in Latin America. By 1939, for example, there were 900,000 German residents or immigrants in Brazil. There was also Brazil's long eastern coastline which provided many superb locations, such as Rio, Santos and Recife, where Abwehr agents could keep an eye on Allied shipping passing offshore. While President Getulio Vargas paid lip service to US hemisphere defences, he told German Ambassador Pruter that he would allow German agents to work in Brazil. Germany saw Brazil as a bulwark against American influence.

Hermann Bohny

German Naval Attaché Captain Hermann Bohny now became the main controller of agents in the vast country. His main agent was "Alfredo" who had entered Abwehr service in Brazil in June 1940. Both Canaris and Dönitz, head of the U-boat fleet, were keen to know about Recife, particularly the Pan Am airfields and the US South Atlantic Fleet's patrols which sortied from the port. These and other tasks were given to German immigrant businessman Alfred Kempter, who had emigrated to Brazil in the 1920s and joined the Abwehr in 1939. Unlike most of his colleagues in Latin America, Kempter was not a patriot and worked solely for money. In February 1940 he and his business partner, Herbert Müller, set up a convenient front in Rio: the Rapid Information Ltd. Müller also joined the service and began to supply the Abwehr with accurate and frequent intelligence of shipping, convoys, cargoes and US activities. Dönitz was pleased with the agents' work. By December 1941, Kempter and Müller had sent 400 radio messages and even more mailed ones to the Hamburg Ast. Kempter was awarded the War Service Cross (1st Class) for his work.

Kempter's "König" network set to work trying to help the U-boats cut the British shipping lines around the Cape of Good Hope. In May 1941 the merchantman M/V *Rodney Star* was sunk as she left Buenos Aires, and that same month a Norwegian tanker was also sunk with the help of

Kempter's intelligence. Kempter and his agents contributed to the toll of 101,600 tonnes (100,000 tons) of Allied shipping sunk per month during 1941: a deadly toll that threatened Britain's ruin. Kempter was invaluable because he provided all sorts of intelligence including tide and water conditions along the Brazilian coasts, and the quality of the anti-submarine netting that protected British shipping in Brazilian ports.

Incompetence

Another effective agent was Albrecht Engels, who headed an import firm and who had been in the service of the Abwehr since the 1930s, when he recruited the Brazilian-born German harbour master of Rio – Herbert von Heyer – who proved invaluable to Engel's network. Engels also recruited a similar agent in Recife where Allied ships bunkered and US planes were refuelled. Less effective than either of his colleagues was a Polish-born "German" by the name of Josef Starzicny who was, as a consequence, not as well paid as the other network controllers and could not attract good agents. He was incompetent, too, since his messages were written in such poor

ABOVE: Rio de Janeiro as shown in 1939. This is the federal district that housed the entire governmental apparatus of Brazil. Rio was also the centre, as was the rest of Brazil, of German espionage in Latin America.

English that the Hamburg Ast could not decipher them. But Starzicny lived well in a luxurious villa in Copacabana with his Brazilian mistress. The Abwehr warned their agent about this woman but he refused to part with her.

When the USA entered the war in 1941 Brazil became anti-Nazi, and by March 1942 all German agents, except for Engels and Kempter, had been swept up. Agents were arrested and tortured by the Brazilian Secret Police (Starcizny had kept too many notes and written records). Brazil actually declared war on Germany in August 1942, by which time the intelligence war in Latin America drew to an end, with only a few Abwehr pockets left across the vast continent. As with many other Nazi espionage operations, it had experienced both success and failure, though overall it must be regarded as rather amateurish. As such, it stood little chance once US counter-espionage activities commenced after December 1941.

Chapter 10

Other Services

I T SAYS SOMETHING FOR THE DIVIDED NATURE OF THE THIRD REICH that in addition to the enormous SD-Sipo and Abwehr organizations, there also existed a number of additional "agencies" operating in the same field. They ranged from the efficient F-Service (the Forschungsamt) which monitored Allied telephone conversations, and the B-Dienst, the Navy's deciphering section, to the more ineffectual INF III, an intelligence agency run by Ribbentrop's Foreign Office (the AA). The INF III had been established in April 1941 to rival the existing intelligence services of the SS and the Wehrmacht High Command, and to extend Ribbentrop's influence in Berlin's corridors of power. Under the leadership of Andor Hancke, the INF III was forbidden to engage in active espionage, but was to speed up the reporting of intelligence and sensitive information from the various embassies, legations and consulates. Hancke's agents were given diplomatic cover and recruited resident German businessmen or journalists in their respective countries to act as sub-agents. They also used the representatives or

LEFT: Ribbentrop, the archetypal Nazi, in the uniform of an honourary SS colonel. His close relationship with the SD did not stop the ambitious foreign minister from creating his own intelligence service.

the offices of German companies as cover for espionage activities.

In neutral Sweden the INF III agent was the German Legation's press attaché, Dr. Paul Grassmann, who had been in Sweden since 1933. He was a journalist who had sought to use the Swedish explorer Sven Hedin's international fame to keep the USA neutral in 1939.[1] Grassmann had also been part of the scheme to redirect the flow of international news into Sweden from British to German sources. A propaganda tool that proved successful throughout 1940–43. Grassmann was an avid attendant at the Swedish Foreign Office press conferences and newspaper gatherings, where he picked up intelligence of varying quality. One of his most important agents was Herbert Lickfett, the Swedish representative for the I.G. Farben chemical company. Lickfett had excellent sources within Swedish industry and from these contacts garnered plenty of intelligence on Allied production and industrial matters. I. G. Farben collaborated closely with the Abwehr's economic section. During 1936–37, the Germans worried about the Scandinavian countries and the possibility that they might ally themselves to France or Britain in the advent of war. Lickfett reassured the AA that there were no organizations in any of the Scandinavian countries that

ABOVE: *A mobile post van in wartime Berlin. These vans were often used as a useful cover for the Funkabwehr in its surveillance of enemy radio activity inside Germany, and in German-occupied territory.*

advocated arming or planning for war, or indeed supported cooperation with the West should a war break out. In Copenhagen, the German press attaché, Georg Duckwitz, was the INF III agent in Denmark. He had a good network working for him, including two Swedish ship owners, one resident in Bergen and the other in Gothenburg – who both kept their eyes and ears open for shipping intelligence. He also employed a rich titled lady who kept an eye on the Danish royal court. Duckwitz will be better remembered as the man who tipped off the Danish resistance movement about the Gestapo raid against the Danish Jews. As a result, the majority of Denmark's 6000 Jews escaped unscathed across the water to Sweden.

It is difficult to estimate the practical worth of INF III's intelligence gathering, since it only duplicated German efforts which would have been better handled by the Abwehr. The same can be said for the AO (Auslands Organization) representatives abroad, who were too conspicuous as local Nazi Germans to be credible agents or spies. In the Swedish city of Gothenburg, the AO representative had been instrumental in organizing a network throughout western Sweden, which no doubt kept a close eye on Allied agents and their Swedish sympathizers.

Intelligence organizations that overlapped in their responsibilities meant duplication of effort. On 4 September 1939 Josef Gottlob, an avid radioman and translator who had been working for the SD since 1937, was called into Walter Schellenberg's Berlin office to be told to set up the

SD's own enciphering service. Gottlob set up RSHA VI Section A6 – the Radio Observation Post – with himself, now promoted to major, in charge. The core of this organization was a group of Austrian cryptographers; specialist army officers who had been forced into German service after March 1938. They were led by Colonel Andreas Figl. Figl was highly experienced in the art of cryptanalysis, having founded the Imperial Austro-Hungarian Military Cipher Bureau in 1911, which had seen several major successes during the World War I. It was an SD officer, Dr. Albert Langer, who had first recruited Figl to serve the SD as its resident cipher expert. Despite this strong abundance of talent, the SD Radio Observation Post (RPO) was not a major success. Schellenberg distrusted Gottlob, who in turn proved an inept leader. Figl did not achieve the level of success expected of him, either. He only produced minor

BELOW: *Germany had an extensive telephone surveillance service, with stations scattered across Germany, such as this one, that monitored millions of calls every week.*

breakthroughs, cracking the ciphers of the neutral and smaller countries. In 1943 Gottlob was removed to the SD station in Madrid and the RPO, having failed to break any significant Allied ciphers, was employed in devising ciphers for the SD instead.

A Mountain of Effort, a Molehill of Intelligence

The postal censorship system was another surveillance service that proved overrated and which wasted the German intelligence effort. Until February 1944, German postal censorship was run by the Abwehr, after which it came under SD control. It employed thousands of workers and officials in 24 Telegraph and Postal Control Stations scattered across Greater Germany and Nazi-occupied Europe. The Control Station in Frankfurt-am-Main in November 1941, for example, employed 97 Abwehr officers, 120 officials and 2600 civilian censors. Frankfurt was the checking point for post between Germany and Switzerland and German-occupied France. The station checked through between 120,000 and 150,000 letters and telegrams per day, yielding mainly economic intelligence, such as a shortage of mercury in the USA, levels of Portuguese exports to Britain and British difficulties in getting hold of really good-quality hemp. By September 1944, the station had been reduced drastically as there were only 20,000 letters/telegrams arriving each day. The conclusion must be that these resources would have been better employed elsewhere, such as deciphering enemy messages.

During the 1930s, the Reichsposte not only ran the postal and telegraph services but the telephone system in Germany as well. Because the security of the system was of the utmost importance, the Reichsposte began to investigate the new electronic scrambling technology then in development. Kurt Vetterlein became the chief of this "research section", the Forschungsstelle, which worked in the huge brick Reichsposte building on Ringstrasse in Berlin. Vetterlein and his small staff concentrated on breaking into the scrambled radio telephone line across the Atlantic

The station chewed through between 120,000 and 150,000 letters and telegrams

to New York, but it was not until late 1940 that they made any progress.

Vetterlein found the perfect spot to eavesdrop on the Allied telephone conversations across the Atlantic: the north Dutch coastal resort of Noordwijk, where his staff moved to, occupying an entire youth hostel. Calls were intercepted by two rhombic antennae on the hostel's roof, which were then de-scrambled by specially built machines. By the autumn of 1941 these calls were being intercepted and recorded as they were being made. Most of the important ones, like the telephone calls between Anthony Eden, W. Averell Harriman (US Ambassador to Moscow) or Churchill with Roosevelt's advisor, Harry Hopkins, were relayed to Schellenberg in Berlin, who in turn, having "spiced them up", sent them to Hitler. Most of the intercepted traffic, however, was of a mundane kind, revealing some interesting facts of economic rather than political or military significance. The Allies realized the scrambler, which was used for fast communications, was insecure, and took steps to restrict the types of information sent over it. The conclusion, therefore, is that Vetterlein's operation was another massive waste of effort.

"Eyes in the Sky": Aerial Reconnaissance

As was mentioned earlier, World War I produced a most effective weapon of surveillance with the development of aircraft. During the inter-war period these flimsy machines became sturdier, faster, more reliable and increased their range and altitude. Their use for espionage work soon became apparent.

In 1930 a veteran aviator Theodor Rowehl became a paid agent of the Abwehr, and was given the task of using his Junkers W.34 aircraft to spy on Poland and other potential enemies of Germany. The W.34 had an operational ceiling of up to 12,700m (42,000ft), and proved so successful that Rowehl soon had a staff of expert pilots and five aeroplanes. His "Experimental Post for High Altitude Flights" became the Abwehr's "eyes in the sky", and flew missions over the USSR and Poland without being detected. In 1936,

Canaris agreed to transfer Rowehl to Göring's command, where Rowehl's new boss proved both generous and supportive. The "Special Purpose Squadron" operated under Luftwaffe intelligence and its chief, General Josef "Beppo" Schmid. However, Rowehl still consulted with Canaris about which targets were to be photographed. In addition to a squadron at Staaken, Schmid had an additional one established in Budapest to fly over the Balkans and Near East. Rowehl's squadron flew over the Sudetenland in 1938, giving the Germans very accurate intelligence about Czech defences, and in September 1939 the squadron did the same over Poland. These aerial photographs were instrumental in aiding the Wehrmacht's swift victory. By September 1939 Rowehl commanded three squadrons with 12 aircraft each. While his aerial reconnaissance won him praise during the Norwegian campaign of 1940, the OKH complained that similar efforts in France did not pay off as well, since Rowehl's pilots had only taken photographs of the frontier areas of eastern France.

The long-range aerial spies' finest hour came before and during the Russian campaign. In 1937, one of Rowehl's spy planes had been shot down over Russia, but the Kremlin did nothing but protest lamely about a violation of international treaties. The Soviets probably did not want to draw attention to the fact that they were conducting similar flights themselves. By 1940–41, Rowehl had 50 planes and some 300 personnel working for him. The planes were converted long-range bombers which had special equipment that pumped a mixture of oxygen and nitrate into the engines to improve their high-altitude performance. Each plane was equipped with three specially manufactured Zeiss cameras, each with a roll of film containing 180 exposures. One camera took vertical pictures while the other two, one to port, the other to starboard, took pictures at an angle. Once the planes landed the cameras were rushed to Oranienburg where the films were developed. The images were then handed over for analysis to expert evaluators using magnifying glasses and special optics. They could determine which shadows, smudges and strange forms on the photographs were of military interest. During late 1940 and early 1941, reconnaissance missions flying from bases at Kirkenes, Plovdiv, Bucharest and Cracow photographed the whole of western Russia in detail, revealing a wealth of useful intelligence for the invading forces.

BELOW: A German aerial surveillance aircraft engaged on a spying mission "somewhere in southern Europe", probably in the Mediterranean theatre.

ABOVE: A German aerial photograph of damaged Soviet aircraft lined up on an airfield near the frontier with German-occupied Poland during the early stages of Operation Barbarossa, July 1941.

From the middle of 1943, Germany's use of large-scale photographic reconnaissance went into decline. Rowehl resigned for personal reasons that December and his squadrons became "Bomber Wing 200", a conventional Luftwaffe unit. Another surveillance agency was thus wound up.

Although the AA's INF III intelligence service left something to be desired in terms of results, the same could not be said of the AA's interception or surveillance service: Pers Z. The strange name came from its cover title from 1936: the Personnel or Administration Office. It was led by Captain Curt Selchow, who had previously worked at the Imperial German Military Radio section during World War I. In 1933 Pers Z had a staff of 30. At its peak during the middle of the war it employed 300 staff, of whom 50 were cryptanalysts and the rest were administrative staff.

By 1939 the Pers Z had cracked the main diplomatic codes of some 34 countries, including all the main powers (Japan, France, Britain, USA, Italy) and Spain. Up to June 1940, the Pers Z concentrated its efforts on France and thereafter worked on Italy. It only devoted a tenth of its efforts on the USA prior to December 1941 and the attack on Pearl Harbor.

The ability to read American diplomatic traffic proved invaluable to the Germans. In 1940 the Pers Z had broken the main diplomatic code of the US State Department, which revealed some interesting intrigues on the part of the neutral Americans. Robert Murphy, special US envoy to French North Africa, had held talks with the French commander-in-chief in North Africa, General Maxime Weygand, where the Frenchman had asked for US military aid if he decided to break with Vichy and declare for de Gaulle. The Vichy Government, angered at Weygand's double-dealing and fearful of German reprisals should they not act, had the commander sacked and returned to France (where he was arrested by the SS and imprisoned until May 1945). The Pers Z also revealed through US State Department signals, that Roosevelt had given Stalin a generous offer of support against Hitler, on 8 October 1941. This offer was leaked to the German papers, who had a field day with this juicy piece of embarrassing "news". Despite this proof that the Germans, somehow, had access to confidential US diplomatic intelligence, the State Department chose not to change its codes.

The Pers Z also read Turkish diplomatic traffic, which was invaluable for several reasons. It had not been able to break the almost impenetrable Soviet diplomatic codes, which were of an exceptionally high quality and equivalent to their military ones. They were often produced on so-called one-time code pads, which meant they were written out and processed with a different code every time they were sent. Decoding them was time consuming and required a large staff of clerks to do the job. Only the USSR had the resources and patience for this kind of code making. It was the only state security conscious enough to introduce this as standard, and as a result its codes proved almost unbreakable. There were ways of circumventing this, however, which is where the Turks entered the picture. Turkey, having fought Russia on and off for over two centuries, had a good network of agents and sent only its most sophisticated diplomats and shrewdest officers to Moscow. They were therefore well informed about events in the USSR, and after 22 June 1941 were Germany's eyes and ears behind Soviet lines. The same was true of the Bulgarian Legation in Moscow.

The F-amt

Of all the surveillance or other intelligence services in the Third Reich, the most impressive was the Forschungsamt (Research Office) – F-amt – founded by Gottfried Schapper[2] in 1933 with the assistance and blessing of Hermann Göring, his old World War I comrade. Schapper had wanted to attach the F-amt to the office of the Reich Chancellery, but Hitler chafed at any single individual having a monopoly on intelligence which was channelled to him. Göring overcame Hitler's phobia, and at the same time extended his own intelligence powers by attaching the F-amt to his position as Prussian Minister of the Interior and head of the Luftwaffe. Göring repaid Schapper poorly by appointing Lieutenant-Commander Hans Schimpf to head the F-amt instead of him. But Göring probably found Schimpf easier to deal with, since he was a likeable and humourous man of a sunny disposition and an experienced naval cryptographer with Abwehr links. Perhaps Göring felt he was also more experienced than Schapper.

Whatever Göring's reasons for his appointment, the F-amt moved into the attic of the Reich Ministry of Air's building in Berlin. Its staff comprised only six men, including Schapper, with Schimpf in charge. By July 1933 its staff had risen to 20 employees: radio and telegraph surveillance staff, cryptographers and evaluators. The Defence Ministry, close by on Bendlerstrasse, had been tapping phones since 1925, so the Forschungsamt used these facilities and the Post Office censors as well. The F-amt was now quite adept at tapping phones, listening to radio messages and other forms of surveillance, giving Göring a powerful weapon against both domestic and foreign enemies. In 1934–35, the Forschungsamt, having grown in size, had to acquire an entire building block, the Schiller Colonnades (116–124 Schillerstrasse). There, former apartments were converted into offices while the massive basement room was occupied by some 50 teleprinter machines of the D1 section; the F-amt's transcription service. The F-amt stayed at the Schiller Colonnades until it was bombed out in 1944. Schimpf killed himself over an unhappy love affair in 1935, but Göring bypassed Schapper yet again by appointing the younger brother of one of his cronies: Prince Christopher von Hessen. Göring had a soft spot for noblemen, but Schapper did the real work, and it was during Hessen's absence on active service from 1939 that Schapper was in charge. He was formally appointed head of the Forschungsamt on Hessen's death in February 1944.

The F-amt

Schapper had to get Göring's formal approval to tap phones and the reich marshal looked at each individual case and either signed with a capital "G" if he approved, or an equally forceful "Nein" if he did not. By 1942, the F-amt had 15 phone-tapping stations throughout Greater Germany,[3] and the same number scattered across occupied Europe. In Germany it ran 500 permanent telephone taps and 500 more across the rest of Europe. The F-amt rented rooms, flats and even requisitioned space from Reichsposte offices. In Paris and Copenhagen it simply took over existing tapping services. At its height during 1943 the F-amt had 6000 employees, i.e. a thousand times the number of a decade earlier! Nothing could illustrate the frightening growth of the totalitarian state's surveillance of its own population and that of Europe.

The F-amt's radio surveillance service expanded from one single post at Beelitz, operated under the aegis of the Reichsposte, to seven stations in Greater Germany and five in the rest of German-occupied Europe. It concentrated on radio broadcasts, plus the radio transmissions of the major banks, merchant ships and firms involved

Bureau IV was very successful, since it broke three-quarters of all diplomatic codes

in large industrial projects. With the expansion of the Reich, F-amt set up another central station in Vienna. It required few staff; only mechanics to keep the printers running day and night copying all the telegraph, radio and transmitter traffic being monitored.

At the Berlin headquarters, the monitoring of telegram traffic needing translation fell under the responsibility of F-amt D2. This section had staff that translated telegrams in foreign languages from local telegram offices or post offices. Bureau IV, under Georg Schröder, meanwhile, dealt with messages in diplomatic codes. Schröder, something of mathematical genius, had a staff of 240 and a mass of Hollerith machines to intercept and decode the messages. The F-amt Bureau IV was very successful and broke three-quarters of all diplomatic codes used by the embassies and legations in Berlin. This enabled the bureau to read half of all the diplomatic messages leaving and entering Germany. During the war it read 3000 intercepts every month. It broke the higher diplomatic codes of France, Italy and Britain. In the British case this did not include the FO's highest code, nor indeed any of the Soviet ones save for those used by the Soviet arms industry.[4] Bureau IV was probably the most efficient of all the code-breaking institutions of the Third Reich.

Radio and Telegram Surveillance

Bureau III had to sift through the flood of information pouring into the F-amt and send what it could for evaluation on to Bureau V. The latter was divided into several branches to deal with this avalanche of intelligence. Branch 11 (Foreign Politics), for example, went through 2400 decrypted messages, 42,000 clear text ones, 11,000 broadcast transcripts, 150 newspapers and then, to top it all, the enormous Havas[5] and Reuters traffic every day. Bureau XII had to deal with 20,000 messages. Once this was done Bureau V's chief, Walter Siefert, had the unenviable task of compressing this oceanic tide of intelligence into some 60–150 reports. These were written on light brown paper (a quaint touch since

the Nazi Party's colour was brown), known as the Forschungsamt's Brown Sheets, which were distributed to the various ministries by courier.

Schapper, however, was not interested in exchanging intelligence with the young, pushy and aggressively ambitious Schellenberg, especially as the SD provided nothing in return for the F-amt's intelligence. Göring, though, could use the F-amt to spring nasty surprises on his domestic and foreign enemies. In the case of Ribbentrop, for example, he

ABOVE: Göring, shown here in 1933 before he grew bloated, was a cunning Nazi leader who had a unique intelligence source at his disposal in the Forschungsamt, which he put to good use against his enemies at home and abroad.

would withhold information, only to produce additional information during meetings with Hitler and leave Ribbentrop in a high state of nervous tension and impotent fury. During the Munich Crisis of 1938, the F-amt tapped the Prague-to-London

telephone cable to great effect. The F-amt intercepted a call from Czech President Eduard Benes to his ambassador in London, Jan Masaryk, stating that he and his government, whatever the British claimed, refused to yield one more inch of Czech territory to save Europe from war. Göring duly showed these transcripts with some glee to the British, which did not endear the Czechs to the British Government.

During the summer of 1939, the F-amt tapped all phones (including both private and office lines) belonging to prominent foreigners in Berlin, such as businessmen, journalists and diplomats. This yielded some important intelligence. For example, during the sham German negotiations with the Poles in 1939, the call from the Polish Government forbidding its Berlin ambassador, Josef Lipski, to negotiate in any fashion with the Germans, was recorded. This was then served up as good propaganda for domestic, if not foreign, consumption. During the war, important intelligence on the USSR, Iran, the Middle East and various neutral countries was secured through F-amt's tapping. However, Hitler and his cronies only took to heart what they wanted or chose to believe.

ABOVE: It was at the top of this building, the Luftwaffe HQ in Berlin, that Göring housed the Forschungsamt during its modest beginnings in 1933. It soon outgrew its cramped Luftwaffe quarters and had to move to a separate building.

This crippled even the efficient intelligence efforts of the Forschungsamt.

The B-Dienst

Few individuals were as important to the German intelligence effort as Wilhelm Tranow, the indefatigable head of the English section at the Germany Navy's Radio Monitoring Service, the Funkbeobachtungsdienst, better known as the B-Dienst for short. During World War II the B-Dienst was under the command of Captain Heinz Bonath. It was Tranow, however, as head of the most important section of the service, who was the man with the greatest and most important role of all the B-Dienst's officers.

By reconstructing the massive British Telegraph Code, Tranow, in 1936–37, became an uninvited but most interested observer of the Royal Navy's exercises in the Atlantic and of its operations along the Yangtze River in China. In addition, his colleague, Lothar Franke, broke all the three main French Navy codes and did the same with its exercises and operations. It was at this time that the service was christened B-Dienst, and it maintained a liaison officer with the Abwehr until 1938. During the lean years between 1928–33, this section of German Navy Intelligence was tiny and stationed in Kiel. It only moved back to Berlin with the rise of Hitler, who promptly made more resources available to the German Navy and the B-Dienst. In 1935, due to the Royal Navy's mistakes, Tranow managed to break not only the Naval Code but also the supposedly unbreakable Naval Cipher as well. In this way the B-Dienst could familiarize itself with the British Navy's phraseology, terms, definitions and codenames for ships and ports. B-Dienst's staff had increased from 30 in 1936 to three times that number in the summer of 1939, and by 1937 some 252,000 messages had been intercepted and decoded by 14 stations. The B-Dienst's total staff with these outstations numbered 500, with Tranow's English section taking the lion's share of both staff and resources. In 1940, in his forlorn quest for an alliance with Britain, Hitler forbade the B-Dienst to spy on the Royal Navy. Tranow, having spent years spying on Germany's most serious naval rival, was not going to stop at this important moment of the war. He ignored Hitler's order and continued, with the connivance of his superiors, to break the British codes.

Wilhelm Tranow's colleague, Lothar Franke, broke all three main French Navy codes

Early Results and Expansion

It was thanks to Tranow personally and his tireless staff that the German Navy knew the entire disposition of the Royal Navy at the outbreak of the war. On 11 September 1939, B-Dienst's English Section picked up radio messages that a convoy was being assembled in the Bristol Channel – *U-31* was sent to intercept it. Five days later *U-31* sank SS *Aviemore* and the deadly war of the Atlantic had begun, with the B-Dienst playing a decisive role in it. On 17 February 1940, the U-boat fleet sank two ships out of Oporto, Portugal, and on 30 August, again acting on B-Dienst intelligence, it sank five vessels of convoy SC 2 out of Canada. A seemingly deadly blow was struck at the B-Dienst when the Royal Navy, on 20 August 1940, changed its codes leaving the B-Dienst high and dry. But Tranow spurred on his section to break back into the British codes, and within seven weeks they had broken 850 code groups. By early 1941 the B-Dienst knew of 700 ship names and 1200 vocabulary words. By this time the B-Dienst, like the other services, had swollen in size. The B-Dienst now possessed 44 stations across Europe from Kirkenes in the Arctic North to Montpellier on the balmy shores of the Mediterranean. In the West lay the Brest station, so important to the war in the Atlantic, and in the East the station of Feodosia in the Crimea. In total a staff of 3900 staff manned these stations, and in Berlin alone were another 1100 staff members to man the B-Dienst's Main Office.

Breaking American codes

The entry of the USA into the war increased the service's workload, but also its flow of intelligence. US Navy codes provided few challenges up to April 1942, but then the Americans began using mechanical and electric ciphering machines. The B-Dienst was unable to break those ciphers but continued, despite frequent changes, to decipher Royal Navy codes. Another asset was the B-Dienst's breaking of the four-digit Anglo-American code, nicknamed "Frankfort", in March 1942. "Frankfort" yielded a rich harvest. On 30 October the B-Dienst alerted Dönitz to the SC 107 convoy out of Newfoundland. Dönitz sent in the wolfpack[6] and 15 British merchantmen were sunk. The Grand Admiral heaped well-deserved praise upon Tranow and the entire B-Dienst.

In late February 1943, the B-Dienst found out that two Allied convoys (SC 122 and HX 229) would leave New York harbour on 5 and 8 March, respectively. Dönitz collected an impressive wolfpack of 17 U-boats and ordered them to patrol off the American east coast in a vast semi-circle

formation, so that any vessel could be detected and destroyed. During a three-day battle between the convoy escorts and the wolfpack, SC 122 and HX 229, were savagely mauled by 44 U-boats from wolfpacks Sturmer, Dranger and Raubgraf – the greatest U-boat concentration achieved in the entire war. A total of 22 ships were lost. But tragic though the loss of merchant ships and their crews was, of ultimately greater significance was that throughout the entire battle, the U-boats had failed to sink or damage a single escort vessel, whilst seven of their own number had been damaged, with two U-boats being sunk later by Allied aircraft on their way back to base. Nevertheless, this huge loss of shipping shocked the Allies and made them wonder if they had not, after all, lost the Battle of the Atlantic to the U-boats. Determined to keep their supply lines to Britain open, the Americans poured their gigantic resources into the battle to crush the U-boat threat once and for all. Improved radar, faster cruisers, destroyers and minelayers, more and better depth charges, greater air surveillance and

LEFT: The U-boat "wolfpacks", ably assisted by the code breakers of the B-Dienst, almost succeeded in cutting Britain's precarious trans-Atlantic convoy lifeline.

the use of sonar soon turned the tide of battle. Hammer blow after hammer blow fell on Dönitz's U-boat fleet. The Allies changed the Frankfort code and Tranow's analysts were unable to break into it. In November 1943, Berlin was heavily bombed by the Allies and the B-Dienst's GHQ was hit – the service's invaluable records and archive went up in flames. The GHQ, or what remained of it, was moved to a small village outside Berlin. Further irreversible blows to the B-Dienst followed. The Royal Navy, finally concerned about its code security, began to use one-time pads, which made its code unbreakable. It also began to use a grid location system rather than coordinates of longitude and latitude. The B-Dienst was now blind and so were the U-boats at sea, whose efficiency declined drastically as a result. The B-Dienst lost its remaining staff to frontline duty. According to Dönitz, it had provided the German Navy with half of its operational intelligence. This was a truly remarkable record for the German intelligence services operating during World War II.

Chapter 11

The Secret War Within

"The Secret Service is a service of Gentlemen"[1]

W. Canaris (1939)

"You should not let yourself be lulled to sleep by him. Seeing the two of you together, one would take you for bosom friends. You won't get anywhere by handling him with kid gloves."[2]

R. Heydrich to Schellenberg in early 1942, on the latter's relations with Canaris.

THE NAZI INTELLIGENCE SERVICES SPENT MUCH OF THEIR TIME and energy in competition with one another. Inter-service rivalries were one of the ways Hitler kept control of organizations that ran his totalitarian state, and he encouraged it. This method of working assuaged Hitler's paranoia and reduced the risk of power blocs developing to rival the Nazi Party, but it also bred a climate of mutual suspicion and fear among those whose first priority should have been the fight against the Third Reich's external enemies. In the intelligence war, the great struggle as far as many in the German services were concerned was not the fight between Canaris' Abwehr and MI5 and the SIS under Menzies: it was the power struggle between the Abwehr and the SD-Sipo, with the Gestapo in tow. As the years went on and this rivalry grew more entrenched, it became indicative of a wider struggle, between the National Socialist regime and its foremost enemy within – the conservative Wehrmacht – about who was to control the future of Germany. By 1944 the SD-Sipo had won the battle against Canaris and the Abwehr, but at the cost of wrecking Germany's intelligence and espionage services. The same was

LEFT: Heydrich, the pupil and eventual enemy of Canaris. Both came to unpleasant ends: Heydrich at the hand of an Allied assassin and Canaris by the hands of the SS in 1945.

true of the SS and the Nazi Party's hollow victory over the Wehrmacht after the attempted coup in July 1944. Certainly the enemy within had been given a deadly blow, but the Nazi empire was already crumbling and rotting from the inside. By destroying the independence of the Wehrmacht and its intelligence branch, the Abwehr, the Nazis had only gained a Pyrrhic victory and hastened their own downfall.

Canaris and Heydrich had a most complicated and twisted relationship. It seems likely from his rapid and rather mysterious dismissal from the German Navy that Heydrich's subsequent entry into the SS and specialization in intelligence as chief of the SD was due in no small part to Canaris – his former mentor. What Canaris and his fellow conservative officers were hoping for, perhaps, was that Heydrich would stay loyal to their creed and act as an agent of influence within the new and sinister organization. Their calculations went disastrously wrong. Heydrich, whose loyalty was primarily self-serving, joined the SS with a sincere wish to further his own career under the protection of his new boss, Heinrich Himmler. What Canaris had created was in fact was a powerful new force in the world of German intelligence, that would become a deadly rival and threat to his own organization in pursuance of its own ends. Canaris and Heydrich had come to working arrangement in 1936 it was true, but such an arrangement only worked if both parties were straightforward about their intentions. Canaris may have been sincere about keeping the pact with the SD to divide intelligence responsibilities, but Heydrich continued to whittle away at the Abwehr, gathering evidence of its shortcomings, mistakes, dubious operations and even more dubious contacts and activities. It was obvious that Heydrich was determined, sooner or later, to carry out a coup against the Abwehr, with perhaps the ultimate aim of removing the admiral from his post.

Heydrich's Empire

Heydrich was many things, but he was no fool and was ruthlessly efficient and well organized in a state that was, thanks to Hitler's sloppiness and lack of trust, sometimes the very epitome of a disorganized chaos. Heydrich had never been a dedicated Nazi. He was something far worse: he was an amoral, ambitious careerist who would employ any method or crime to reach his goal. That is why Hitler made him Reich Protector of Bohemia-Moravia with instructions to get the Skoda, Brno and Plzen arms factories to produce maximum amounts of weapons. Heydrich, neither a racist nor a dedicated Nazi, had no time for ideological/racist nonsense if it stood in the way of results; results that would further his career. His ultimate goal was never in doubt: replace Himmler as head of the SS, after which the highest of ambitions – including perhaps leading the Third Reich itself – might have then been in his reach. The Protectorate was to be the proving ground. Heydrich improved work conditions and pay in the Czech factories, suppressed the general Nazi terror against the population, while at the same time stepping up successful measures to crush the resistance movement. He was successful on all fronts. The factories hummed with activity to the benefit of the German war effort, the population appreciated the new conditions and the resistance went into decline. In London, the Czech-exiled government decided that Heydrich had to be killed before he made the entire population a nation of Nazi collaborators.

Heydrich had no time for ideological/racist nonsense if it stood in the way of his career

The second reason why the Reich Protector needed to be liquidated was that he was also a threat to the Czech intelligence services' infiltration of, and contacts with, the Abwehr. Heydrich remained head of the SD and was a natural spymaster. He knew the expertly run Czech intelligence services had an agent, "Franta", high up in the Abwehr, but he did not know how high up. The only thing he knew was that this "traitor" had been supplying the Czechs with intelligence since 1936. Heydrich respected and liked the Czechs as Germanized Slavs, and he was sure that he could make them, in time, loyal members of Hitler's Greater Germany. But before that happened "Franta" had to be found and liquidated.

In the Czech resistance organization, the UVOD,[3] only Captain Vaclav Moravek knew "Franta's" real identity. His colleagues, Lieutenant-Colonels Masin and Balaban, did not. On Heydrich's orders the SD-Sipo were to find them, capture them alive and force them to reveal their agent's identity. The Gestapo stormed Masin's secret radio station. They caught Masin but Moravek climbed out of a window, and escaped by sliding down a 14m (45ft) aerial antenna. He lost a finger in the process, but made good his escape and warned London of events. Masin was not so lucky. Despite the Gestapo torture, the tough Czech colonel did not divulge any information to his tormentors and was later shot. On 22 March Moravek, together with other UVOD members, were discovered in a Prague park. They tried to escape but Moravek was shot dead.

Unmasking "Franta"

Nevertheless, Heydrich discovered, through other sources, that "Franta" was Paul Thümmel, a Saxon aristocrat and veteran Nazi Party member. But far more incriminating and threatening was Thümmel's position as the deputy chief of the Prague Ast, and the fact that he had powerful friends in Berlin. That meant a link to Canaris, which could possibly mean that the admiral had, at the very least, connived at these contacts. With enough evidence, or so he

ABOVE: (from left to right) Hans Frank, Himmler, Himmler's ADC Karl Wolff (a rival of Heydrich) and Heydrich in Prague in 1941 – a grand array of SS power in the Nazi state.

believed, Heydrich invited Canaris on 21 May 1942 to Hradcin Castle in Prague for "consultations". Heydrich did not mince his words: the Abwehr was a nest of traitors, conspirators and cowards. It had to be brought under the SD's control and purged of all treacherous elements. Canaris fiercely defended his organization and his operatives, including Thümmel, against any such accusations, and refused to place the Abwehr under Heydrich's command. The "consultations" must have deteriorated into a furious argument that probably left both men as bitter enemies. They had always been rivals, but now their struggle intensified and both were playing for the highest of stakes.

London had now decided to act and two Czech agents, Kubris and Gabcik, were dropped in Bohemia with orders to plan the assassination of Heydrich. That seemed an easy task since Heydrich, believing the Czechs would not dare to kill him, was driven round in his staff Mercedes only accompanied by his chauffeur, SS-Oberscharführer Klein. Heydrich, a complete fatalist, could never be accused of being a coward.

Gabcik and Kubris chose to kill Heydrich in Prague, at the Troja bridge, where the traffic usually ground to a halt. The early morning of 27 May 1942 was overcast and unsettled as Klein and Heydrich drove past. On an observer's signal Gabcik ran out in the street and opened fire with his Sten gun, but it jammed. Kubris, seeing this, lobbed a hand grenade into the car. Heydrich was wounded by the blast, and set off after his assailants with a drawn Luger, but managed only to stagger a few feet before collapsing. A tram filled with Czech commuters passed him but no one lifted a finger to aid the wounded man. Only when some constables came past was a cart requisitioned and the bleeding Heydrich taken to hospital. He later died of blood poisoning, unlamented by the Czechs and many Germans, on 4 June 1942, and was taken back to Berlin for a full state funeral.

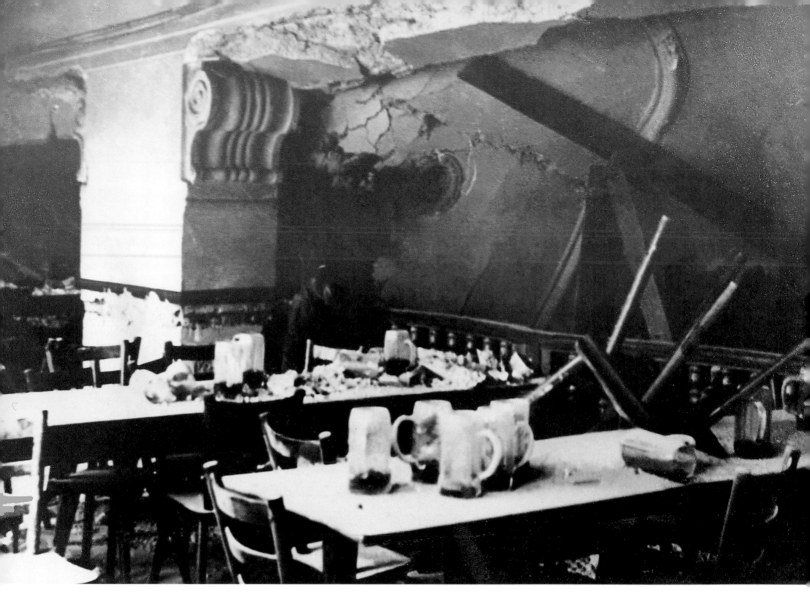

ABOVE: The scene at the Bürgerbräukeller after the assassination attempt by a communist, George Elser, in November 1939 against Hitler. The bomb killed seven Nazi Party members. Elser was shot by the SS in 1945.

Hitler sent Heinz Pannwitz, one of SS General Heinrich Müller's nasty young Gestapo henchmen, to investigate and punish those guilty of the assassination. Pannwitz lured one of the conspirators, Karel Curda, to betray Gabcik and Kubris for 10 million Czech Crowns (£125,000 or $600,000) – a colossal sum of money. The agents were holed up in an Orthodox church in Prague, and the building was stormed by the Waffen-SS. Gabcik and Kubris fought to the death. Frustrated that the perpetrators had alluded him, Pannwitz took his revenge on the village of Lidice and one other village (the assassins had links to both places), murdering up to 3000 innocent Czech civilians for the murder of Heydrich. Meanwhile, Heydrich had been given a state funeral. Canaris feigned sincerity when he said that Germany had lost a good and great man through a dastardly assassination. SS-General Sepp Dietrich was more blunt on hearing of Heydrich's death: "Thank God that sow is gone to the butchers." Canaris must have privately and

secretly shared the delight. His most deadly enemy was gone, the Abwehr's contacts with the Czechs had been saved, and his organization's existence secured – for a while.

There is a possibility that there was more to this opportune removal of a hated and odious figure, since Heydrich's most deadly and sworn enemies were not among the ranks of the Czechs, but the Germans. After the unpleasant meeting at Hradcin Castle in Prague a few days before Heydrich's assassination, Canaris must have known that the Abwehr's days were numbered unless he took drastic action. The admiral may have been willing to collaborate with the Czechs to destroy Heydrich, or at least act as a sleeping partner and make it clear to the Czechs that the

Abwehr would not look too hard into the resistance's doings, and was willing to tell them as much as they could about Heydrich's routines.

It may also be uncoincidental that by the autumn of 1942 Canaris had put out very delicate and cautious feelers to the British SIS about cooperation against the Nazi regime. Canaris even proposed, through his Spanish contacts who had good channels to London, that he meet with Menzies in some neutral country of the SIS chief's choosing. Neither Donovan of the OSS nor Menzies followed the official Allied line of stonewalling and cold shouldering the German resistance and its representatives. Donovan had, after all, given Allen Dulles a brief to welcome such contacts in order to find out what was going on behind the scenes in Germany. Menzies believed that such a meeting was of great importance, and that collaboration with the Abwehr had much to offer. A true spy chief does not have any scruples, nor can he afford the luxury of discarding the most improbable schemes. The British Government, however, told Menzies to ignore Canaris' approach and the Foreign Office, the SIS's formal master, vetoed the idea for fear of offending the Soviets. Hugh Trevor Roper, one of Menzies' subordinates, was all for dealing with the Abwehr if for no other purpose than finding out what the German intelligence services were up to. But his superior, Kim Philby, opposed any collaboration between the SIS and Abwehr. After all, it would not serve the purposes of his real master: Stalin.

The Abwehr's Role in German Resistance

What could not have been made of such a partnership? The German Widerstand (resistance movement) was more widespread than anyone at the time could have managed, but what it gained in size was cancelled out by its ineptness and inaction.

The Abwehr was one of the main centres of the German Widerstand movement. Canaris lent his support both to it and to his subordinates' intrigues, especially the openly Nazi-hating Colonel Hans Oster and his deputy, Hans von Moltke. The latter was the main Abwehr contact of the Widerstand

Hitler wanted to invade Czechoslovakia but the German Army was against it

abroad and it was he, in a letter to his English friend, Lionel Curtis, in March 1943, who put their endeavours in context: "People outside Germany do not realize the handicaps under which we labour and which distinguish the position in Germany from that of any other of the occupied countries: lack of unity, lack of men, lack of communications."[4]

Seeking Foreign Help

During mid-August 1938, Edwald von Kleist met the young Berlin correspondent of the London *Morning Post*, Duncan Colvin, for talks at the Casino Club in the Bendlerstrasse: the nerve centre of conservative establishment Germany. Kleist was quite open with Colvin, telling him that Hitler wanted to invade Czechoslovakia but that the German Army was against it. General Ludwig Beck had told Kleist to tell Colvin that any failure by Britain to make a determined stance against Hitler would only mean one thing: war. During the subsequent Munich crisis (in late 1938) Major Gerhard von Schwerin had told his friend and British contact, Kenneth Strong, the Assistant British military attaché in Berlin, that the accord Neville Chamberlain had signed with Hitler was not worth the paper it was written on. Britain, argued Schwerin, needed to make a tough stance against Hitler or see the whole of Europe engulfed in war. On 23 April 1939, British Prime Minister Neville Chamberlain introduced peacetime conscription. At the same time Fabian von Schlabrendorff, sponsored by Canaris, had meetings in London with several Conservative Party backbenchers, including Winston Churchill. He had to admit that there was little hope of a German coup against Hitler succeeding. His visit was kept secret, but a senior Foreign Office official, Frank Roberts, noted with some contempt that the German resistance expected Britain to save them from Hitler. Schwerin was also in London in the spring of 1939 and saw some very prominent British people, including Director of Naval Intelligence Admiral Godfrey, through whom he urged the British to talk tough with Hitler. When

he returned to Berlin he was promptly dismissed from the Abwehr by Field Marshal Keitel for over-stepping his brief and talking politics with British intelligence. In late May 1939 Hans Robinsohn, one of the leaders of the October Third Club (Hamburg),[5] also had meetings with the SIS in London.

All these groups and approaches to the British had two things in common. Firstly, Canaris and the Abwehr were involved in one way or the other either protecting or encouraging them. This is without doubt. But the other undeniable fact is that there was a lot of talk and very few results from all this activity. Canaris was not, however, the instigator or leader of these plots and remained in the background. During 1938 and 1939 some of the military planned to assassinate Hitler, but nothing came of these plans. The plans of 1938 foundered because there was no war and the conspirators felt very demoralized that the British had remained inactive. During the autumn of 1939 there was an attempt on Hitler's life at the Bürgerbräukeller in Munich on 6 November by a communist named Georg Elser. Army plans were then thwarted by the SS who stepped up its security measures around Hitler. During the first years of the war Canaris was too busy with other matters to see the conspiracies through to their logical conclusion, i.e. the death or overthrow of Hitler. But his previous plots would come back to haunt him.

ABOVE: The folly of driving in an occupied country in an open-topped vehicle. The remains of Heydrich's car after the Czech hit squad had thrown a hand grenade into the back seat, fatally wounding the Reich Protector.

The real surprise regarding Canaris is not that he fell from grace in early 1944, but that he was not removed from his position much earlier, given his opposition to Hitler and involvement in various plots against the Führer. It was claimed that the Gestapo and SD had accumulated some 10 volumes dealing the wrongdoings of the Abwehr and its delinquent chief. It was claimed that Canaris saved his skin by being in possession of intimate and highly damaging secrets about both Himmler and Heydrich. This may have been true, but while Heydrich could not wait to liquidate the "little admiral", Himmler was hesitant. His decision seems at first puzzling since SS power would have been increased by the elimination of Canaris. Himmler had, however, his own very secret reasons for not wanting to crush the head of the Abwehr. He too, despite his nickname of "Loyal Heinrich", was in fact an ambitious and complex character.

In the autumn of 1942 came a series of events that began the process which unravelled the whole intricate web of intrigue and conspiracy that surrounded Canaris. The Devil is in the details, it is claimed, and the smallest detail can lead to the fall of the mightiest. In Canaris' case it was the Abwehr's failure to support one of its agents and his generosity towards the persecuted. When a currency fraud was being investigated in Prague, the Gestapo rounded up a number of suspects, one of whom divulged that the Abwehr was involved. It was well known that the Abwehr financed many of its operations with black market trading, especially with currency transactions since it was in need of genuine currency in addition to the counterfeits it used. The acting Portuguese Consul in Munich, Wilhelm Schmidhuber, who was also an Abwehr agent, was arrested by the Gestapo on suspicion of being the ringleader of this currency scam. He was arrested in October 1942 and the Abwehr failed to step in and save him. Unfortunately Schmidhuber knew far too much for the Abwehr to treat his fate with such nonchalance. Schmidhuber had helped a number of Jews to escape (he worked under the part-Jewish Hans von Dohnanyi, who had used Abwehr funds to help Jews escape from German-occupied Europe). Even without "intensive interrogation" Schmidhuber talked, and the more he told the worse it looked for Canaris. And worse was to follow.

Canaris pointed out that he would hardly remove a loyal Abwehr man for doing his job

Torch – Intelligence Failure

In November 1942, a large invasion fleet landed an Anglo-American army on the coast of North Africa in Operation Torch. General Alfred Jodl had believed that the Allied invasion force was aimed at French West Africa (Senegal) or even Malta, but not Morocco and Algeria. When the landing did take place in November 1942 – a month after Schmidhuber's arrest – the Germans, including Hitler, were taken completely by surprise. Captain Herman Wichman, chief of the Hamburg Ast, had discovered the true destination of Torch but his message to the OKW via Tirpitz Ufer had somehow got lost on its way. Jodl was certain who was to blame when he claimed, in ominous terms, that "once again Canaris has let us down through his irrationality and instability".[6] Once praised for his work, Canaris and his intelligence network increasingly became a scapegoat for Germany's deteriorating military situation. Canaris and other conspiratorial officers were urged by supporters that it was time to stop talking and begin to act before it was too late. Canaris began to feel the heat and wanted, most uncharacteristically, to have Schmidhuber assassinated to shut him up. Emil Bonhöffer, a senior member of the Widerstand, and Hans von Dohnanyi, were horrified at such talk from the one German leader who abhorred such activities. But it reflected Canaris' increasing problems and fears for the Abwehr's security.

Canaris Under Pressure

In February 1943, a sour-faced Kaltenbrunner called at Tirpitz Ufer to scold Canaris about another failing link in the Abwehr chain. Kaltenbrunner claimed that the Vienna Ast chief, Count Marogna-Rewitz, was in touch with Anglophile political groups in Admiral Horthy's Hungary. He deserved not only to be removed from his post for this obvious treason, but also investigated and punished as swiftly as possible. Canaris would not listen to this SS nonsense, and sarcastically pointed out that he would hardly remove a competent and loyal Abwehr man for doing his job. The whole point of intelligence, the admiral pointed out to the tall SS chief, was to be in touch with everyone in order to gather as much information and intelligence as possible, especially about the enemy's intentions. Kaltenbrunner was not pleased with the dressing down, especially as his own claims in the field of intelligence work were particularly weak. Once Kaltenbrunner had left, Canaris ordered his subordinate Oster to begin the destruction of all incriminating documents from the files at Tirpitz Ufer and Zossen, HQ "Zeppelin". Many of these files not only contained documents on the Widerstand movement, but also contained evidence that could be used in the prosecution of Nazi leaders once their regime had been overthrown. The documents could seal the fates of senior Abwehr personnel if they were discovered

LEFT: *A high-ranking SS officer (centre) shows Himmler (left) and the SD/RSHA chief Ernst Kaltenbrunner (right) around Mauthausen concentration camp. Kaltenbrunner was hanged by the Allies in October 1946.*

by the Nazis. Unfortunately for the Abwehr, Canaris' order to destroy this incriminating material was to come too late.

Manfred Röder, who had investigated and prosecuted the Red Orchestra agents,[7] presented himself at Tirpitz Ufer on 5 April 1943, with an arrest warrant for Hans von Dohnanyi. It was the first, but not the last, time the Gestapo would dare to invade the Abwehr's headquarters. Röder was up the stairs and down the narrow corridors before anyone could warn Dohnanyi that the Gestapo prosecutor – truly a man to be feared – was heading towards his office. Dohnanyi was taken unawares as Röder and his assistant, the stony faced Captain Franz Sonderegger, walked into his office. Oster entered Dohnanyi's office telling Röder that if his subordinate, Dohnanyi, was guilty of anything then they should arrest him as well. Dohnanyi wanted to present the files on the Widerstand as deliberate disinformation that would be fed to the enemy. Unfortunately, Oster misunderstood Dohnanyi's signals, panicked and ended up trying to conceal documents. The hawk-eyed Sonderegger saw what Oster was up to and reported what he had seen to Röder. Dohnanyi ended up in Sachsenhausen concentration camp, where he died, while Oster was forced to leave the Abwehr in late 1943 – he retired to his sister's estates at Schnalitz.

The Gestapo Closes In

One document that Dohnanyi had drawn up was the X-Report of the talks between Dr. Josef Müller, Abwehr lieutenant, and the Abwehr's special contact with the Vatican back in 1939–40. Müller and his Papal contact, Father Lieber, had wanted Dohnanyi to destroy the document, but the latter had wanted to keep the report for posterity. On 22 September 1944 the Gestapo raided Zossen and found among numerous papers the X-Report. Dr. Müller was given a one-way ticket to one of the Nazis death camps because of Dohnanyi's wretched report. Müller had in fact already been arrested by the Gestapo on the

Conclusion

ALL THE INTELLIGENCE SERVICES OF WORLD WAR II had their share of spectacular successes and failures, none more so than the German ones. However, taken as an overall assessment of those services, the Abwehr and SD must be rated, objectively, as failures for several reasons. Firstly, their counter-intelligence system failed to root out and destroy many enemy spy rings in occupied and neutral Europe, despite the enormous efforts made on the German side. Prime examples of this failure are the successes of the Red Orchestra and Red Three. The Orchestra was able to operate deep inside the Reich and inside the heart of German-occupied Europe for well over a year before it was exposed and destroyed. Both the SD and Abwehr counter-intelligence officers involved in the Soviet agents' detection made some very clumsy and elementary mistakes. The Orchestra's exposure had as much to do with Moscow's mistakes as with the Abwehr and SD's persistence. The Red Three, despite German penetration of Switzerland, were never caught and liquidated by the Germans. Instead, it was the Swiss who had to deal with this Soviet spy ring, and then only after the damage to the German position on the Eastern Front had been done. Similarly, German espionage efforts abroad were compromised by incompetence and amateurish clumsiness, especially the Abwehr's efforts to penetrate Britain, which spectacularly backfired when the Germans came to believe and act upon the information being fed them by SIS double agents. The German failures to meet and counteract the invasions of North Africa, Italy and France had much to do with faulty intelligence and disinformation provided by deep-penetration double agents in the pay of the enemy.

How could these poor results have come about? The most important reason was the dismantling of

ABOVE: *Adolf Hitler, the head of the Nazi state. His failure to impose unity and order within the German intelligence community contributed to his eventual defeat.*

Germany's intelligence services after World War I, which forced the Abwehr to rebuild itself during the inter-war years while its main opponents (France, Britain, Poland and the USSR) could simply continue their intelligence work as before. When Canaris

ABOVE: *Canaris (second from left) and Heydrich (third from left) had an uneasy relationship, though initially the admiral had been a sponsor of the young Reinhard.*

arrived at the Tirpitz Ufer in 1935, Germany's enemies were well ahead of her in the intelligence field, and despite the admiral's best efforts the gap was never closed. In fact, as time went by the gap widened rather than narrowed. Another key factor in Germany's intelligence failure was the constant division of effort and constant infighting between the SD, Abwehr and the other services that operated in Nazi Germany. The German intelligence services should have been united, serving a common purpose and with a greater demand for efficiency than was the case in the governmental chaos that was the Third Reich. Ultimately the responsibility for this shambles can only rest with Adolf Hitler, who unlike the Allied leaders had neither a knack nor an understanding for intelligence work. His deliberate creation and fostering of the SD as a separate Nazi intelligence service was a deeply flawed mistake and a wasted effort. His failure to impose unity and order in the intelligence services go a long way to explain his eventual defeat.

By contrast, General Reinhard Gehlen's outstanding intelligence service on the Eastern Front, the FHO, was an example of what could be achieved when there was a talented, utterly dedicated, efficient and apolitical leader at the helm of a streamlined intelligence service. Despite smaller resources than either the SD or Abwehr, Gehlen produced impressive results when it came to general flows of information, sabotage operations and agent infiltration, even though his Soviet target was one of the best-guarded and security conscious state on the face of the earth. Otto Skorzeny's bloodless and brilliantly executed operations also showed the potential of the German intelligence services, and the work of the Brandenburgers was also impressive.

The realities of Hitler's spectacular personal weaknesses, however, coupled with the general rotten state of the Third Reich, meant that Gehlen's, as well as the senior intelligence services' successes, were entirely wasted. Like Stalin, Hitler only wanted to listen to and make use of intelligence that confirmed his own preconceptions and prejudices. That is no way to conduct a war and even less the actions of a man determined to win a war. For all its vaunted reputation for ruthlessness and Teutonic efficiency, the Third Reich was in intelligence terms a creaking, poorly captained old vessel that leaked from every side. It was riddled with traitors, informers and double agents of the enemy who were more than willing to work against the hated Nazi regime. Heroes or villains, these agents inside the Third Reich did contribute greatly to the Allied victory over Hitler, and perhaps we should be grateful for their assistance.

Footnotes

INTRODUCTION
1 Means "slipshod" or sloppy in south German or Austrian.

CHAPTER 1
1 Philip Knightley, *The Second Oldest Profession*, p1.
2 Joseph E. Persico, *Roosevelt's Secret War*, p95.
3 By 1914 some 170 million to Germany's 65 million.
4 Amazingly they were to repeat this mistake, again, in 1939–40 by building the Maginot Line and deploying a third of their over-stretched field army in these forts.
5 Alfred von Tirpitz (1849–1930), Imperial Minister of Marine 1897–1916. Forced to resign in 1916 because of his advocacy of unrestricted submarine warfare that would inevitably bring in the USA into the war.
6 As we saw earlier, the ND had posted officers to each major port in Britain
7 See P. Knightley, who, like many modern writers out to denigrate the importance of the intelligence services and the value of intelligence to national security, has down-played these fears. These fears, however, were based on fact and the ND was not, as Knightley seems to claim, some small and unprofessional shoestring operation but a formidable and valued section of the total German war effort.
8 This is one of the main arguments in Thomas Pakenham's *The Boer War* (London, Cardinal, 1991). A shortcoming the British were willing to remedy since they had no wish for a repeat of the Boer War.
9 Was this the germ that grew into MI5's double-cross system during the next war?
10 Born in 1859, Cumming was forced to leave active duty due to an unhappy tendency of being violently seasick as soon as he stepped on a ship and had become, by 1909, instead the head of SIS (MI6), which was under FO control and whose headquarters were housed on Northumberland Avenue in London.
11 Mata Hari continues to fascinate, and the discussion whether she was a spy or not rages on. Personally, I feel she was probably a French double agent in the making (as she had volunteered her services to the French) and that she was shot simply to silence her. Dead agents, especially double agents, tell no embarrassing tales.
12 The civilian who found the balloon would answer the questionnaire and then, when the wind conditions were right, would float it back across the frontline.

CHAPTER 2
1 Mikael Rosquist, *Spionage i Sverige* (Stockholm, 1988), p7.
2 Abwehr means defence, which sounded better than Secret Service (Nachrichtendienst) as in the old days of the Kaiser.
3 L. Farago, *The Game of the Foxes*, p5.
4 Oshima was so pro-German that the Japanese Foreign Office jokingly referred to him as the German Ambassador in Berlin.
5 Soviet Authority for "Corrective" Labour.
6 People's Commissariat of State Security.
7 See chapter 7.
8 Dimitrov eventually became the communist dictator of Bulgaria. His companions were not so lucky as they were expendable, and ended up in a Siberian death camp.
9 He was a Baltic German nobleman born in Latvia.
10 P. Leverkuehn, *German Military Intelligence*, p77.

11 Poznan, West Prussia and Upper Silesia, while the port city of Danzig (Gdansk) was made into an international city under the control of the League of Nations.
12 This is my personal abbreviation used for convenience.
13 Hitler was merciless with enemy spies. For an example see Chapter 7.
14 Hated no doubt because the Czech state was dominated by Slavs where Germans were the underdogs. That Czechoslovakia was democratic, prosperous and an ally of the USSR did not make the Czechs any more popular with Berlin.
15 W. Schellenberg, *The Schellenberg Memoirs*, p56.
16 The KdP represented the German minority in Slovakia.

CHAPTER 3
1 N. West, *MI6*, p1.
2 C. Whiting, *Hitler's Secret War*, pxi.
3 Sir Mansfield Cumming (1918–23) and Admiral Hugh Sinclair (1924–38).
4 R. Manvell & H. Fränkel, *The Canaris Conspiracy*, p25.
5 C. Whiting, *Hitler's Secret War*, p.xii.
6 There seem to be a good reason to accept the allegation that Canaris, who was a married man with two daughters, was a predatory and practising homosexual with one known affair – with the Italian SIM chief, General Amé's chauffeur – and possibly others. But this diversion from the norm of ordinary society seems to be nothing unusual among spies, who have their above-average quotas of homosexuals, perverts, nymphomaniacs, sexual deviants of all sorts and sex maniacs among their ranks. If you didn't belong to one of the above categories and you were a spy, then there was something decidedly "fishy" about you. Sex has always been a weapon and a shield for agents of either sex.
7 H. Woodhead, *The Third Reich: The Shadow War*, p4.
8 During the seventeenth and eighteenth centuries Prussia invited French Hugenots (Protestants), Dutchmen, Italians and Jews to settle in their thinly populated and backward state to improve the economy.
9 Canaris had contracted a milder form of malaria in South America, hence his loss of weight.
10 It was claimed later that Canaris had killed the monk but this seems out of character.
11 Padfield, *Himmler*, p.111.
12 Göbbels loathed his small stature, swarthy Latin looks, clubfoot and generally less than handsome figure.
13 There is no proof who Hitler's paternal grandfather really was, as Alois Hitler, his father, was born out of wedlock. Himmler's actions were also strange.
14 See Chapter 11.
15 It was claimed that Heydrich had several affairs at the same time, and that his dismissal from the navy rankled with him for the rest of his life. A careless officer who spoke out of place about the Deputy SS-Reichsführer's dismissal found himself on his way to a KZ camp.
16 See Chapter 7 for details of Gehlen's spy organization on the Eastern Front, the FHO (Fremde Heere Ost), from early 1942.
17 Heydrich's wife, Lisa von Osten, was viewed as a bad influence upon him while Erika Canaris was a good one upon the admiral.

CHAPTER 4

1 See Chapter 1 for the pre-war intelligence war between Poland and Germany.

2 KZ (Konzentrationslager): Concentration Camp.

3 In late November Stalin staged a similar incident at Mainila on the Russo-Finnish frontier, where the Finns were treacherously accused of firing on a Soviet border post as a justification for the unprovoked invasion of Finland.

4 PIS: Polish Intelligence Service. This is my shorthand name and not one that was commonly used, like SIS or NKVD.

5 The Greater Dortmund area had therefore a population larger than that of Norway in 1939, or about three million.

6 W. Schellenberg, *Memoirs*, p81. His remarks were prophetic and made quite an impression upon Schellenberg. All Germans feared that this unjustified war would be lost and rebound badly upon Germany.

7 Finland was a Grand Duchy in personal union with Imperial Russia through the tsar. The Whites were led by the legendary Field Marshal (then General) Count Gustav Mannerheim. The victory prevented Finland from being incorporated into Lenin's Soviet Federal Russian State in 1918. Iceland was under Danish rule and only became an independent republic in 1944. Norway and Sweden had been in union until 1905 when Norway, unilaterally, declared its independence. These two states and Denmark were monarchies.

8 See Christer Jörgensen and Chris Mann, *Hitler's Arctic War*. (New York, St. Martin's Press, 2002) for details of the war in the North (1939–45).

9 See Chapter 5 on the adventures of Jeff and Mutt – the Norwegian double agents in Britain.

10 *Norsk National Socialists Parti* – a small Norwegian Nazi party quite separate from Quisling's NS (*Nasjonal Samling*).

11 Kempf was born in 1904. He was a shipping inspector for the Hugo Stinnes Shipping Line, and a Luftwaffe pilot during the Polish campaign. He arrived in Germany in October 1939 and was involved in the *Altmark* incident that triggered Hitler's invasion of Norway. Kempf was head of Abwehr I M in Oslo 1939–42.

12 His reports.

13 Overvåkningpolitiet.

14 He was an Austrian socialist refugee who had second thoughts and willingly became one of Benecke's main agents.

15 All attributes of a good female agent.

16 These operations against the Netherlands are examined in Chapter 8 on "Special Operations".

17 Rönne was accused of withholding intelligence on Allied intentions prior to D-Day.

CHAPTER 5

1 C. Whiting, *Hitler's Secret War*, p143.

2 P. Fleming, Operation Sea Lion, p177.

3 The famous Bürgerbräukeller.

4 Another suspicious fact was that Hitler, who would ramble on in his speeches, cut this one short and left early for an urgent "appointment" in Berlin.

5 British Union of Fascists.

6 Italy was still outside the war and remained officially "non-belligerent" until June 1940

7 P. Fleming, *Operation Sea Lion*, p178. Hitler made the remarks in October 1941 but they applied even more accurately, given Sea Lion, to the year before.

8 We have no way of knowing whether these facts about this "Mata Hari" are factual.

9 It seems that the idea worked. Mussolini's foreign minister, Count Ciano, was a frequent customer and probably revealed his real views of the Germans, of whom he was not overly fond. Heydrich had met the buxom redhead Kitty while out on one of his late-night excursions on the prowl for some sex. He immediately took a shine to Kitty, whom he made the Brothel Mama.

10 Vera, with her blue eyes and jet-black hair, did not look much like a typical Norwegian and the spelling of her name was Swedish not Norwegian. Furthermore Mrs Erikson – a German widow once married to a Swede – could hardly pass off as the woman's aunt.

11 Popov almost immediately reported this to the SIS station chief in Belgrade and offered to become a double agent for the SIS (MI6).

12 G. Peis, *The Mirror of Deception*, p175.

13 Some claim he was a Swedish-speaking Finn.

CHAPTER 6

1 There are four language groups in Switzerland: the Germans, French, Italians and in the southeast corner of the country the Roman-speaking population. The Germans, by virtue of numbers and economy, have been the dominant group in the multilingual and divided country, which is a federal state from necessity.

2 See Chapter 5.

3 My own shorthand abbreviation, not used at the time.

4 *Bureau Ha* was officially Section NS1 of the SAI, but the *Ha* was answerable to Guisan only and not part of the SAI. Its headquarters was Villa Steig in the pleasant suburb of Kastanienbaum, outside Lucerne.

5 This was probably General Ludwig Beck or Colonel Hans Oster of the Abwehr.

6 Soviet Military Intelligence.

7 Hitler's chief Nazi ideologist.

8 This group of Ic officers was to prove a determined group of anti-Hitler conspirators, and was behind the bomb plot attempt on Hitler in early 1943.

9 See Chapter 6.

10 *Servizio Italiana Militare* or Italian Military Intelligence

11 V.E. Tarrant, *The Red Orchestra*, p187.

12 P. Grose, *Gentleman Spy*, p188.

13 Means "Father of the Turks".

14 Papen, quite rightly, viewed Ribbentrop as a parvenu phoney who cheated and lied his way to the top.

15 Moyzisch was in fact part Jewish but accepted into the SD.

16 Operation Bernhard had been launched by the SD to forge British five-pound notes on an industrial scale in order to wreck the financial system of Britain.

17 See Chapter 5.

CHAPTER 7

1 The NKVD had a far more pervasive grip on every aspect of life in the USSR, where the totalitarian state had been "perfected" in all its majestic horror – this was not achieved in Hitler's Germany until after June 1944 – and where the state controlled the economy. Cover companies and trading could not be conducted in the USSR by German spies like their Soviet adversaries, such as Leopold Trepper, could in Nazi-occupied Europe.

2 Typical of this is the existence of three separate German military intelligence services – the Abwehr, the FHW (under General Liss) and FHO (under Colonel Kinzel) – when one was more than enough, and that should have been the Abwehr but headed by Gehlen and not Canaris.

3 K. Strong, *Men of Intelligence*, p94.

4 Two persuasive yet unfounded lies were spread by Moscow to justify this unprovoked aggression. One was that it would provide the USSR with additional defensive territory and the other, an even more preposterous lie, that the Soviets had popular support for "incorporating" the Baltic states into the Soviet Union. The German invasion exposed these claims as the lies they were – Army Group North sliced through the region in a matter of weeks, and the supposedly pro-Soviet population greeted the Germans as

liberators. This says something about the oppression Stalin's vicious rule brought to these states, as the Germans were not usually very popular otherwise with the Baltic peoples.

5 Soviet Secret Police – People's Commissariat of State Security – see glossary for details of name in Russian.

6 The Lithuanian President Smetonas had managed to escape to Germany while Konstantin Päts (Estonia) and Latvia's Ulmanis were sent to Siberia.

7 Short for Estonian Nationalist Insurgency Army.

8 Harrison E. Salisbury, *The 900 Days*, (p.221) called the Estonian nationalists "traitors, Nazi sympathisers, cowards and panic mongers" for not supporting their brutal and bloodthirsty Soviet occupiers against the Germans. No doubt had Salisbury written his book now his views would have been quite different, in the light of Estonia's independence in 1991 and the revelations about the Soviet occupation.

9 Leader of the Cossack Host.

10 After the disbanding of the Nightingale commandos Skonprynka simply joined the UPA inside the Ukraine, where Bandera's men ended up fighting both their now German occupiers and the Soviet partisans alike. Skonprynka was killed in action against regular Soviet Army and NKGB troops outside Kiev in 1951.

11 P. Leverkuehn, *German Military Intelligence*, p166.

12 Hitler should have reflected upon the British setbacks at the hands of "niggers', i.e. the Zulus and Ashanti, and the Italian debacle in 1896 at the hands of the Ethiopians at Adowa (Adua). Even so-called primitive peoples could humiliate the Europeans.

13 Stavka: title of the Imperial Russian Army's General Staff and later that of the Red Army.

14 A Soviet Front was the equivalent to a German Army Group.

15 All the communist leaders, like the agents they were, had cover names. Leon Bronstein "Trotsky", Vlamdir Uljanov "Lenin" (the man from Lena), Josef Vissarionovitch Djugashvili – the man of steel – "Stalin", and so forth.

16 Gosplan was the authority that drew up the Soviet Union's five-year plans.

17 General Andrei Vlasov, commander of the Soviet Second Shock Army, had been captured on 13 July 1942 at Volkhov when Stalin's offensive to relieve Leningrad failed. Vlasov agreed to collaborate with the Germans and set up the Russian Liberation Army (ROA), which sought to gain Russian support against the communist regime.

18 The Communist Party of the Soviet Union, or CPSU for short.

19 He had a wife and two children.

20 Supreme Military Council.

21 RNNA – *Russkaia Natsionalnaia Narodnaia Armia*.

22 Derived from the name of a Muslim warlord who fought the Russian conquest of the Caucasus in the nineteenth century.

23 His firm, "Riepert Imports and Exports', set up office at 192 Rue Royale and its neighbour was Simexco, a reputable firm according to Piepe's German sources.

24 German Secret Field Police.

25 Organization Todt: a construction corps set up to assist the Wehrmacht in various building projects.

26 A "cobbler" produced "shoes" (false documents).

27 With the coming of Hitler the GRU was forced to move its operations from Berlin to the Netherlands and Paris instead.

28 KPD (German Communist Party – Kommunistische Partei Deutschlands).

29 Communist International – centred in Moscow to spread a world revolution.

30 The Abwehr called a ring or apparat (GRU term) an orchestra, with a conductor (leader), pianists (radiomen) and the players (the spies). The name Red Orchestra (Die Rote Kapelle) was a term coined by Piepe in talks with Rohleder.

31 Mathieu posed as a member of the Belgian Resistance.

32 "Arier" was recruited by the GRU in February 1938 and Scheliha only worked for money not conviction.

CHAPTER 8

1 Present day Tanzania.

2 Germans settled for hundreds of years in Central and Eastern Europe as colonists, including the Russian-Germans commonly called the Volga-Germans.

3 See Chapter 4.

4 The Germans wanted to capture the Dutch Government and Queen Juliana in order to force them to head a legal administration under the benevolence of a German protective administration, like that of the Czech state of Bohemia and Moravia or Denmark. It was not to be and the Netherlands, like Norway, resisted fiercely but ineffectually and was brought under direct German military occupation.

5 It was two miles from the German frontier and 450 yards long, which carried the railway from Goch in Germany to the western part of Holland.

6 The equivalent to the French *Gendarmes* and under military command and the Ministry of Interior.

7 See Chapter 9 under Yugoslavia.

8 Among these were Abwehr officers to sort captured partisan documents and interrogate captured partisan officers, as well as special "Savdil" (signals) troops who would go through codes and destroy Tito's central communications. The Bosniaks (Muslim Bosnians) were also part of the assault force.

9 There had not been enough transport aircraft to take all the SS paratroopers in one single attack.

10 The Secret Field Police under Abwehr command.

11 Count Adrian von Fölkersam – Baltic German aristocracy – born in Riga. His grandfather served in the Imperial Russian Navy, he was student at Berlin, joined the Brandenburgers in 1939 but decided to switch to Skorzeny's commandos in 1943 because the Brandenburgers were being squandered. Fölkersam was a true nobleman of only 23 and just as recklessly brave as Girg. He was killed, much to Skorzeny's grief, in action on the Eastern Front on 18 January 1945.

12 Only 8 dead and 26 wounded on both sides had been lost during Panzerfaust.

13 His coup was only marred by the fact that Horthy's removal from power enabled the SS butcher, Eichmann, to begin the deportation of Hungarian Jews to Auschwitz from October.

14 After the collapse of the Reich Skorzeny was acquitted of war crimes for Greif and fled, via Paris, to safety in Spain.

CHAPTER 9

1 Section D became the SOE during the summer of 1940 but the chief of SOE, the tough Labour minister Hugh Dalton, never got the support he needed from other departments, especially the cautious FO which wanted to avoid a break with Romania at all costs until it was inevitable. Nothing came of the plans to sabotage the Danube route or the oilfields, which remained open and producing their precious black gold until August 1944, when they were occupied by the Russians. Repeated Allied bombing raids failed to make an impact on the dispersed oilfields.

2 Lupescu (Wolf) was a Bessarabian Jewess and deeply unpopular with the anti-Semitic Iron Guard. The royal couple settled in Estoril outside Lisbon.

3 See Chapter 1.

4 Romania is a Latin state with a strong French and Italian influence, while Slav Bulgaria looked to Russia for guidance, protection and influences. They had fought wars with each other in 1912–13 and 1915–17, with Bulgaria on the losing side on both occasions.

5 Boris III refused to hand over Bulgaria's 50,000 Jews since Bulgaria gave equal protection to its Muslim minority. In this he had the overwhelming support of his subjects who, unlike the anti-semitic Romanians or Hungarians, opposed German racial policies. But this is set against Bulgarian atrocities against the population of Greek Thrace, which were savage. Boris III could have been killed by the SD or the NKVD, both seeing him as an obstacle to their respective power's dominance over Bulgaria.

6 The King, George IV, was Anglophile by family (since he was related to the British royal family) and by political sentiments – in this he probably reflected the sentiments of most of his countrymen. General Ioannis Metaxas, Greece's military dictator, admired Mussolini and the Germans but he was determined to resist the Axis threat against Greece with all available means.

7 The Germans had to undertake anti-partisan operations because of the Italians' reluctance to undertake such. It should be noted that the SD-Sipo (after 1943) dominated the cities, while the Whermacht-GFP in cooperation controlled the Greek countryside.

8 Blume had participated in the Nazification of the police in Dortmund and had headed the 7a Sonderkommando Einsatzkommando (Vilna HQ). During his unit's rampage across Western Russia Blume butchered over 1000 Slavs and Jews. But he refused, to his "credit", to shoot women and children, and after 11 months of "distinguished" service Blume was recalled to Berlin.

9 Internal Macedonian Revolutionary Organisation, a terrorist organization which had sought since 1900 to make Macedonia either independent or part of Bulgaria. Neither aim was achieved, since Serbia grabbed Macedonia in 1913 and after 1918 it remained part of Yugoslavia.

10 Organization Todt: set up by Dr. Todt to build roads, railways and other facilities used by the Wehrmacht.

11 Hoettl, *The Secret Front*, p172.

12 See Chapter 8.

13 Son and heir to King Fuad I who reigned from 1936 until he was unseated by a military coup led by the Abwehr contact Colonel Nasser in 1952.

14 The stretch of the great Saharan Desert that runs through Egypt and stretches all the way to southern Libya and the oasis of Kufra. Almaszy, an extrovert bisexual of varying tastes, loved the fast jet-set life of the rich and infamous in Cairo, and it was with great regret that as a neutral he was forced to leave his post with the Anglo-Egyptian Survey Team in September 1939 and return to Budapest.

15 Gamal Abdel Nasser (1918–70), the charismatic leader of Egypt between 1956 and his premature death in 1970. He participated in the 1948 war against Israel and led Egypt to defeat in 1956 and 1967 against the same enemy. Anwar al-Sadat or as-Sadat, (1918–81) was Nasser's right-hand man who took power in 1970 and signed the peace treaty with Israel in 1977. Murdered by fundamentalist terrorists in 1981. Their contacts with the Abwehr is almost never mentioned as part of their past histories.

16 See David Fraser, *Knight's Cross: A Life of Field Marshal Erwin Rommel* (London, Harper Collins, 1994) for a full biography. For the more technical side of this amazing soldier's career see Christer Jörgensen, *Rommel's Panzers: Rommel and the Panzer Forces of the Blitzkrieg, 1940–1942.* (Staplehurst, Spellmount, 2003).

17 "Are you out of your mind, man?" or "Blimey-what a crazy idea!'

18 Ritter – the Rider or Cavalryman (which his name means in German) – had his last ride as Abwehr agent and Tirpitz Ufer had enough of him. He had bungled one too many times and was cashiered when his hoped-for diplomatic posting to Brazil was not granted, since his name was linked too deeply with Abwehr espionage. Canaris, ever the loyal employer, wanted him posted to North Africa but there were no openings. Ritter ended the war in

charge of a Flak (AA) artillery regiment. The born survivor Ritter re-emerged, yet again, as a member of Gehlen's BND (West German Intelligence Service or Bundes Nachrichten Dienst), no doubt to wreck havoc with their operations.

19 Charles Whiting, *Hitler's Secret War*, p73.

20 C. Whiting, *Hitler's Secret War*, p76.

21 The SAS (Special Air Service) and LRDG (Long Range Desert Group) were set up during the campaign in North Africa to attack the German lines of communication and launch sabotage raids.

22 Hadji is a title of some respect in the Islamic world since the holder of such an honour indicated that this man had undertaken a Hadj or Pilgrimage to the Holy City of Mecca.

23 LIU – Letter Interception Unit or Postal Censors.

CHAPTER 10

1 For Abwehr II operations in Asia, Hedin was used a source of intelligence, maps, optimal routes, topographical information and a host of information, which this German sympathizer readily agreed to furnish his German "friends" with.

2 Schapper had joined the NSDAP by 1920, which made him an Old Comrade (Alte Kamerade) of the party. He had joined the Defence Ministry Cipher Centre in 1927, and it was in February 1933 that Schapper put the idea of a Research Office to Göring, who jumped at the chance.

3 Germany as it extended to the borders of 1937, including Austria, Sudetenland, the Czech lands, western Poland and some western parts of the USSR added in 1941. In other words, a bloated version of the Third Reich expanded out of all recognition.

4 Given the importance of the Urals industrial area this was no mean achievement.

5 French News Agency based in Paris.

6 Nickname for a U-boat battle group.

CHAPTER 11

1 C. Whiting, *Hitler's Secret War*, p3.

2 ibid, p145.

3 Czech Central Command of Internal Resistance.

4 Klemens von Klemperer, *German Resistance against Hitler*, p4.

5 Set up in Hamburg in 1924 to counteract the Weimar Republic being toppled by nationalist extremists such as Hitler, and which had 60 members and subsequently continued to work in Germany against the Nazis. Robinsohn, as a German Jew, was not safe in Germany and fled to Denmark. The Club had links with the Abwehr and other parts of the Widerstand.

6 L. Paine, *The Abwehr*, p163.

7 See Chapter 7.

8 Had the content of these exchanges been known to the Gestapo then Canaris would have been arrested and removed from his post a year earlier, since it showed clearly that he and Beck were plotting against Hitler.

End Notes on Sources

(Full details of literature in the Bibliography)

Chapter 1
David Kahn, *Hitler's Spies*, pp29–38. Good background to the ND and its links with the General Staff.; Julia Keay, *Sanningen om Mata Hari*, pp143–146, 148, 154. Makes clear Kalle made no mistake when he sent message to Paris uncoded. Nigel West, *MI6*, pp3–13. Best source on SIS; Philip Knightley, The *Second Oldest Profession*, pp1, 10–12, 26–30, 33–40, 42–48. The title alone says everything about his ideas about spying and intelligence work.; Nigel West. *MI5*, pp37–47. By 1918 MI5 had a permanent staff of 800; of captured German spies only some 11 were executed – nine of them shot in the Tower of London. Kenneth Strong, *Men of Intelligence*, pp5–15. Nicolai was branded as a traitor by the Nazis for writing and publishing a book on his wartime intelligence service.

Chapter 2
W.L. Shirer, *The Rise and Fall of the Third Reich*, pp407, 458, 462–463, 564, 569, 627; M.Bloch, *Ribbentrop*, pp34–37, 43–47, 60, 98, 107, 115-119. Göring told Hitler bluntly that Ribbentrop's knowledge of the world was limited to the sale of alcohol, since he was a mere champagne salesman while Unity Mitford told here admirer, Hitler, that the appointment of Ribbentrop as German ambassador in London, the most vital post of the AA, was a "sick joke". Hitler, for some reason, took to the boring, boorish Ribbentrop whose whole character was totally unsuited to deal with the sophisticated and cynical British. A. Gill, *An Honourable Defeat*, pp38–44, 81-86; P. Padfield, *Himmler*, pp105–113, 128–139, 146–161, 196–202, 219–223, 226–231, 250–251; P.R. Black, *Ernst Kaltenbrunner*, pp70, 73–79, 82–87, 93–101, 118–120; W. Hoettl, *The Secret Front*, pp20–33; E. Crankshaw, *Gestapo*, pp63–71, 83–92; C. Andrew & O. Gordievsky, *KGB*, pp234–238, 254–256. They make the claim that Stalin ordered that no intelligence efforts be made against Germany which, given the conduct of the GRU in the affair of the Red Orchestra, was probably right. S. Koch, *Double Lives*, pp56–61, 108–121, 127–145; W.G. Krivitsky, *In Stalin's Secret Service*, pp183–209. In this Soviet spymaster's opinion the Germans were the unwitting tools of Stalin's machinations against the Red Army generals. M. Burleigh, *Germany Turns Eastwards*, pp3–7, 22, 86–93, 133–136; W. Schellenberg, *Memoirs*, pp40–49, 51–57, 63–67; H. Woodhead, *The Third Reich: The Shadow War*, pp13–26; I. Colvin, *Chief of Intelligence*, pp25–28, 46–52; A. Brissaud, *Canaris*, p31. Canaris did not condone the use of female agents in the "service" and was shocked and disgusted with Sosnowski's callous and ruthless used of female agents who he, the cad that he was, sacrificed while he survived. L. Paine, *Abwehr*, pp8–15, 31–45; A. Cave Brown, *The Secret Servant*, pp177–186; R.M. Smelser, *The Sudeten Problem 1933–1938*, pp168–188; L. Farago, *The Game of Foxes*, pp3–8; N. West, *MI5*, pp101–113, 114–117; P. Knightley, *The Second Oldest Profession*, pp89–99.

Chapter Three
P. Leverkuehn, *German Military Intelligence*, pp195–200; C. Whiting, *Hitler's Secret War*, pp3–21; P. Padfield, *Himmler*, pp105–113, 196–198; W. Hoettl, *The Secret Front*, pp20–22, 67–77; E. Crankshaw, *Gestapo*, pp24–26, 88–90. Captain Best, captured during the Venlo incident, described Gestapo Müller as a "very

decent little man" and infuriated Heydrich by asking Müller who this excitable young officer was. E.H. Cookridge, *Gehlen*, pp37–79; W. Schellenberg, *Memoirs*, pp29–31. Schellenberg found Heydrich both odious and dangerous as a superior.

Chapter 4
Eddy Bauer (ed), *Andra världskriget. Holland och Belgien ockuperas*, (Stockholm, Bokorama, 1983), pp29–30, 36; T. Pryser, *Hitler's hemmelige agenter*, pp23–26, 31–34, 36–38, 53; P. Leverkuehn, *German Military Intelligence*, pp65, 77–78, 82–87, 98–103. The PIS papers were found in Fort Legionov by chance in October 1939. K. Strong, *Men of Intelligence*, pp71–87; W. Shirer, *The Rise & Fall of the Third Reich*, pp564, 569, 627–630, 675, 719–720; P. Padfield, *Himmler*, pp265–266; W. Schellenberg, *Memoirs*, pp69–70; I. Colvin, *Chief of Intelligence*, pp42; A.L. Lie, *Gåten Marina*, pp17–29, 42–69, 70–113, 121–218.

Chapter 5
C. Whiting, *Hitler's Secret War*, pp49–61, 63, 126–140; D.A. Johnson, *Germany's Spies and Saboteurs*, pp78–83, 84–87; R. Wheatley, *Operation Sea Lion*, pp 122–124. Preparations for sending Einsatzkommandos to Britain began in August 1940 when Britain was divided into six districts for each Einsatzgruppe. By 7 September 1940, a list of names with suspects (left-wingers, communists, trade unionists, conservatives, generals, prominent politicians, free masons and so forth) comprising 2700 names had been completed, with the first name being: W.S. Churchill, Downing Street, Prime Minister. No doubt the terror that Poland had suffered would be inflicted upon Britain as well. P. Fleming, *Operation Sea Lion*, pp63–127, 166–177, 178–190. Each side was wholly ignorant of the other's intentions, as shown by the Invasion Warning Sub-Committee's (IWSC) persistence in believing that the Germans would invade East Anglia rather than the south coast. G. Peis, *The Mirror of Deception*, pp21–30, 33–49, 85–101, 157–164, 171–178. It was Peis who found out that Jebsen "Artist" and Wulf Schmidt "Tate" came from the same north German village. N. West, *MI5*, pp248–263, 264–275; C. Whiting. *Hitler's Secret War*, pp112–125; I. Colvin, *Chief of Intelligence*, pp117–118, 121–123. Abwehr reports from Britain gravely exaggerated British military and economic strength, and the SIS concluded that the Abwehr was a genuine asset for the British war effort. L. Paine, *The Abwehr*, pp71–106, 125–149; J.E. Persico, *Roosevelt's Secret War*, pp19–31, 138–141. Persico is very critical of Kennedy's conduct and statements during his singularly disastrous diplomatic posting in London. As for Hoover, he does not come out well in this, either, since his personal dislike of Dusko Popov "Tricycle" – whom Hoover described as a Balkan playboy – interfered with his professional judgement and thus deprived the US of any early warning of the Pearl Harbor attack by the Japanese.

Chapter 6
On Switzerland: C. Whiting, *Hitler's Secret War*, pp85–103; P.R. Black, *Ernst Kaltenbrunner*, pp120–121; C. Leitz, *Nazi Germany and Neutral Europe during the Second World War*, pp10–11, 14, 15–16, 19–20, 24–25; J.M. Pakcard, *Neither Friend nor Foe*, pp10, 12–14, 16,

71, 73, 75, 78, 80–82; J. Kimche, *Spying for Peace*, pp6–9, 11, 13, 16–18, 25, 27–30, 32–39, 46–48, 64, 73, 78–88, 90–95, 97–99, 101–103, 106–111; J. Vader, *The Lucy Spy Ring* (*Purnell's History of the Second World War*, Vol. XVIII), pp1373–1374; P. Grosse, *Gentleman Spy*, pp162–163, 168–177, 178–191; J.E. Persico, *Roosevelt's Secret War*, pp251–252, 287; D.A. Waters, *Hitler's Secret Ally*, pp133–137, 139–140, 153, 156–160. Both Persico and Waters are far too critical of Switzerland, ignoring the country's active yet covert intelligence war against Nazi Germany. G. Peis, *Mirror of Deception*, pp138–139. Peis is deeply critical of the Abwehr's incompetence and waste of agent material, calling this operation and the attempted subversion of South Africa Circus Abwehr. I share his critical attitude. V.E. Tarrant, *The Red Orchestra*, pp148–188

On Turkey: P. Leverkuehn, *German Military Intelligence*, pp2–10, 12–26; F.G. Weber, *The Evasive Neutral*, pp1–2, 20–49, 108–111, 127–129, 133–139. Weber is very critical of Turkey's conduct during the war and views its occupation of the International Zone protecting the Dardanelles and Bosporus in 1936 as no better than Hitler's occupation of the Rhineland. I share his critical attitude and have only this to add: Turkey has steadfastly refused to acknowledge its mass murder and deliberate genocide of 1.5–2.5 million Armenians and other Ottoman Christians during World War I. L.W. Moyzsich, *Operation Cicero*, pp30–47, 49–64, 66–82, 84–105, 107–128, 130–203; Elyasna Bazna, *I was Cicero*, pp5–55, 61–110; Report by OSS Agent Theodore A. Morde 5–6 October 1943 in J. Heideking & Christof Mauch (ed), *American Intelligence and the German Resistance to Hitler*, pp130–142; K. von Klemperer, *German Resistance to Hitler*, pp329–331; R. Denniston, *Diplomatic Decrypts, the Foreign Office and Turkey 1942–44* (Stroud, Sutton Publishing, 1997), pp129–131, 134–137, 139. Denniston shows that the Cicero success backfired on the Germans once they had taken possession of the reports that Cicero had sent, which helped them decipher the German diplomatic ciphers.

On Spain and Portugal: M. Bloch, *Operation Willi*, pp2–3, 22, 24, 68 77, 82 86, 97, 101 109, 136, 138 141, 145, 154 161, 163 171, 172–181, 182–190, 201, 214–216. Bloch, the greatest living expert on Windsor, presents a most impressive detective work to unravel the many layers of deceit, conspiracy and plots that surrounded the duke. He has also covered the affair from a Spanish point of view and presents much documentary material not hitherto used before. P. Preston, *Franco*, pp160, 168, 172, 207, 349, 357, 393. The Spanish Foreign Office supplied the Germans with attaché reports from the USA and Britain during the war which proved most helpful to assess bomb damage, production figures and a host of intelligence. The Spanish Embassy in London was a hive of German espionage and frequently used by the Abwehr to spy on Britain. It cultivated the Spanish Ambassador José Lequerica in Paris, and prominent defeatists such as Pierre Laval and Marshal Pétain. The Spanish kept the Germans well informed about the state of moral collapse inside the French Government that proved most helpful for German policy towards their defeated foe. C. Leitz, *Nazi Germany and Neutral Europe during the Second World War*, pp144–155, 167–169; G. Hills, *Rock of Contention*, pp420–423; J.M. Packard, *Neither Friend or Foe*, pp127, 213–217, 223–227, 288–291, 346–349. Like the accidental death of General Sikorski at Gibraltar, Leslie Howard's end over the Bay of Biscay in April 1943 has been the subject of much speculation that perhaps he was shot down because the Germans thought his manager was Churchill. In fact Göbbels hated Howard for his propaganda film *Pimpernel Smith*, where he savaged the Nazis, including Göbbels, and the propaganda minister swore revenge. Another reason was that T.M. Sheppington, Shell Manager in Lisbon, was on board and the SD believed, mistakenly, that the businessman was in reality head of Lisbon SIS. After the KLM flight from Lisbon to Bristol was shot down, Göbbels gloated in *Der Angriff* that the Pimpernel had been silenced forever. C.B. Burdick, *Germany's Military Strategy and Spain in World War II*, pp24–29, 32, 36–41, 58, 67–68, 77, 80–81, 94–95, 98, 103–119, 121–128, 150.

Chapter 7
P. Leverkuehn, *German Military Intelligence*, pp155–162, 164–166, 167–172; M. Cooper, *The Phantom War*, pp121–123; H. Höhne & H. Zolling, *The General was a Spy*, pp11–26; H.E. Salisbury, *The 900 Days*, pp150–157, 163, 187, 220–221, 224–225; E.H. Cookbridge, *Gehlen*, pp77–79, 83–87, 89–103, 104–112, 119–120, 121–123; G. Gorodetsky, *Golikov*, in H. Shukman (ed), *Stalin's Generals*, pp77–81. Golikov, a political general and unimaginative Soviet bureaucrat, was chosen by Stalin to feed him with "acceptable" GRU intelligence that fitted his disastrous preconceptions and prejudiced views: i.e. that Hitler would not unleash a two-front war and all rumours of a German invasion was a British plot. Between the pair of these incompetents the USSR almost perished at Hitler's hands. A. Knight, *Beria*, pp88–93, 95–97, 101–109, 110–114, 121–123, 126, 130–131. Beria was the Soviet equivalent of Heydrich: cold, ruthlessly calculating, utterly amoral, ideologically uncommitted, and devoted only to his career and his ambition to step into his chief's shoes at the earliest opportunity. Beria also shared Heydrich's avaricious sexual appetites, but the SS chief had the decency of only inflicting his sexual desires upon grown women while his vile Soviet counterpart had a taste for pubescent girls. K. Strong, *Men of Intelligence*, pp88–90, 92–95; V.E. Tarrant, *The Red Orchestra*, pp9, 11–147.

Chapter 8
P. Leverkuehn, *German Military Intelligence*, pp163–164; W. Hoettl, *The Secret Front*, pp195–226; J. Lucas, *Kommando*, pp10–11, 24–28, 43–45, 48–50, 71–74, 77–86, 103–126; C. Foley, *Commando Extraordinary*, pp 51 85, 103 118, 127 149, 153–157; G. Peis, *Mirror of Deception*, pp145–146.

Chapter 9
Balkans: P. Leverkuehn, *German Military Intelligence*, pp133–154; Ian Colvin, *Chief of Intelligence*, pp135, 137; Mark Mazower, *Inside Hitler's Greece*, pp24, 163–16, 169, 212–214, 219–230,233.

Middle East: Günter Peis, *Mirror of Deception*, pp31–33, 131–137, 143; P. Leverkuehn, *German Military Intelligence*, pp10–26; C. Whiting, *Hitler's Secret War*, pp66–78, 83–84; J. Eppler, *Operation Condor*, pp31–37, 57–68, 80–105, 198–240.

Latin America: S.E. Hilton, *Hitler's Secret War in South America 1939–1945*, pp33–34, 49, 80–81, 196, 214, 216–217. Best and most detailed source on German espionage in Latin America. N. West, *MI5*, p365; David A. Johnson, *Germany's Spies and Saboteurs*, pp105–115; H. Woodhead, *The Shadow War*, pp77–81.

Chapter 10
D. Kahn, *Hitler's Spies*, pp109–128, 163–178, 201–209.

Chapter 11
C. Whiting, *Hitler's Secret War*, pp3–5, 148–151; K. von Klemperer, *German Resistance to Hitler*, pp119–121, 159, 172–174 , 242, 315–316; Anton Gill, *An Honourable Defeat*, pp215–218, 257: R. Manvell & H. Fränkel, *The Canaris Conspiracy*, pp130–131, 146–150, 163–165, 177, 195–197; L. Paine, *The Abwehr*, pp163–165, 174, 184–188. In 1944 Canaris was 57 years old, prematurely aged and out of influence in both government and opposition circles, concludes Paine.

Bibliography

Abshagen, Carl Heinz, *Canaris: Patriot und Weltbürger*. (Transl. by Alan M.Brodrick) (London, Hutchinson, 1956).

Abtey, Jacque and Unterberg-Gibhardt, *Fritz, 2eme Bureau contre Abwehr* (Paris, 1966).

Aline, Countess of, *The Spy Wore Red. My Adventures as an Undercover Agent in World War II* (London, Bloomsbury, 1987).

Andrew, Christopher, and Gordievsky, Oleg, *KGB. The Inside Story* (London, Harper Collins, 1990).

Agrell, Wilhelm, *Venona. Spåren från ett underrättelsekrig* (Lund, Historisk Media, 2003).

Anon., *Gestapo i Norge* (Oslo, Norsk Kunstforlag, 1972).

Aronson, Schlomo, *The Beginnings of the Gestapo system. The Bavarian Model 1933* (Jerusalem, Israeli U.P, 1969).

Baker, Ralph, *The Blockade Busters* (London, Chatto & Windus, 1976).

Barnhart, Michael A., *Japanese Intelligence before the Second World War. The Best Case Analysis*. In Ernest May (ed), *Knowing One's Enemies. Intelligence Assessment before the Two World Wars* (Princeton, Princeton U.P, 1984).

Bartz, Karl, *Die Tragödie der deutschen Abwehr* (Salzburg, 1955).

Bartz, Karl, *The Downfall of the German Secret Service* (London, 1956).

Bauer, Eddy (ed), and Världskriget, Andra, *Holland och Belgien ockuperas* (Stockholm, Bokorama, 1983).

Bernhardsson, Carl Olof, *Spionpolisen går på jakt* (Stockholm, Natur och Kultur, 1952).

Black, Peter R., *Ernst Kaltenbrunner. Ideological Soldier of the Third Reich* (Princeton, Princeton U.P, 1984).

Blackstock, Paul W., *Agents of Deceit* (Chicago, 1966).

Bloch, Michael, *Operation Willi. The Plot to Kidnap the Duke of Windsor July 1940* (London, Weidenfeld & Nicolson, 1984).

Bloch, Michael, *Ribbentrop* (London, Transworld, 1994).

Bokun, Branko, *Spy in the Vatican 1941-1945* (London, Tom Stacey, 1973).

Böhme, Klaus, *Svensk polis och Gestapo*. In Bo Hugenmark (ed), *I orkanens öga. 1941-osäker neutralitet*. (Stockholm, Probus, 1992)

Bowder, George C., *Hitler's Enforcers. The Gestapo and SS security service in the Nazi revolution* (Oxford, O.U.P, 1996).

Brissaud, André, *Canaris. The Biography of Admiral Canaris, Chief of German Military Intelligence in the Second World War* (London, Weidenfeld & Nicolson, 1970).

Budiansky, Stephen, *Battles of Wits. The Complete story of codebreaking in World War II* (London, Penguin, 2000).

Budick, Charles B., *Germany's Military Strategy and Spain in World War II* (Syracuse, Syracuse U.P., 1968).

Burleigh, Michael, *Germany turns eastwards. A Study of Ostforschung in the Third Reich* (London, Pan Macmillan, 2002).

Calic, Eduard, *Reinhard Heydrich* (New York, William Morrow, 1985).

Carlgren, Wilhelm M., *Svensk utrikespolitk* (Stockholm, Allmänna Förlaget, 1973).

Carr, Raymond, *Spain 1808–1975* (Oxford, Clarendon, 1982).

Cave-Brown, Anthony, *The Secret Servant: The Life of Sir Stewart Menzies, Churchill's Spymaster* (London, Sphere Books, 1989).

Chase, Allan, *Falange* (New York, 1943).

Colvin, Ian, *Chief of Intelligence* (London, Victor Gollancz, 1951).

Cookridge, E.H., *Gehlen. Spy of the Century* (London, 1972).

Cookridge, E.H., *Inside the S.O.E.* (London, 1966).

Cooper, Matthew, *The Phantom War. The German struggle against Soviet partisans 1941–1944* (London, Macdonald & Jane, 1979).

Crankshaw, Edward, *Gestapo. Instrument of Tyranny* (London, 1966).

Cruickshank, Charles, *S.O.E in Scandinavia* (Oxford, O.U.P, 1986).

Davies, Philip H.J., *The British Secret Services* (Oxford, ABC-Clio, 1996).

Delarue, Jacques, *The History of the Gestapo (Translated by Mervyn Savill)* (London, MadDonald, 1964).

Delmer, Sefton, *The Counterfeit Spy. The Untold Story of the Phantom Army that Deceived Hitler* (Ldonon, Hutchinson, 1973).

Denham, Henry, *Inside the Nazi Ring. A Naval Attaché in Sweden 1940-1945* (London, John Murray, 1984).

Douglas, Gregory, *Gestapo Chief. The 1948 interrogation of Heinrich Müller from secret US intelligence files* (Los Angeles, R.James Bender Publishing, 1995).

Duggan, John P., *Neutral Ireland and the Third Reich* (Dublin, Gill & MacMillan, 1985).

Dulles, Allen W., *Germany's Underground* (New York, 1947).

Dulles, Allen W., *The Craft of Intelligence* (New York, 1963).

Englich, Kurt, *Den osynliga fronten. Spioncentral Stockholm* (Stockholm, 1985).

Eppler, John, *Operation Condor. Rommel's Spy* (London, Futura, 1987).

Fest, Joachim, *Plotting Hitler's Death. The German Resistance to Hitler 1933–1945* (London, Phoenix, 1997).

Fjørtoft, Kjell, *Lille-Moskva. Det glemte krigen* (Oslo, Gyldenfal, 1983).

Flaherty, Thomas H. (ed.), *The Third Reich. The Heel of the Conquero* (New York, Time Life Books, 1991).

Flaherty, Thomas H. (ed.), *The Third Reich. War on the High Seas* (New York, Time Life, 1990).

Fleming, Peter, *Operation Sea Lion. The Outstanding Account of the Nazi Invasion Plans for the British Isles 1940* (London, Pan Books, 1984).

Flyghed, Jan, *Rättstat i kris. Spioneri och sabotage i Sverige under andra världskriget* (Stockholm, Fedreatius, 1992).

Foley, Charles, *Commando Extraordinary. Otto Skorzeny* (London, Cassell, 1994).

Frick, Lennart and Rosander, Lars, *Det vakande ögat. Svensk underrättelsetjänst under 400 år* (Lund, Historisk Media, 1998).

Gehlen, Reinhard, *The Service* (New York, 1972).

Gill, Anton, *An Honourable Defeat. The Fight against National Socialism in Germany, 1933–1945* (London, Mandarin, 1995).

Giskes, Hermann J., *Abwehr III F. London calling North Pole* (London, William Kimber, 1953).

Grose, Peter, *Gentleman Spy. The Life of Allen Dulles* (New York, Houghton-Mifflin, 1994).

Gruber, Gerry S., *The Life and Times of Reinhard Heydrich* (London, Hale, 1980).

Grundt-Larsen, Jörgen, *Modstandbevaegelsens Kontaktudvalg i Stockholm 1944–45* (Odense, 1976).

Guillaume, Gilbert, *Mes Missiones face a l'abwehr. Contre-espionnage 1938–1945* (Paris, Plon, 1973).

Harris, John, and Trow, M.J., *Hess, The British Conspiracy* (London, André Deutsch, 1999).

Heideking, Jürgen, and Mauch, Christof (ed), *American Intelligence and the German Resistance to Hitler. A Documentary History* (Oxford, Westview Press, 1996).

Herwig, Holger M., *Imperial Germany.[Secret Service].* In Ernest R.may (ed), *Knowing One's Enemies. Intelligence Assessment before the Two World Wars* (Princeton, Princeton U.P., 1984).

Hilton, Stanley E.., *Hitler's Secret War 1939–1945. German Military Espionage and Allied counter espionage in Brazil* (Baton Rouge, Louisiana State U.P, 1981).

Hingley, Ronald, *The Russian Secret Police. Muscovite, Imperial Russian and Soviet Political Security Operations 1565–1970* (London, Hutchinson, 1970)

Hoettl, Wilhelm, *The Secret Front. The Inside Story of Nazi Political Espionage* (London, Phoenix Press, 2000). Originally published 1954.

Höhne, Heinz and Zolling, Hermann, *The General was a Spy. The Truth about General Gehlen and his spy ring* (Translated by Richard Barrry). (London, Pan Books, 1972).

Irving, David, *The German Atom Bomb* (New York, 1968).

Johansen, Erik, *De illegale. Om spiongae, undergrundskoer, stikker likvideringer og ilegal presse under besaettelsen* (Copenhagen, Centrum, 1983).

Johnson, David A., *Germany's Spies and Saboteurs* (Osceola, MBI Publishing, 1998).

Kimche, Jon, *Spying for Peace. General Guisan and Swiss Neutrality* (London, Weidenfeld & Nicolson, 1961).

Kleist, Franz Rintelen von, *The Dark Invader. Wartime Reminiscences of a German Naval Intelligence Officer* (London, Frank Cass, 1998). Originally published 1933.

Klemperer, Klemens von, *German Resistance against Hitler. The Search for Allies Abroad* (Oxford, Clarendon, 1992).

Knightley, Philip, *The Second Oldest Profession* (London, Pan Books, 1986).

Koch, Stephen, *Double Lives. Stalin, Willi Münzenberg and the Seduction of the Intellectuals* (London, Harper-Collins, 1995).

Krivitsky, Walter G., *In Stalin's Secret Service* (New York, Engiman Books, 2000). Originally published 1939.

Kurowksi, Franz, *Deutsche Kommandotruppes 1939–1945. Brandenburg und Abwehr in weltweiten Einsatz* (Stuttgart, Motorbuch Verlag, 2000).

Leitz, Christian, *Economic Relations Between Nazi Germany and Franco's Spain 1936–1945* (Oxford, Clarendon, 1996).

Leverkuehn, Paul, *German Military Intelligence* (London, Weidenfeld & Nicolson, 1954).

Lundberg, Lennart, *Under kriget. Svenska spioner och hjältar i skuggan av andra världskriget* (Gothenburg, Treböcker, 1997).

MacDonald, Cullum A., *The Venlo Affair*, in *European Studies Review*, Vol. VIII (October 1978), pp445–464.

McKay, C.G., *From Information to Intrigue. Studies in Secret Service Based on the Swedish Experience 1939–45* (London, Frank Cass, 1993).

Mader, Julius, *Hitler Spiongeneralen sagen aus* (Berlin, Verlag der Nation, 1970).

Manvell, Arnold Roger, *SS and Gestapo. Rule by Terror* (London, Pan Books, 1972).

Manvell, Arnold Roger, and Fränkel, Heinrich, *The Canaris Conspiracy. The Secret Resistance to Hitler in the German Army* (London, Heinemann, 1969).

Marres, Juliette, *Nazi Overlords. Holland May 1940–May 1941.* (*Purnell's History of the Second World War*, Vol. V, pp451–458) (London, Phoebus, 1980).

Masterman, John, *The Double Cross System in the war of 1939–1945* (London, Yale U.P., 1972).

Merson, Allan, *Communist Resistance in nazi Germany* (London, Lawrence & Wishart, 1985).

Meurling, Per, *Spionage och sabotage i Sverige* (Kristianstad, Kristianstad boktryckeri, 1954).

Moyzisch, L.C., *Operation Cicero* (London, Wingate, 1956).

Nicolai, Walter, *The German Secret Service* (London, 1924).

Norway, Department of State, *The Gestapo at Work in Norway* (London, 1943).

Øksendal, Asbjørn, *Gulltransporten* (Oslo, Aschehoug, 1974).

Øksendal, Asbjørn, *Operasjon Lapwing. Kompani Linge sprenger Rørosbanen. Den største jernbanesabotasje i Norge under krigen* (Oslo, Grøndahl, 1973).

Øksendal, Asbjørn, *Operasjon Oleander. Gestapo i Trondhjem och Leksvik affaeren 1942–44* (Trondheim, Nordanfjelske forlag, 1968).

One's Enemies. Intelligence Assessment before the Two World Wars (Princeton, Princeton U.P., 1984).

Onodera, Yuriko, *Telegram till Tokyo*. In Bo Hugenmark (ed.), *I orkanens öga. 1941-osäker neutralitet* (Stockholm, Probus, 1992). Øvrebø, Ludvig, *Hjemmestyrkene i Elverum* (Elverum, n.d.).

Ottessen,Kristian, *Theta. Theta. Et bald fra motstandskampens historie 1940–1945* (Oslo, Universitetsforlaget, 1983).

Overton Fuller, Jean, *The German Penetration of SOE. France 1940–1944* (London, William Kimber, 1975).

Padfield, Peter, *Himmler. Reichsführer SS* (London, Papermac, 1991).

Paine, Lauran, *The Abwehr. German Military Intelligence in World War Two* (London, Robert Hale, 1984).

Papeleux, Léon, *L'amiral Canaris entre Franco et Hitler. La rôle de Canaris dans les relatiosn germano-espagnoles (1915–1944)* (Tournai, Casterman, 1977).

Payne Best, S., *The Venlo Incident* (London, 1950).

Peis, Günter, *The Mirror of Deception. How Brtain turned the Nazi Spy Machine against itself* (London, Weidenfeld & Nicolson, 1977).

Persico, Joseph E., *Roosevelt's Secret War. FDR and World War II Espionage* (New York, Random House, 2001).

Peyron, Ulf, *Fallet Horney. Drama utan slut* (Stockholm, Norstedts, 1985).

Popov, Dusko, *Spy-counterspy. The Autobiography of Dusko Popov* (New York, 1974).

Porch, Douglas, *The French Secret Services: from the Dreyfus Affair to the Gulf War* (London, Macmillan, 1996).

Preston, Paul, *Franco. A Biography* (London, Harper-Collins, 1993).

Pryser, Tore, *From Petsamo to Venona: Intelligence Services in the Nordic Countries* from *Hot to Cold war*, Scandinavian Journal of History, Vol. XXIV (1999), pp75-89.

Pryser, Tore, *Hitlers hemmelige agenter. Tysk etterretning i Norge 1939–1945* (Oslo, Universitetsforlaget, 2001).

Read, Anthony, *Operation Lucy: Most Secret Spy Ring of the Second World War* (New York, Coward, McCann & Geoghan, 1981).

Reile, Oscar, *Geheime Ostfront. Die deutsche Abwehr im Osten 1921–1945* (Munich, Welsermühl, 1963).

Richardson, Gunnar, *Beundran och fruktan. Sverige inför Tyskland 1940–1942* (Stockholm, Carlsson, 1996).

Rosquist, Michael, *Spionage i Sverige* (Stockholm, 1988).

Salisbury, Harrison E., *The 900 Days. The Siege of Leningrad* (London, Papermac, 1986).

Schwarze, Erika, *Kodnamn Onkel* (Stockholm, Månpocket, 1995).

Shirer, William L., *The Rise and Fall of the Third Reich. A History of Nazi Germany* (London, Pan Books, 1964).

Skodvin, Magne (ed.), *Norge i krig. Fremmedåk og frihetskampe 1940–1945. Vol. II. Berit Nøkleby, Nyordningen* (Oslo, Aschehoug, 1985).

Soltikow, Michael, *Im Zentrum der Abwehr: mein Jahre bei Admiral Canaris* (Güthersloh, Prisma, 1986).

Stevenson, William, *A Man Called Interpid* (London, Sphere Books, 1977).

Strik-Strikfeldt, Wilfred, *Against Hitler and Stalin. Memoir of the Russian Liberation Movement 1941–45.* (Transl. David Footman) (London, Macmillan, 1970).

Strong, Kenneth, *Men of Intelligence. A Study of the Roles and Decisions of Cheifs of Intelligence from World War I to the present day* (London, Cassell, 1970).

Taylor, Simon, *Germany 1918-1933. Revolution, counter-revolution and the rise of Hitler* (London, Duckworth, 1983).

Tennant, Peter, *Touchlines of War* (Hull, University of Hull Press, 1992).

Vader, John, *The Lucy Spy Ring. Switzerland-Germany 1939–1944* (Purnell's History of the Second World War, Vol. XIII, pp1373-1374) (London, Phoebus, 1980).

Vaksberg, Arkady, *The Prosecutor and the Prey. Vyshinksy and the 1930s Moscow Show Trials* (London, Weidenfeld & Nicolson, 1990).

Volkogonov, Dimitri, *Stalin. Triumph and Tragedy* (London, Weidenfeld & Nicolson, 1991).

Watt, Donald Cameron, *How War Came. The Immediate Origins of the Second World War, 1938–1939* (London, Mandarin, 1990).

Weber, Frank G., *The Evasive Neutral. Germany, Britain and the Quest for a Turkish Alliance in the Second World War* (London, University of Missouri Press, 1979).

Weiner, J.G., *The Assassination of Heydrich* (New York, 1969).

West, Nigel, *MI5: British Security service operations, 1909–1945* (London, Triad Grenada, 1983).

West, Nigel, *MI6: British Intelligence service operations, 1909–1947* (London, Weidenfeld & Nicolson, 1983).

Wheatley, Ronald, *Operation Sea Lion. German Plans for the Invasion of England 1939–1942* (Oxford, Clarendon, 1958).

Whiting, Charles, *Heydrich: Henchman of Death* (Barnsley, Leo Cooper, 1999).

Whiting, Charles, *Hitler's Secret War. The Nazi Espionage Campaign Against the Allies* (Barnsley, Leo Cooper, 2000).

Woodhead (ed.), Henry, *The Third Reich. The Shadow War* (New York, Time Life Books, 1992).

Index

Italic page numbers refer to illustrations

Picture credits